Asia Bible Commentary Series

DANIEL

Asia Bible Commentary Series

DANIEL

Kevin S. Chen

General Editor
Andrew B. Spurgeon

Old Testament Consulting Editors
Joseph Shao, Havilah Dharamraj, Koowon Kim

New Testament Consulting Editors
Steve Chang, Finny Philip, Samson Uytanlet

© 2025 Kevin S. Chen

Published 2025 by Langham Global Library
An imprint of Langham Publishing
www.langhampublishing.org

Langham Publishing and its imprints are a ministry of Langham Partnership

Langham Partnership
PO Box 296, Carlisle, Cumbria, CA3 9WZ, UK
www.langham.org

Published in partnership with Asia Theological Association

ATA
QCC PO Box 1454–1154, Manila, Philippines
www.ataasia.com

ISBNs:
978-1-78641-269-0 Print
978-1-78641-270-6 ePub
978-1-78641-271-3 PDF

Kevin S. Chen has asserted his right under the Copyright, Designs and Patents Act, 1988 to be identified as the Author of this work.

All rights reserved. No part of this publication may be reproduced, stored in a retrieval system or transmitted, in any form or by any means, electronic, mechanical, photocopying, recording or otherwise, without the prior written permission of the publisher or the Copyright Licensing Agency.

Requests to reuse content from Langham Publishing are processed through PLSclear. Please visit www.plsclear.com to complete your request.

Scripture quotations marked (ESV) are taken from The Holy Bible, English Standard Version® (ESV®), copyright © 2001 by Crossway, a publishing ministry of Good News Publishers. Used by permission. All rights reserved. Scripture quotations marked (NIV) are taken from the Holy Bible, New International Version®, NIV®. Copyright © 1973, 1978, 1984, 2011 by Biblica, Inc.™ Used by permission of Zondervan. Scripture quotations marked (NASB) are taken from the New American Standard Bible®, Copyright © 1960, 1962, 1963, 1968, 1971, 1972, 1973, 1975, 1977, 1995, 2020 by The Lockman Foundation. Used by permission. Scripture quotations marked (NRSV) are taken from the New Revised Standard Version Bible, copyright © 1989 National Council of the Churches of Christ in the United States of America. Used by permission. All rights reserved. Scripture quotations marked (RSV) are taken from the Revised Standard Version of the Bible, copyright © 1946, 1952, and 1971 National Council of the Churches of Christ in the United States of America. Used by permission. All rights reserved.

British Library Cataloguing-in-Publication Data
A catalogue record for this book is available from the British Library
ISBN: 978-1-78641-269-0

Cover & Book Design: projectluz.com

Langham Partnership actively supports theological dialogue and an author's right to publish but does not necessarily endorse the views and opinions set forth here or in works referenced within this publication, nor can we guarantee technical and grammatical correctness. Langham Partnership does not accept any responsibility or liability to persons or property as a consequence of the reading, use or interpretation of its published content.

For Joel.
As you grow up,
may your energies and gifts be increasingly directed towards
the kingdom that will never be destroyed.

CONTENTS

Commentary

Series Preface xi
Author's Preface xiii
Acknowledgments xv
List of Abbreviations xvii
Introduction 1
Commentary on Daniel 3
Selected Bibliography 167

Topics

What's in a Name? 9
Dreams and Visions 19
A Biblical Perspective on Music 41
Second Exodus in the Prophets and in Daniel 54
The Structure of Daniel 82
Biblical Allusions in the Book of Daniel 123

SERIES PREFACE

What's unique about the Asia Bible Commentary Series? It is a commentary series written especially for Asian Christians, which incorporates and addresses Asian concerns, cultures, and practices. As Asian scholars – either by nationality, passion, or calling – the authors identify with the biblical text, understand it culturally, and apply its principles in Asian contexts to strengthen the churches in Asia. Missiologists tell us that Christianity has shifted from being a Western majority religion to a South, Southeastern, and Eastern majority religion and that the church is growing at an unprecedented rate in these regions. This series meets the need for evangelical commentaries written specifically for an Asian audience.

This is not to say that Asian churches and Asian Christians do not want to partner with Western Christians and churches or that they spurn Western influences. A house divided cannot stand. The books in this series complement the existing Western commentaries by taking into consideration the cultural nuances familiar to the Eastern world so that the Eastern readership is not inundated with Western clichés and illustrations that they are unable to relate to and which may not be applicable to them.

The mission of this series is "to produce resources that are biblical, pastoral, contextual, missional, and prophetic for pastors, Christian leaders, cross-cultural workers, and students in Asia." While using approved exegetical principles, the writers strive to be culturally relevant, offer practical applications, and provide clear explanations of the texts so that readers can grow in understanding and maturity in Christ and Christian leaders can guide their congregations into maturity. May we be found faithful in this endeavor and may God be glorified!

Andrew B. Spurgeon
General Editor

AUTHOR'S PREFACE

Writing a book is a journey, and sometimes this journey can be framed in terms of the author's broader life journey. This is certainly the case for me and for this book. I write from the perspective of a second-generation Chinese-American, who for much of my life did not take special interest in my parent's heritage. It's not that I didn't care at all—as a kid, I enjoyed Chinese food, getting red envelopes for the Lunar New Year and other special occasions, and traveling to Taiwan to visit relatives. But I went to Chinese school on Friday nights begrudgingly, and I couldn't understand the purpose of my church's insistence that our English-speaking youth group occasionally attend combined services with the adult, Mandarin-speaking congregation.

I stopped going to Chinese school after sixth grade, and as the years went on, it looked as though I would never study Chinese again. Yet about twenty years later, a few years into my teaching career, I was invited to teach Chinese students through a translator. I accepted, and I came away with a newfound desire to study Chinese so that I could serve these students better. One thing led to another, and soon I was not only learning to teach in Chinese but also to read Chinese, primarily through grading student papers. In addition to learning how to do these core teaching tasks, I also realized that I would be more effective if I understood my students' background better, which sparked a new interest in Chinese culture and Chinese church history.

Several years after my initial foray into this particular context of Asian ministry, my desire to increase my involvement kept growing, and I became a full-time Chinese theological educator by joining the faculty of a Chinese seminary. My five years of service there greatly deepened my understanding of and calling towards Chinese theological education. I am grateful that my current institution allows me to teach in both English (which I also enjoy) and Chinese and so continue this journey that I hope will last for the rest of my life.

This book has allowed me to merge two great passions of mine: Old Testament Studies and ministry in Asian contexts. Recognizing that this commentary is for a broader Asian audience, I have also made a concerted effort to draw out connections to other Asian cultures. This has often required me to do additional research, which was sometimes the case even when making connections to Chinese culture. Even so, I must confess my own limitations and gladly defer to those who know more, as there are likely places where what I have written falls short. For these faults, I can only ask for the mercy of God and of the reader. Nevertheless, I have learned so much from the book of Daniel and treasure it much more now, and I pray that this book will strengthen you on your journey of faith, too.

Kevin S. Chen

ACKNOWLEDGMENTS

I would like to thank Langham and Asia Theological Association for this special opportunity to contribute to the Asia Bible Commentary Series. It is both a great honor and a delight to be included in this exciting and significant project. Thank you, Andrew Spurgeon, for your initial interest in my participation and for your support and guidance throughout the entire writing process. Thank you also to Bubbles Lactaoen for your administrative assistance. Thanks is also due to those who reviewed earlier versions of this book and have thus made it better than it would have been.

    I would never even have gotten connected with Andrew if it were not for a tip from Jerry Hwang over breakfast at the annual meeting of the Evangelical Theological Society in November 2022 in Denver, Colorado. Thank you, Jerry! I still remember that I happened to be studying the Aramaic portion of Daniel at that time and was reading it when Jerry arrived at the hotel breakfast area for our appointment that morning. I soon would learn from Andrew that the Asia Bible Commentary Series needed an author for Daniel. Surely all of this came about because of the kindness and wisdom of God, who since then has further supplied strength and grace to complete this commentary. 感謝主!

LIST OF ABBREVIATIONS

BOOKS OF THE BIBLE

Old Testament

Gen, Exod, Lev, Num, Deut, Josh, Judg, Ruth, 1–2 Sam, 1–2 Kgs, 1–2 Chr, Ezra, Neh, Esth, Job, Ps/Pss, Prov, Eccl, Song, Isa, Jer, Lam, Ezek, Dan, Hos, Joel, Amos, Obad, Jonah, Mic, Nah, Hab, Zeph, Hag, Zech, Mal

New Testament

Matt, Mark, Luke, John, Acts, Rom, 1–2 Cor, Gal, Eph, Phil, Col, 1–2 Thess, 1–2 Tim, Titus, Phlm, Heb, Jas, 1–2 Pet, 1–2–3 John, Jude, Rev

BIBLE TEXTS AND VERSIONS

Divisions of the canon

NT	New Testament
OT	Old Testament

Ancient texts and versions

LXX	Septuagint
MT	Masoretic Text

Modern versions

ESV	English Standard Version
KJV	King James Version
NASB	New American Standard Bible
NIV	New International Version
NRSV	New Revised Standard Version

Journals, reference works, and series

ANE	Ancient Near East
BBR	*Bulletin for Biblical Research*
BHS	*Biblia Hebraica Stuttgartensia*

BibSac	*Bibliotheca Sacra*
CBQ	*Catholic Biblical Quarterly*
HALOT	Hebrew and Aramaic Lexicon of the Old Testament
JBL	*Journal of Biblical Literature*
JPS	Jewish Publication Society
JSOT	*Journal for the Study of the Old Testament*
OTE	Old Testament Essays
TOTC	Tyndale Old Testament Commentary
VT	*Vetus Testamentum*
WBC	Word Biblical Commentary
WTJ	*Westminster Theological Journal*

INTRODUCTION

Set in Asia amidst the rise and fall of mighty empires, the book of Daniel casts a vision of the one and only "kingdom that will never be destroyed" (2:44). This everlasting kingdom is God's kingdom, which will be ruled by "one like a son of man" (7:13) and yet is manifested at times in human history according to God's power and sovereign will. As such it speaks directly to Asian Christians and churches whose primary citizenship is in heaven and yet who also have an earthly citizenship under the authority of a particular human kingdom. Whether in history or today, such kingdoms can be unpredictable and sometimes even violent. Daniel and his three friends knew the tensions of such dual citizenship and showed what faithfulness can look like in challenging circumstances. They also knew what it was like to have lost their earthly homeland, which some Asians today know too well. Nevertheless, Daniel and his friends lived lives that brought glory to the one true God. They even witnessed God performing miracles that both delivered them from danger in a foreign land and demonstrated that he is "God of gods and Lord of kings" (2:47).

The book of Daniel is also characterized by prophecies of the future, beginning in Daniel 2 and continuing throughout the book. The acceptance or rejection of predictive prophecy has been a major factor in relation to the dating, authorship, and audience of the book. Traditionally, biblical accounts of divine revelation of the future were accepted at face value. However, the rejection of predictive prophecy by critical scholars affected their assessment of the dating, authorship, and original audience of prophetic books, including Daniel (cf. Cyrus, Isa 45:1). Rather than presupposing that Scripture is authoritative and reliable, these scholars tend to view such passages as prophecies after the fact (*vaticinium ex eventu*), which means they do not believe that they were genuinely predictive prophecies at all. Thus the predictions of future world empires in Daniel, including the especially precise predictions in Daniel 11, are seen as history that is being passed off as prophecy. The result is that critical scholarship assigns a second century BC date for the book of Daniel.

In contrast, this commentary affirms the authority and reliability of the Bible, including its predictive prophecies and other divine revelations of the future. Thus not only are the narratives in Daniel taken as historically reliable, but Nebuchadnezzar's revelatory dreams and Daniel's visions are viewed as being the result of divine revelation. Although the book of Daniel does not directly mention its author, there is evidence within the book that Daniel is at least as likely as anyone else to have written this book. First, Daniel was directly involved in almost every single incident in the book (Daniel 3 excepted). Second, Daniel was a man of learning who read widely and knew literature well (1:4, 17, 20; 9:2). Third, Daniel "wrote down" the vision that he had in Daniel 7 (v. 1). Fourth, at the end of the book, Daniel is instructed to "roll up and seal the words of the scroll until the time of the end" (12:4), which can be taken as a reference not only to Daniel 10–12, but to the whole book of Daniel (see commentary).

As for the date of the book, its latest time reference is the third year of Cyrus (Dan 10:1), which means that the book had to be completed after 536 BC. Daniel was part of a group that had been exiled in 605 BC, and so he could have been in his eighties by this time. We do not know the date of Daniel's death, but we can estimate that the book of Daniel was written ca 530–520 BC to the Israelites of that time. It should be acknowledged that some evangelical scholars hold to a later date for the book along with non-Danielic authorship for various reasons. Although this is not my view, I hope for charity on this difficult question.[1]

---

1. For such an evangelical scholar, see Wendy Widder, *Daniel: A Discourse Analysis of the Hebrew Bible*, Zondervan Exegetical Commentary on the Old Testament (Grand Rapids: Zondervan, 2023), 27–31.

DANIEL 1

FAR FROM HOME

On December 10, 1949, Chiang-kai Shek, leader of the Republic of China (ROC), boarded a plane at a military airport in Chengdu, Sichuan, bound for the island of Taiwan. He and the Kuomintang (KMT) party had lost the civil war with the Chinese Communist Party (CCP) and were retreating. My paternal grandparents also left China in 1949 because my grandfather Chen Diwei (陳第維) was part of the KMT. He and my grandmother Cao Lihua (曹麗華) left behind their extended families, never to return to their native Hunan. Sometimes I wonder what my grandparents must have felt in Taiwan when the Cultural Revolution was going on in the 1960s and 1970s, especially since my grandmother's extended family were easy targets as educators and landowners who had obvious KMT ties. Communication was risky back then and not nearly as convenient as today, but when my father visited these relatives many years later, they confirmed the suffering that they endured. And this only begins to scratch the surface of the pain of war, social upheaval, and living in exile far from home.

Set in West Asia, the book of Daniel also involves war, social upheaval, and the experience of being exiled far from home. The southern kingdom of Judah had fallen to the Babylonians in 586 BC. Two groups of exiles had already been deported, and the last group of exiles was deported at this time. These exiles had to live in a foreign country that had its own king, people, language, and culture. Tragically, the Israelites had lost the Promised Land along with their status as an independent nation. The centuries-long rule of the house of David was over, and the Babylonians had destroyed the temple, the physical center and national symbol of the worship of the Lord.

Yet the existential crisis that these Israelites faced was also a theological crisis. Had the Lord abandoned them? Were his words, including the Davidic covenant, still valid? Was Israel's story coming to an end? Was the Lord truly sovereign over the nations and their gods, especially at this time? Where was history going? The book of Daniel provides strong answers to these questions – not only for exiled Israelites, but also for all of God's people who are "exiles" seeking their final home (Heb 11:13–14).

After providing the historical setting (vv. 1–2), Daniel 1 describes the Babylonian training program in which Daniel and his three friends participate (vv. 3–7), Daniel's refusal to defile himself with the royal food (vv. 8–14), and the successful outcome (vv. 15–21).

1:1–2 JERUSALEM FALLS AND JUDAH IS EXILED

The opening two verses of Daniel establish the historical setting for the book in condensed fashion: Nebuchadnezzar, king of Babylon, came against Jerusalem during Jehoiakim's reign, besieged the city, and plundered the temple. Although there are some difficulties in chronology (see below), this brief account can still be helpfully supplemented by 2 Kings 23–24. Jehoiakim was a son of Josiah and succeeded his brother, Jehoahaz, in 609 BC when Jehoahaz was taken captive by Pharaoh Neco (2 Kgs 23:30–34; cf. 2 Chr 36:1–4). Pharaoh Neco replaced Jehoahaz with Jehoiakim, who paid Neco tribute and ruled for eleven years (2 Kgs 23:35–36). Not long after the Babylonians defeated the Egyptians at Carchemish in 605 BC, Jehoiakim became Nebuchadnezzar's vassal, but Jehoiakim rebelled after three years (2 Kgs 24:1; cf. 2 Chr 36:6).

The chronological difficulty arises from the report in Daniel 1:1, which says that Nebuchadnezzar came against Jerusalem in Jehoiakim's "third year." This seems to be one year too early given historians' dating of his reign as beginning in 609 BC and the battle of Carchemish taking place in 605 BC (cf. Jer 46:2), which would have preceded Nebuchadnezzar's coming against Jerusalem.[1] One common explanation is that the "third year" in Daniel 1:1 starts counting with Jehoiakim's first full year, not his accession year (e.g., Jer 25:1), and that Daniel 1:1–2 describes a siege in 605 BC that is not explicitly mentioned in 2 Kings 24 (whereas 2 Kgs 24:10–11 describes another siege during Jehoiachin's rule).[2] Still other proposals for construing these historical records exist, with some tending towards harmonization (my preference) and some seeing irreconcilable differences.[3] In any case, it is possible to maintain the historical reliability of these biblical accounts without being dogmatic on every last detail.

---

[1]. Paul R. House, *Daniel*, TOTC (Downers Grove: InterVarsity, 2018), 46.
[2]. E.g. see Michael B. Shepherd, *Daniel in the Context of the Hebrew Bible* (Lang: New York, 2009), 70–71, 126 (note 21); Ernest C. Lucas, *Daniel*, Apollos Old Testament Commentary (Downers Grove: InterVarsity, 2002), 37, 50–52.
[3]. For the latter, see John Collins, *Daniel, A Commentary on the Book of Daniel.* Hermeneia (Minneapolis: Fortress, 1993), 131–132.

What is clear is that the author of Daniel in this condensed prelude has highlighted key elements for the purposes of the book of Daniel: Nebuchadnezzar's involvement, a siege of Jerusalem, and the plundering of temple vessels. Nebuchadnezzar is a main character in the subsequent narrative (Daniel 1–4), and the temple vessels reappear in Daniel 5:2–3, 23. Whereas the detail about Nebuchadnezzar taking "some of the articles from the temple of God" and bringing them to "the treasure house of his god" suggests the supremacy of Nebuchadnezzar's god, Daniel 1:2 is clear that the Lord gave these vessels and Jehoiakim "into his hand." Indeed, over and above all that was happening geopolitically in that region, the Lord was justly angry with Judah and was punishing them for their sins (2 Kgs 23:26–27; 24:3–4, 20). Exile had been threatened as far back as Moses (Deut 4:25–28) and more recently by Jeremiah, whose account provides more details on Jehoiakim's sins (Jer 25:1–4; 26:21–23; 36:20–31). The prophet Isaiah had specifically predicted that Jerusalem's treasures would be taken to Babylon (2 Kgs 20:17; Isa 39:6), just as Daniel 1:2 describes (cf. 2 Kgs 24:13).[4]

Within the Bible's own vision of reality, Babylon is not simply the historical kingdom that Nebuchadnezzar ruled at that time but is linked to and even rooted in Babel and its infamous tower (Gen 11:4–9), since "Babylon" and "Babel" are translations of the same Hebrew word (*babel*). Besides this lexical identity, like Nebuchadnezzar and his son Belshazzar, the builders of the tower were proud and sought their own glory, but they were ultimately thwarted by the Lord, the true "king of kings" (cf. Dan 2:37, 47). Historical Babylon in the OT thus continues in the line of those groups of people who are united against God and his people (cf. Gen 3:15). The uncommon designator of "the land of Shinar" in Daniel 1:2 (see KJV, ESV) reinforces this connection between Babylon and the Tower of Babel (Gen 11:2). Such a broadened significance for Babylon is also supported by Isaiah 40–55, where Israel's deliverance from Babylon is equated with an eschatological "Second Exodus" (e.g., Isa 43:14–21; 48:20–21; cf. 11:11–16; see also, "Second Exodus in the Prophets and in Daniel," pp. 54–55).

---

4. Cf. Jennie Grillo, "From a Far Country: Daniel in Isaiah's Babylon," *JBL* 136 (2017): 363–380.

1:3–7 DANIEL AND HIS THREE FRIENDS BEGIN TRAINING FOR BABYLONIAN SERVICE

The preceding context sets the stage for Daniel and his three friends, who enter a training program set up by Nebuchadnezzar. The group of Israelite captives taken in 605 BC included some "from the royal family and the nobility" (v. 3).[5] The royal family likely refers to the house of David. Nebuchadnezzar commanded Ashpenaz, "chief of his court officials" (or "eunuchs"; see KJV, ESV), to bring from this subgroup promising young men who were healthy, handsome, and intellectually gifted to be trained for three years to serve in the king's palace (vv. 4–5). The concentrated use of wisdom terminology in verse 4 ("showing aptitude for every kind of learning, well informed, quick to understand") paves the way for the theme of wisdom in the book of Daniel, including multiple contests of wisdom that will demonstrate the superior wisdom of Daniel and of the Lord.

The prophecy of Isaiah concerning temple articles being taken to Babylon (2 Kgs 20:17; Isa 39:6) also predicted that some of Hezekiah's sons (descendants of David) would become "eunuchs in the palace of the king of Babylon" (2 Kgs 20:18; Isa 39:7). Although there is some debate about whether the term *saris*, which can mean "eunuch" or "official," refers to eunuchs in Daniel 1:3, 7–11, 18 (see NIV), the close correspondence to 2 Kings 20:17–18 and Isaiah 39:6–7 suggests the essential fulfillment of Isaiah's prophecy.[6]

According to Daniel 1:4, the main content of this training program is "the language and literature of the Babylonians." Within the book of Daniel, the "language" of the Babylonians is Aramaic (see 2:4, NASB, ESV), but some scholars point out that the study of Babylonian literature would likely have involved additional languages (for example, Akkadian and Sumerian) as well as learning to read a cuneiform writing system.[7] Commentators agree that this training was probably not a neutral Babylonian education but was part of an attempt to produce conformity to Babylonian thought and culture. Goldingay poignantly refers to the attempt to "Babylon-ize" these promising Israelites.[8] The use of education to shape the minds of youth and control society has been repeated many times since, including in Asia today.

---

5. Cf. Shepherd, *Daniel in the Context of the Hebrew Bible*, 71.
6. For an argument against the meaning of "eunuch," see Collins, *Daniel*, 134–135.
7. Anathea E. Portier-Young, "Languages of Identity and Obligation: Daniel as Bilingual Book," *VT* 60 (2010): 108; Dale Ralph Davis, *The Message of Daniel: His Kingdom Cannot Fail*, Bible Speaks Today (Downers Grove: InterVarsity, 2013), 31; Lucas, *Daniel*, 53.
8. John Goldingay, *Daniel*, WBC (Dallas: Word, 1989), 15.

For example, though declining in enrollment and government funding, a representative North Korean school in Japan posts portraits of Kim Jong Il and Kim Il Sung, along with a map of a unified Korea with its capital as Pyongyang. Students are taught the greatness of North Korea and communism and, conversely, that the South Korean government is illegitimate.[9] Historically, communist "reeducation" was also attempted in several Asian countries.[10] University students in some places in Asia today may be required to take courses that promote philosophies that serve the government's self-interest to maintain power and control.

The reference to Babylonian language in Daniel 1:4 (see the Babylonian names listed in v. 7) also prepares the reader for the bilingual nature of the book, which is written in Hebrew (1–2:3; 8–12) and Aramaic (2:4–7:28). Additional foreign words from Persian, Akkadian, and Greek increase the multilingual flavor of the book.[11] This multilingual environment and exilic context is unique to Daniel in the biblical canon. Many Asian countries are highly multilingual, such as India, the Philippines, Indonesia, Malaysia, and Singapore, and multilingual people may be especially able to relate to the dynamics of multilingualism in the book of Daniel.

For the Israelite young men in training, the king provides "food and wine from the king's table" (v. 5). While presumably of high quality, these provisions create conflict for Daniel (see v. 8 below). Daniel and his three friends, Hananiah, Mishael, and Azariah, are explicitly mentioned for the first time in verse 6 as being among the group of trainees. Yet as soon as their names are listed, verse 7 describes how their Hebrew names are changed by the chief official to Babylonian ones: Belteshazzar, Shadrach, Meshach, and Abednego, respectively. Each of these Hebrew and Babylonian names have their own meaning. The Hebrew names bear witness to Yahweh (Daniel = "God is my judge"; Hananiah = "Yahweh is gracious"; Mishael = "Who is what God is?";

---

9. Esteban Flores, "Indoctrination or Education? Inside North Korean Schools in Japan," *Harvard International Review* 39, no. 1 (2018): 9–12.
10. Hoang Minh Vu, "Recycling Violence: The Theory and Practice of Reeducation Camps in Postwar Vietnam," in *Experiments with Marxism-Leninism in Cold War Southeast Asia*, ed. Matthew Galway and Marc Opper (Canberra: ANU, 2022), 219–238; Thomas Clayton, "Building the New Cambodia: Educational Destruction and Construction under the Khmer Rouge, 1975–1979," *History of Education Quarterly* 38 (1998): 1–16.
11. Cf. Collins, *Daniel*, 18–20; Portier-Young, "Daniel as Bilingual Book," 108; Benjamin Noonan, "Daniel's Greek Loanwords in Dialectal Perspective," *BBR* 28 (2018): 575–603; Benjamin Suchard, "The Greek in Daniel 3: Code-Switching, Not Loanwords," *JBL* 141 (2022): 121–136.

Azariah = "Yahweh helps"), whereas the Babylonian names refer to other gods (Belteshazzar = "Bel, protect his life"; Shadrach and Meshach are uncertain; Abednego = "servant of Nabu").[12] The pressure to conform to Babylonian culture not only includes their new environment and training program, but also the additional pressure on their Israelite identity as worshipers of Yahweh through masking this identity with Babylonian names. (For more on these names, see "What's in a Name?" below.)[13]

Whether Babylonian education, Babylonian food, or Babylonian names, there is intense pressure on the Israelite captives to assimilate wholesale to their new environment. Rotohka highlights the pressures of assimilation on South Asian Christians, who often need to secure employment but want to avoid participating in rampant corruption.[14] We should also recognize that not all acts of assimilation are morally equivalent, since Daniel 1:8 shows Daniel refusing to defile himself with royal food, but neither rejecting outright his Babylonian name nor his Babylonian education (see discussion on 1:17, 20 below).

---

12. Collins, *Daniel*, 140–141; Goldingay, *Daniel*, 5, 17–18; Portier-Young, "Daniel as Bilingual Book," 108–109.
13. To give a modern example, Tariq Aziz, a Chaldean Catholic with a Christian name (Mikhail Yuhanna, or "Michael John"), "adopted his Muslim-sounding name to avoid offending more rigid Arab counterparts." See Philip Jenkins, *The Lost History of Christianity: The Thousand-Year Golden Age of the Church in the Middle East, Africa, and Asia – and How It Died* (New York: HarperOne, 2008), 169.
14. Angukali Rotohka, "Daniel," in *South Asia Bible Commentary*, ed. Brian Wintle (Grand Rapids: Zondervan, 2015), 1085.

WHAT'S IN A NAME?

As noted above, Daniel and his three friends' names are changed from Hebrew names that are reminders of the true God, Yahweh, to Babylonian names that reference Babylonian gods. Whereas Daniel's Hebrew name continues to be used frequently throughout the book of Daniel, his Babylonian name, "Belteshazzar," reappears several times, always in connection with Nebuchadnezzar, who calls him by this name (Dan 4:9, 18–19; 5:12; cf. 2:26; 4:8). After Babylon falls to the Medes and Persians in Daniel 5, the name "Belteshazzar" does not appear anymore. On the other hand, the author of the book of Daniel almost always refers to Daniel as "Daniel" (4:19 excepted) and usually mentions this original name whenever the alternate name, "Belteshazzar," is used. Furthermore, Daniel refers to himself as "Daniel" (e.g., 7:15, 28; 8:1, 15, 27; 9:2) and is addressed by Gabriel and other messengers as "Daniel" (9:22; 10:11–12; 12:4, 9). At the same time, there is no record of Daniel or his three friends directly protesting their Babylonian names.

The original Hebrew names of Daniel's three friends, "Hananiah," "Mishael," and "Azariah," are used a few more times in the context following Daniel 1:6–7 (vv. 11, 19; 2:17), but their Babylonian names, "Shadrach," "Meshach," and "Abednego," resurface in Daniel 2:49 and fittingly dominate Daniel 3 and their confrontation with Nebuchadnezzar, including when the author is narrating (vv. 13, 16, 19, *passim*). The idolatrous meanings of these Babylonian names and the pressure that they exert highlights the faithfulness and courage of these men in refusing to worship the golden image in Daniel 3. Despite the Babylonian names that are imposed upon Daniel, Hananiah, Mishael, and Azariah, their words and deeds testify to their unchanged core identity as exclusive worshipers of Yahweh, the God of Israel and the nations, the one true God.

Yahweh's own name also has an origin story (Exod 3:6–15), as do many biblical names. Similarly, personal names in many Asian cultures are more than labels or identifiers. My own Chinese name, *Sheng Han* (聲漢), means "sound of Han [China]" and was chosen by my paternal grandfather (see Daniel 1, "Far From Home," above).[1] In *Learning Our Names*, Asian co-authors E. David de Leon, La Thao, Sabrina Chan, and Linson Daniel tell the fascinating stories behind each of their names.[2] David de Leon explains that his Spanish surname arises from Spain's rule over the Philippines and further cites the 1849 decree that ordered Filipinos to standardize their surnames for the sake of official record keeping by selecting surnames from a catalog provided by the

Spanish government (*Catálogo Alfabético de Apellidos*).³ Outside Asia, the imposition of surnames parallels African slaves in the Americas, whose descendants often have surnames shared with the cultural and linguistic conventions of those who had enslaved them. Without direct involvement from a Western power, Suharto's suppression of Chinese Indonesians that began in the mid-1960s included legislative pressure to abandon their Chinese names.⁴

Co-author La Thao explains that her first name is not actually, "La," but the Hmong word, "Lag," meaning "sickle."⁵ This name represents the livelihood of her parents and many Hmong people as farmers, though she herself is not a farmer. Co-author Sabrina Chan explains both the meaning of her Chinese name, 思穎 (Sz-ying, "thinking well"), and the humorous origin of her English name, Sabrina, as being intended by her parents to refer to a Hong Kong restaurant called "Selena's" but was confused with the Audrey Hepburn movie, *Sabrina*.⁶ Co-author Linson Daniel describes how his Indian immigrant parents chose his first name from a phone book and how his last name used to be "Thomas" (his father's first name, according to the customs of his parents' region), but was changed to "Daniel" to match his father's last name and the practice of their new environment.⁷

Unlike the biblical Daniel and his three friends, the names of these four co-authors are not overt reminders of Yahweh, but indicators of personal identity, family history, and cultural background. Yet what shines through Daniel and his friends back then and through the global church in its glorious diversity today is the culturally embodied, core identity that we uphold as brothers and sisters in Christ and as children of the living God (Hos 1:10; Rom 9:26), who all have the hope of being given yet another "new name" (Isa 62:2; Rev 2:17; 3:12).

---

1. My brother's Chinese name, *Sheng Yang* (聲洋), means "sound of the ocean [foreign]") and was chosen by my mother to match my Chinese name.
2. Sabrina S. Chan, Linson Daniel, E. David de Leon, La Thao, *Learning Our Names: Asian American Christians on Identity, Relationships, and Vocation* (Downers Grove: InterVarsity, 2022), 4, 12–18.
3. See https://issuu.com/filipinasheritagelibrary/docs/catalogo_alfabetico_de_apellidos?e=18015266/13622223.
4. Benjamin Bailey and Sunny Lie, "The Politics of Names among Chinese Indonesians in Java," *Journal of Linguistic Anthropology* 23 (2013): 25–26.
5. Chan, Daniel, de Leon, Thao, *Learning Our Names*, 15.
6. Chan, Daniel, de Leon, Thao, *Learning Our Names*, 16.
7. Chan, Daniel, de Leon, Thao, *Learning Our Names*, 17.

1:8–14 DANIEL REFUSES TO DEFILE HIMSELF AND PROPOSES A TEN-DAY TRIAL PERIOD

The conflict that dominates the rest of Daniel 1 concerns the royal food and wine provided for Daniel and the other Israelite students. These provisions are mentioned in verse 5, but Daniel refuses to partake of them because he does not want to "defile himself" (Hitpael *ga'al*). Why would such eating and drinking defile Daniel? Many solutions have been proposed, with three of the most common being that the food was unclean according to the Mosaic law, the food had been offered to idols, or that partaking would have effectively pledged full allegiance to the king.[15] In my view, the verb "defile" (*ga'al*) suggests unclean food (see Mal 1:7), though the royal wine cannot be accounted for as easily. Lucas further raises the possibility that multiple factors are involved.[16] Although it is difficult to confirm whether the provisions from the king's table were offered to an idol (whereas apparently the vegetables mentioned in v. 12 were not), Daniel may have felt the need to take a stand against this instance of assimilation. Davis insightfully highlights Daniel's "setting [*sim*] on his heart" not to defile himself in verse 8 as a response and act of resistance to the chief official "setting" (*sim*) new names for Daniel and his three friends in verse 7.[17] There may also be a hint that Daniel takes this stand to exemplify his obedience to Deuteronomy 6:6: "These commandments that I give you today *are to be on your hearts*" (ital. added). In any case, Daniel's refusal reveals how he did not passively succumb to his environment but rather maintained his convictions and engaged in conflict respectfully and wisely, as will be seen below.

Daniel's refusal to partake of these royal provisions and their possible connection to idolatry relates to Paul's teaching about food sacrificed to idols in 1 Corinthians 8–10, though the Mosaic distinction between clean and unclean food is less of a consideration for Christians. In this passage, Paul explains that eating or not eating is not the primary issue, but whether eating will cause another person to stumble (1 Cor 8:4, 8–13). At the same time, believers are to "flee idolatry" (1 Cor 10:14) and avoid any fellowship with demons (1 Cor 10:19–28). To eat or not to eat continues to be an important issue for Christians in some Asian contexts. In South Asia, Finny Philip explains that food that has been offered to various gods is believed to be sacred, which can create challenges to Christians if this food (for example, sweets) is

---

15. Davis, *Message of Daniel*, 31–32.
16. Lucas, *Daniel*, 54.
17. Davis, *Message of Daniel*, 31.

later offered to them.¹⁸ Like Daniel, Christian faithfulness in some cultural contexts can involve complex questions of eating, even though we are free from Mosaic dietary laws. For Adam and Eve, it was clear what could and could not be eaten, but the answers to these questions are not always obvious for Christians today.

Yet Daniel does not merely refuse the royal food and drink but proactively seeks a solution that will respect the interests of various parties. Rather than immediately escalating the situation, he first asks the chief official for permission not to defile himself (v. 8). The biblical author subsequently makes the important point that God granted favor to Daniel before this official (v. 9). Thus God is with Daniel and is helping Daniel as he respectfully takes this stand. In the Bible and in life, finding favor in another's eyes is something that we cannot control but is still under God's control (e.g., Gen 43:14; Ruth 2:2, 10; Esth 5:1–2). House further points out that the terms translated in the NIV as "favor" (*hesed* or "steadfast love") and "compassion" (*raham*) in Daniel 1:9 appear in the classic statement of the Lord's character in Exodus 34:6–7.¹⁹ As such, these words suggest the Lord's covenant faithfulness both to Daniel and to Israel, even during the Babylonian exile.

Rather than answering Daniel harshly, the chief official explains his fear of the king, who commanded the official to serve this food and drink and who might punish or even execute the official if the Israelite youths are not well taken care of (v. 10). Kwong draws a parallel to Chinese tradition, which connects eating rich food to fatness, strength, and health (cf. v. 15).²⁰ The official's response suggests that the king's primary motive in the matter of food may not necessarily have been to "defile" Daniel and the others but to make sure they were well fed. In this tight space between the king's purposes, the official's self-preservation, and Daniel's own convictions, Daniel proposes a ten-day trial period for him and his three friends to satisfy at least temporarily the interests of all parties involved (vv. 11–14). Instead of partaking of the royal food and wine, he suggests that they eat vegetables and drink water for ten days (v. 12). After this period, he invites the guard (cf. vv. 11, 16) to compare them with those who are eating the royal meals and then make his own decision (v.

---

18. Finny Philip, "1 Corinthians," in *South Asia Bible Commentary*, ed. Brian Wintle (Grand Rapids: Zondervan, 2015), 1569.
19. House, *Daniel*, 53–54.
20. Andrew P. C. Kwong, (鄺炳釗), *Daniel*, Tien Dao Bible Commentary (Hong Kong: Tien Dao, 1989), 65.

13). The text tells us that God had already given Daniel favor before the chief official (v. 9), and by God's grace, the guard agrees to this proposal (v. 14).

There is much that can be learned from how Daniel handles this difficult situation. On the one hand, we can see his courage and faithfulness to the Lord in refusing to defile himself through the royal meals. On the other hand, we can also see his wisdom in thinking not only of his own convictions, as legitimate as they are, but also considering the interests of the chief official and the king, even if these interests are not as noble as his. Daniel's wisdom here is thus intertwined with patience, humility, faith, creative thinking, and love. At the same time, it is not as though Daniel himself deserves all the credit because it is God who has given him favor before the official (v. 9). The subsequent context further shows that God blesses Daniel's proposal (1:15) and that Daniel's wisdom comes from God (1:17; 2:27–30). Not every difficult situation that we encounter will necessarily be resolved smoothly (see Daniel 3), but our faithfulness and pursuit of wisdom is seen by God and stands as a valuable testimony to those around us.

1:15–21 DANIEL AND HIS THREE FRIENDS SUCCEED AND ARE RECOGNIZED

After the ten-day trial period of a diet of only vegetables and water, the physical appearance and health of Daniel and his three friends is superior to the other Israelite youths (v. 15), and so the guard changes the diet of the whole group to vegetables and water (v. 16). Although the text does not explicitly say so, the Lord evidently blessed Daniel's conviction not to defile himself and his creative proposal to abstain from certain foods. Based on Daniel's three-week fast from "choice food," including "meat and wine," later in the book (see Dan 10:3), he probably did partake of these things on other occasions and hence was not a vegetarian. This further suggests that the vegetarian diet he proposes in verse 12 is not for health reasons and that the health and strength of Daniel and his three friends after ten days is the work of God.[21]

Related to the original objective of the training program to learn "the language and literature of the Babylonians" (v. 4), Daniel 1:17 declares that "God gave" the four of them "knowledge and understanding of all kinds of literature and learning." Whereas achieving success in their studies is likely a familiar concept to Christian students, it is still surprising that God gives

---

21. Kwong, *Daniel*, 66; House, *Daniel*, 55.

them the wisdom to understand "*all kinds* of literature [or books],"[22] which likely includes pagan works. Apparently, there is nothing inherently wrong with learning this kind of material. Despite the content and Nebuchadnezzar's possible ulterior motives, Lucas explains, "Learning about a culture . . . is not the same thing as assimilating to it but is the essential basis for a critical involvement in it."[23]

This passage has significant implications for the value of learning about other cultures, religions, and even "all kinds of literature and learning" (v. 17). Daniel and his three friends do not reject their program of study as evil or a waste of time. Instead, God blesses the efforts of these four Israelites to learn Babylonian material, suggesting that even this learning has value. Certainly, the Bible is our supreme authority and teaches us to learn it first and foremost (Josh 1:8; Ps 1:2), but this does not dismiss other kinds of learning.[24] Indeed, the terminology related to teaching or learning (*lamad*), wisdom (*hokmah*), and books (*sefer*) in Daniel 1:4, 17 in reference to Babylonian learning also appears in Deuteronomy in reference to Scripture (e.g., Deut 4:5–6; 6:1; 11:19; 17:18; 31:24, 26). Evidently, God can be involved with both biblical and Babylonian learning. This befits the all-knowing and gracious God. Though Daniel and his three friends are identified as having natural talent (v. 4), God gives them additional "knowledge and understanding" (v. 17). Of course, their natural talent is also a gift from God. In Daniel's case, he is also given the ability to understand "visions and dreams of all kinds" (v. 19), which will prove important in the rest of the book.

After Daniel, Hananiah, Mishael, and Azariah complete their training, the chief official presents them to Nebuchadnezzar (v. 18), who finds them to be outstanding, not only among their peers (v. 19), but even "ten times better than all the magicians and enchanters in his whole kingdom" (v. 20). Despite the attempt to "Babylon-ize" them, there remains something special about these four Israelites – an additional source of wisdom that surpasses Babylonian wisdom. Nebuchadnezzar may not understand the source of this wisdom, but he will hear a testimony from Daniel in the next chapter about the Lord's perfect wisdom (2:27–28).

---

22. Italics added.
23. Lucas, *Daniel*, 58.
24. In Christian higher education, these principles relate to what has been called "the integration of faith and learning." See David Dockery, *Renewing Minds: Serving Church and Society through Christian Higher Education*, rev. ed. (Nashville: B&H Academic, 2008).

Daniel 1 thus introduces us to Israelite life in Babylonian exile, far from home, through the experiences of Daniel, Hananiah, Mishael, and Azariah. As promising Israelite youths, they are enrolled in a Babylonian training program and face pressures from many sides. Though they do not openly protest their Babylonian names and seem to pursue their studies with diligence, Daniel leads them to avoid defiling themselves by partaking of the royal meals.[25] With God's help, Daniel's considerate and creative solution succeeds, and the four of them enter the king's service with honor. The Lord's faithfulness to Daniel is further revealed by the historical note that Daniel remained "until the first year of King Cyrus" (v. 21), thus outlasting the proud Babylonian empire. Believers living in difficult environments today also have the assurance of the Lord's faithfulness and everlasting kingdom.

---

25. "[T]he point at which those who want to remain faithful to God have to draw a line if there is to be both involvement and effective confrontation will differ from culture to culture, and even from situation to situation within a culture." Lucas, *Daniel*, 59.

DANIEL 2

THE KINGDOM OF THE LAST DAYS

World history has seen several kingdoms that have lasted for centuries and sometimes over a millennium, such as the Roman Empire. Various regions of Asia have had many kingdoms that were centuries long, which are too many to list here. Yet history also reveals that most of these kingdoms no longer exist today. In other words, despite their impressive longevity, they were not eternal. This historical reality suggests that each of the "kingdoms" of the world today, even the most powerful ones, will come to an end. Yet it is one thing for an average person to accept this and quite another for political leaders, particularly if they have delusions of grandeur about themselves and their rule. For example, the radical leader of the Taiping Rebellion (1850–1864), Hong Xiuquan (洪秀全), believed that his destruction of idols and demons in China would establish a utopian peace (*taiping* [太平]).[1]

In Daniel 2, the Babylonian "king of kings" (v. 37), Nebuchadnezzar, has a dream that he wants to have interpreted (vv. 1–3) but without revealing the content of the dream to his wise men (vv. 4–11). Angry at their objection that this is impossible, he issues a command for all of them to be executed, including Daniel, who asks for time to pray with his three friends for divine revelation (vv. 12–23). Their prayer is answered by God, and Daniel goes before Nebuchadnezzar to describe the dream (vv. 24–35) and interpret it (vv. 36–45). As Daniel explains, the dream is about "what will be in the last days" (v. 28, author's translation), namely, "a kingdom that will never be destroyed . . . [and] will itself endure forever" (v. 44). Nebuchadnezzar then elevates Daniel and honors his God as a "Lord of kings" and a "revealer of mysteries" (vv. 46–49).

2:1–3 NEBUCHADNEZZAR HAS A DISTURBING DREAM

The setting for Daniel 2 is that Nebuchadnezzar has troubling "dreams" (v. 1; note singular "dream" in v. 3, and for the rest of the chapter), which he wants

---

1. Carl Kilcourse, *Taiping Theology: The Localization of Christianity in China, 1843–64* (New York: Palgrave Macmillan, 2016), 68–72. For other examples of utopian political visions, see Ambrose Mong, *A Better World is Possible: An Exploration of Western and Eastern Utopian Visions* (Cambridge: James Clarke & Co, 2018), 1–2, including note 3.

to have interpreted (v. 3).[2] As a pagan king, his "wise men" (vv. 12–14) consist of "magicians, enchanters, sorcerers, and astrologers" (v. 2; cf. vv. 10, 27; 1:20).[3] Kwong argues that they are relying on evil spirits and draws a broad parallel to Chinese business owners today, who consult *feng shui* experts when moving their offices to a new location.[4] Nebuchadnezzar's actions recall Pharaoh's "wise men," "sorcerers," and "magicians," who tried to match the miracles performed by Moses and Aaron (Exod 7:11; cf. 8:14–15).

There is an even more striking correspondence to an earlier Pharaoh in Joseph's day, who calls all his "magicians" and "wise men" after he has a "dream" (Gen 41:1) because his "spirit" (Heb.) is "troubled" (Gen 41:8) – just like Nebuchadnezzar's (Dan 2:1, 3). In another parallel between these stories, Daniel is identified as a foreign Israelite (Dan 2:25, "a man from among the exiles from Judah"), and Joseph is identified as a foreign "young Hebrew" (Gen 41:12). Indeed, scholars have pointed out numerous parallels between Daniel and Joseph in these two passages, with some seeing Daniel 2 as dependent on Genesis 41.[5] Widder sees both texts as showing God's sovereignty over all nations, the use of symbolic dreams to communicate effectively with Gentile kings, and the preparation of an interpreter from among God's own people.[6] Joseph's dreams of rule (Gen 37:5–10) contrast with Daniel's interpretation of Nebuchadnezzar's dream, which envisions the end of Nebuchadnezzar's rule and all other human kingdoms (Dan 2:39, 44).

Just as God "was with Joseph" in Egypt (Gen 39:2, 23), he did not abandon Daniel or the Israelites while they were captives in Babylon. Despite Israel's many years of rebellion against God's ways, which resulted in exile, God is continuing to work among them in this foreign land, raising up Daniel to reveal the future to the powerful Nebuchadnezzar. We can be encouraged that

---

2. Lucas believes that the use of the plural "is probably idiomatic." Lucas, *Daniel*, 69. Regarding the timing of these dreams in the "second year" of Nebuchadnezzar's reign, see House, *Daniel*, 59–60. After explaining the chronological difficulty of relating this to the three-year training of Daniel (1:5), House holds that Daniel was still in training when it happened.
3. Deuteronomy 18:10–12 strongly forbids such involvement with dark spiritual power.
4. Kwong (鄺炳釗), *Daniel*, 99. Kwong also mentions heads of state consulting shamans when seeking a successor.
5. Matthias Henze, "The Use of Scripture in the Book of Daniel," in *A Companion to Biblical Interpretation in Early Judaism*, ed. Matthias Henze (Grand Rapids: Eerdmans, 2012), 282–286; Matthew Rindge, "Jewish Identity under Foreign Rule: Daniel 2 as a Reconfiguration of Genesis 41," *JBL* 129 (2010): 85–104; Wendy Widder, "The Court Stories of Joseph (Gen 41) and Daniel (Dan 2) in Canonical Context: A Theological Paradigm for God's Work among the Nations," *OTE* 27 (2014): 1112–1128. Some detailed arguments by Rindge or Widder are unaware of certain dynamics of the Joseph narrative.
6. Widder, "Joseph (Gen 41) and Daniel (Dan 2) in Canonical Context," 1126–1127.

God can still speak to and move the leaders of the world today, for as Proverbs 21:1 (ESV) says, "The king's heart is a stream of water in the hand of the LORD; he turns it wherever he will."

> **DREAMS AND VISIONS**
>
> Nebuchadnezzar's dream in Daniel 2 is the first of many revelatory dreams and visions in the book of Daniel. Whereas a dream is experienced while sleeping, a "vision" can be experienced in a conscious or semi-conscious state and also while sleeping. Daniel refers to Nebuchadnezzar's "dream" as "*visions* that passed through your mind as you were lying in bed" (2:28, ital. added). Nebuchadnezzar likewise refers to his second "dream" as "visions that passed through my mind" (4:5; cf. v. 9, ESV). Daniel himself is given a "vision" at night that tells him what Nebuchadnezzar's first dream/vision is (2:19). Later, Daniel has a dream/vision of his own (7:1–2), which is followed by additional visions (8:1; 10:1). Oppenheim shows how the ANE attests to such visionary experiences, including for rulers such as Ashurbanipal (seventh century king of Assyria) and Nabonidus (sixth century BC king of the Babylonian Empire).[1]
>
> Dreams and visions also feature prominently in some key passages elsewhere in the Bible. The Abrahamic covenant is instituted (Gen 15:18) in connection with Abram's "vision" (Gen 15:1). The Davidic covenant is likewise called a "vision" (2 Sam 7:17; 1 Chr 17:15, ESV; Ps 89:19). Joel predicts that an outpouring of the Spirit on all flesh will result in visions: "Your sons and daughters will prophesy, your old men will dream dreams, your young men will see visions" (2:28). The apostle Peter quotes this text in his Pentecost sermon to explain why believers are speaking in languages they have never learned (Acts 2:17). Although there is no clear indication of a dream or vision at this time (Acts 2:3), several people see visions subsequently in Acts: Ananias (9:10), Paul (9:12; 16:9–10; 18:9; 23:11; 26:19; 27:23–24), Cornelius (10:3), and Peter (10:17, 19; 11:5). Keener points out that the writings of Luke in Acts (not his Gospel account), emphasize dreams and visions, as does the Gospel of Matthew (cf. Matt 1:20; 2:12–13, 19, 22; 17:9; 27:19).[2] Despite "Western academic skepticism," Keener's extensive research – which includes his own experience, along with his wife's (a Central African), as well as others he knows personally – shows the

prevalence of testimony concerning revelatory dreams and visions in the ancient world, church history, and global Christianity.[3] Muslim beliefs and testimonies about dreams are also significant in this regard.[4]

I can add my own testimony. I rarely remember my dreams when I wake up, but in the weeks leading up to the death of my doctoral advisor, Dr. John Sailhamer, I dreamed about him on four separate occasions. I had been planning to visit him, as he had been suffering from dementia for several years, and I had been traveling to visit him every year or so. Before I left for this trip, I didn't make too much of these four dreams other than that they reinforced the plan that I already had. But in retrospect, I think that they were probably serving as divine reminders to follow through with my plan to visit, which was more important than I knew.[5] Not expecting that his passing was imminent, I visited him on New Year's Day, January 1, 2017. Eight days later, he was gone.

Though there are many testimonies that highlight the significance of revelatory dreams, there are probably just as many if not more accounts of seemingly revelatory dreams and visions that ultimately misled and even harmed those who followed them. The aforementioned leader of the Taiping Rebellion, Hong Xiuquan (see the introduction to this chapter), had strange visions in the mental and emotional aftermath of failing his civil service examinations for the third time in 1837. He later claimed that these visions involved being taken to heaven by angels, meeting God the Father and Jesus there, and being given a seal and a sword to drive out demons from heaven and destroy them on earth.[6] The so-called "female Christ" (女基督) of the Chinese cult Eastern Lightning (or, Church of the Almighty God) similarly failed her university entrance exam, had a mental breakdown, and experienced visions.[7] Though without the same negative impact, the famed Chinese evangelist John Sung had strange visions leading up to and during his asylum stay while a student at the Union Theological Seminary.[8]

Whereas the supreme, normative authority of Scripture should always be maintained, both the OT and NT seem to assume the possibility of revelatory dreams and visions (see above) while warning against deceptive ones (Deut 13:1–5; Zech 10:2; Jude 1:8). In Jeremiah 23, the Lord calls the "false dreams" (v. 32) of the false prophets of Jeremiah's day "delusions of their own minds" (v. 26), which he distinguishes from his powerful word (vv. 28–29). In some cases, there may even be demonic influences involved (1 Tim 4:1; cf. Jer 14:14; Ezek 12:24).

Thus Christians must always rely on the Bible as our highest authority for Christian faith and conduct and test everything by it, including dreams and visions. As will be seen below, not every element of Nebuchadnezzar's dream in Daniel 2 has a biblical parallel, but it is still best interpreted in light of extant Scripture (e.g., 2 Sam 7:12–13, 16; Isa 2:2–4; 28:16).

---

1. Adolf Leo Oppenheim, "The Interpretation of Dreams in the Ancient Near East. With a Translation of an Assyrian Dream-Book," *Transactions of the American Philosophical Society* 46 (1956): 249–250.
2. Craig Keener, *Miracles: The Credibility of the New Testament Accounts*, vol. 2 (Grand Rapids: Baker, 2011), 874.
3. Keener, *Miracles*, 870–884.
4. See Nabeel Qureshi, *Seeking Allah, Finding Jesus: A Devout Muslim Encounters Christianity* (Grand Rapids: Zondervan, 2016). Qureshi gives an account of his father's dreams (65–67) and describes the vision and three dreams of his own that led to his conversion (256–273).
5. Keener discusses the role of retrospect in certain cases. Keener, *Miracles*, 880–882.
6. Kilcourse, *Taiping Theology*, 46–49. For other revolts led by those who failed these exams, see Ichisada Miyazaki, *China's Examination Hell: The Civil Service Examinations of Imperial China*, trans. Conrad Schirokauer (New Haven: Yale University, 1981), 121–124.
7. William Bennett, "Where did Eastern Lightning's Leaders Come From?," 2 April, 2014, *China Source*, https://www.chinasource.org/resource-library/articles/where-did-eastern-lightnings-leaders-come-from/. See Emily Dunn, *Lightning from the East* (Leiden: Brill, 2014), 69, 71. On pages 87–88, she discusses the similarities and differences to Hong Xiuquan.
8. Daryl Ireland, *John Song: Modern Chinese Christianity and the Making of a New Man* (Waco: Baylor, 2020), 17–31. Based on groundbreaking research on Sung's student records at the Union Theological Seminary and his previously inaccessible diaries (2–3), Ireland shows that this experience was later re-framed in terms of the fundamentalist-modernist controversy of that time and a personal spiritual awakening unrelated to mental instability (33–50). Certainly, the strange visions and experiences Sung recorded in his diary (17–25) are very different from the gospel-focused, fundamentalist-friendly ones supposedly from the same time recounted in his public testimony (47–48). Note how continents and countries both morph into parts of a human body in two visions (17–18 and 48), but in different ways. Compare 宋尚節 (John Sung), 我的見證 (My Testimony), rev. ed. (Hong Kong: Hong Dao, 1975), 86–89.

2:4–11 NEBUCHADNEZZAR DEMANDS THAT HIS WISE MEN INTERPRET HIS DREAM WITHOUT TELLING IT TO THEM

Although not evident in the NIV, the Hebrew text says that the astrologers answered, "in Aramaic" (v. 4a, NASB, ESV). This linguistic detail serves as a transition to the Aramaic portion of Daniel (2:4b–7:28), which extends beyond what the astrologers say here.

This section of Daniel is the longest Aramaic passage in the Bible (cf. Jer 10:11; Ezra 4:8–6:18; 7:12–26), and its presence marks the book of Daniel as a bilingual book, with roughly equal parts in Hebrew and Aramaic. The use of Aramaic (a lingua franca) by Babylonians further heightens the multilingual setting of the book of Daniel (cf. "the language and literature of the Babylonians," 1:4).[7] Several scholars have emphasized the association of Hebrew with Israel and Aramaic with empire. Portier-Young further explains that the Aramaic in Daniel "evok[es] a history of imperial rule, a complex colonial identity, and the interweaving of Judean (and Jewish) life within the world of empire."[8] She sees the sequence of Hebrew (Daniel 1), Aramaic (Daniel 2–7), Hebrew (Daniel 8–12) in the book of Daniel as serving a rhetorical function by providing a link to the covenant and Israel's past (Daniel 1), depicting exilic life under imperial authority (Daniel 2–6), marking the end of this authority (Daniel 7), and entering a time of a reorientation "in which the claims of empire had dissolved and claims of covenant alone remained" (Daniel 8–12).[9] The placement of the bilingual book of Daniel along with the bilingual Ezra-Nehemiah at the end of the Hebrew Bible not only reflects the historical realities of exile, but also concludes the Hebrew Bible with a linguistic diversification that harmonizes with the worldwide scope of its message. This placement also paves the way for the Greek New Testament.

Hebrew was the mother tongue of the exiles, but Daniel also speaks Aramaic (2:15, 24) and even praises God in Aramaic (2:20–23), offering a foretaste of "all peoples, nations, and *languages*" worshiping the one like a son of man (7:13–14, ESV, ital. added). This eschatological hope is especially inspiring in view of the staggering linguistic diversity of Asia, which includes countries such as Indonesia and India, where hundreds of living languages

---

7. Collins further points out that this literature would have been in Akkadian. Collins, *Daniel*, 138, 156.
8. Portier-Young, "Daniel as Bilingual Book," 103. Her literature review provides examples of such scholars (100–102).
9. Portier-Young, "Daniel as Bilingual Book," 108–115.

are spoken.[10] Some readers may already know how to voice praise to God in several of these languages!

In keeping with her argument above, Portier-Young points out that the first words in the Aramaic section of Daniel support the empire: "May the king live forever!" (2:4b).[11] Though this is probably a customary address used by the astrologers (3:9; 5:10; 6:7, 22), it is also mixed with pretense regarding Nebuchadnezzar and his longevity, a pretense which Daniel "will relativize, even refute . . . in the same language [Aramaic]."[12] Similarly, Goldingay remarks, "There is an irony about the standard courtly greeting," since "the only lasting name and the only lasting reign is the name of God and the reign of God" (2:20, 44).[13]

The astrologers' initial response to Nebuchadnezzar is simple enough, "Tell your servants the dream, and we will interpret it" (2:4). Yet Nebuchadnezzar demands that they tell him "the dream and its interpretation" (vv. 5–6, ESV). If they fail, they will be executed and their houses destroyed. But if they succeed, they will receive gifts and great honor (vv. 5–6). Once again, the astrologers ask Nebuchadnezzar to inform them what his dream is (v. 7; cf. v. 4). Nebuchadnezzar accuses them of stalling ("to gain time") and insists that they tell him what his dream was (vv. 8–9). He suspects that they might conspire to lie about the interpretation, but if they can miraculously describe his dream, he is confident that their interpretation will be reliable (v. 9).

House further points out that the Aramaic phrase translated, "until the times change" (v. 9; cf. ESV; NIV, "hoping the situation will change") should not be equated with a mere delay (as in v. 8), because God "chang[ing] times" (v. 21) involves changing kings.[14] The terms of "change" (*shenah*) and "time" (*'idan*) are notably identical in verses 9 and 21. House also refers to the "king's nervousness."[15] Rotohka further suggests that Nebuchadnezzar may have wondered whether his dream of a statue being shattered was a warning about a

---

10. For Indonesia, see https://www.ethnologue.com/country/ID/; for India, see https://www.ethnologue.com/country/IN/. Both pages are part of SIL's extensive "Ethnologue" website.
11. Portier-Young, "Daniel as Bilingual Book," 110–111.
12. Portier-Young, "Daniel as Bilingual Book," 111.
13. Goldingay, *Daniel*, 53.
14. House, *Daniel*, 62–63.
15. House, *Daniel*, 62.

plot against his life, and he may have suspected that his wise men would only give "their best guess from their manuals" of dream interpretation.[16]

Seow insightfully highlights the theme of time, whether Nebuchadnezzar's inability to "live forever" (2:4), the astrologers' futile attempt to buy time and manipulate time (2:8–9), Daniel's successful request for time (2:16), or God's transcendence and sovereignty over time.[17] Time-related terminology is prominent in Daniel 2 as well as the rest of the book.[18] From an eternal perspective, time is always on God's side, never the side of human kingdoms and their rulers. For this reason, time is ultimately on the side of believers, even when we have to endure much hardship.

In any case, just as Nebuchadnezzar revealed his reasons in verse 9, the astrologers reveal theirs in verses 10–11. From their perspective, what the king asks is impossible. No "man on earth" (Aramaic) can do it, and no king has ever asked for such a thing (v. 10). Moreover, it is "too difficult," and only the "gods" know, but they are far removed from human beings (v. 11). The astrologers are speaking from their pagan worldview and do not know that the God of heaven can and will reveal the secret of Nebuchadnezzar's dream to Daniel, for nothing is too difficult for him (Gen 18:14).

2:12–23 NEBUCHADNEZZAR ORDERS THE EXECUTION OF ALL WISE MEN, AND DANIEL ASKS FOR TIME

The astrologers' objection that the king's request is unreasonable makes Nebuchadnezzar so angry that he issues a command for all the wise men to be executed (v. 12), including Daniel and his three friends (v. 13).

Should this threat to their lives be regarded as persecution, as understood today? The book of Daniel has clear examples of persecution (3:8–12; 6:4–8), but this instance is not one of them because it is not specifically targeted at Daniel, his friends, and their faith, but rather because they are members of the "wise men of Babylon" (2:12). Most of these "wise men" are not worshipers of Yahweh. A modern parallel can be drawn to draconian COVID lockdowns,

---

[16]. Rotohka, "Daniel," 1091. Louis Hartman and Alexander Di Lella refers to their "dream books." Cf. Louis Hartman and Alexander Di Lella, *The Book of Daniel*, Anchor Bible (Garden City: Doubleday, 1978), 144.

[17]. C. L. Seow, "From Mountain to Mountain: The Reign of God in Daniel 2," in *A God So Near: Essays on Old Testament Theology in Honor of Patrick D. Miller*, ed. Brent Strawn and Nancy Bowen (Winona Lake: Eisenbrauns, 2003), 361 (including note 20), 363.

[18]. E.g. *'idan*, verses 8–9, 21; 3:5; 4:16; 7:25; *zeman*, verses 16, 21; 3:7; 4:36; 6:10; 7:12; *'alam*, verses 4, 20, 44; 4:3, 34; 6:27; 7:14. For various Hebrew terms in Daniel 8–12, see 8:14, 17, 19, 26; 9:2, 24–27; 10:14; 11:29, 35; 12:1, 4.

which affected everyone, as long as Christians or other groups were not unfairly targeted. Of course, from the perspective of those suffering, it may not matter much if an order or act is considered to be a form of persecution if the end result is the same. What is consistent in Daniel is the faithful's endurance of suffering, which arises for varied reasons.[19]

Daniel responds to the king's threat with "wisdom and tact" (2:14; cf. 1:17, 20), just as he did earlier regarding the royal food (1:8–13). Rather than reacting impulsively, he gathers information (2:15) and then asks for time to interpret the king's dream (v. 16). He knows that he needs a miracle, and so he calls his three friends together to pray that God will give him revelation so that their lives will be spared (vv. 17–18). Their plea for God's "mercy" continues the theme of mercy, which first appeared in 1:9 when God gave Daniel "steadfast love" and "mercy" (Heb.) before the chief official. The early church also prayed together, especially for important matters (Acts 4:24–31; 12:5, 12; 13:1–3), and so should we today.

The prayers of Daniel and his friends are answered when God reveals the "mystery" of the king's dream to Daniel in a vision at night (Dan 2:19). The repetition of the term "mystery" characterizes Daniel 2 (vv. 18–19, 27–30, 47), which only appears once elsewhere in the book (4:9). The title "God of heaven" (vv. 18–19, 37, 44) emphasizes God's transcendence and sovereignty over earth, humanity, and earthly kingdoms (vv. 10–11, 28, 35, 39; 4:34–35).[20] This title does not appear elsewhere in Daniel, but it appears frequently in Ezra-Nehemiah (Ezra 1:2; 5:11–12; Neh 1:4–5; 2:4, 20; cf. 2 Chr 36:23).

Even before we learn about the content of the king's dream, Daniel's prayer explains its main point: God is to be praised as the all-wise and all-powerful One, who rules over all human kings, reveals secrets (e.g., Nebuchadnezzar's dream and its meaning; cf. Deut 29:29; Isa 48:6), and answers the prayers of his people (Dan 2:20–23). God has "wisdom and power" (v. 20; cf. Job 12:13) that surpasses Nebuchadnezzar's power as well as the astrologers' wisdom, and he has given this wisdom and power to Daniel (2:23).[21] In this part of the narrative, wisdom from God came as a direct revelation, apart from study

---

19. If the royal meals that would have defiled Daniel in 1:8 were not intended to defile him but nourish him as best the Babylonians knew how (1:10), then the royal training program, though it certainly involved heavy pressure, may not have been persecution in this proper sense either.
20. For its relationship to a Phoenician title and diachronic considerations, see James A. Montgomery, *Daniel*, International Critical Commentary (Edinburgh: T&T Clark, 1927), 158.
21. Seow, "Reign of God in Daniel 2," 363.

(cf. 1:4, 17). The exalted "God of heaven" (2:18–19) is also the "God of my fathers" (v. 23, ESV), who is faithful to his covenant with Israel.

Montgomery calls this prayer "entirely to the point of the story," which manifests in human history God's knowledge and "sovereign determination of all political changes."[22] Going further, Hartman and Di Lella argue that this poetic prayer "strikes the keynote of the whole Book of Daniel, that Yahweh is truly the Lord and Master of human history."[23] There will be important prophetic details to come, but this major theme can keep us centered in our study of Daniel. Even when there are exegetical difficulties that we cannot fully resolve, we can be assured that the God of glory "knows what lies in darkness" (2:22).

Collins observes that Daniel 2:20–23 comprises the first of four poems in Daniel 1–6 (the remaining three poems appear in 4:1–3, 34–35, and 6:26–28).[24] Segert's list of Aramaic poetry in Daniel 2–7 omits 4:1–2 and 6:26, but includes 4:10–12, 14–17 (the tree vision), as well as 7:9–10, 13–14, 23–27.[25] Segert further lists 8:23–26, 9:24–27, and 12:1–3 as poetry in the Hebrew part of Daniel.[26] Most, if not all, of these poems are placed at key positions in the narrative and emphasize God's power and everlasting kingdom or, as Segert puts it, "the relevance of religious messages in the visions."[27] The use of poems in narrative for strategic theological purposes is found throughout the OT, from the Pentateuch onwards (Gen 49:1–27; the poems in Numbers 23–24; Judges 5).[28] Aspects of Daniel's doxology in Daniel 2:20–23 even resemble the content of some of these strategic poems (e.g., Exod 15:1–18; Deut 32:1–43; 1 Sam 2:1–10). For example, the celebration of the Lord's "strength" (Exod 15:2, 13; cf. Dan 2:20, 23) in the Song of the Sea concludes, "The LORD reigns forever and ever" (Exod 15:18; cf. Dan 2:21). In Exodus 15:6, his "right hand . . . shattered the enemy" further parallels how the statue

---

22. Montgomery, *Daniel*, 157.
23. Hartman and Di Lella, *The Book of Daniel*, 145.
24. Collins, *Daniel*, 160.
25. Stanislav Segert, "Aramaic Poetry in the Old Testament," *Archív Orientální* 70 (2002): 67. He follows Baumgartner's work on Daniel for the *BHS*, which formats poetry differently from prose.
26. Segert, "Aramaic Poetry in the Old Testament," 69. Cf. G. T. M. Prinsloo, "Two Poems in a Sea of Prose: The Content and Context of Daniel 2.20–23 and 6.27–28," *JSOT* 59 (1993): 93, including note 2.
27. Segert, "Aramaic Poetry in the Old Testament," 77.
28. John Sailhamer, *The Pentateuch as Narrative* (Grand Rapids: Zondervan, 1992), 35–37; John Sailhamer, *The Meaning of the Pentateuch* (Downers Grove: InterVarsity, 2009), 36, 306, 321.

is shattered in Daniel 2:34–35, 44–45. The participial constructions describing divine action in Daniel 2:21–22 ("He changes times"; "he deposes kings and raises up others") follow the syntax and theology of 1 Samuel 2:6–7 ("The LORD brings death and makes alive . . . he humbles and he exalts"). This is itself dependent on Deuteronomy 32:39 ("I myself am he! . . . I put to death and I bring to life, I have wounded and I will heal"). The truth behind "as surely as I live forever" in Deuteronomy 32:40 is assumed in the declaration that the Lord sets up and removes kings in Daniel 2:21 and contrasts with the aforementioned courtly address in Daniel 2:4. Like Nebuchadnezzar's dream (v. 28), these three poems also have an eschatological thrust (Exod 15:17–18; Deut 32:41–43; 1 Sam 2:10).

2:24–35 DANIEL DECLARES TO NEBUCHADNEZZAR HIS DREAM ABOUT THE LAST DAYS

After the thematizing doxological poem in verses 20–23, the plot continues with Daniel calling for a stop to the execution of the wise men because he can interpret the king's dream (Dan 2:24). The official Arioch mentions Daniel's foreign identity as one of "the exiles from Judah" (v. 25), which distinguishes him from the Babylonian astrologers who failed Nebuchadnezzar earlier (vv. 10–12; cf. Joseph in Gen 41:12). As a member of a conquered people, Daniel's "wisdom and power" (v. 23) also disrupt the presumed power dynamic of Babylon over Israel. The mention of Daniel's Babylonian name, Belteshazzar (v. 26), links back to Daniel 1:7 and accordingly serves as a reminder of Daniel's status as a foreign captive.[29] The king's question about whether Daniel can do what he asks (2:26) not only distinguishes him from the other wise men (v. 27), but more importantly highlights the greatness of the "God in heaven," whom Daniel knows and "who reveals mysteries" (v. 28). This "God of heaven" (vv. 18–19, 37, 44) is the God of Israel, the God of Daniel's fathers (v. 23), the God of the temple in Jerusalem, who transcends the fallen temple that Nebuchadnezzar conquered (1:1–2).

While Daniel's poetic prayer highlights God's greatness (2:20–23), the narrative portion is concerned with "what will happen in the last days" (v. 28, author's translation).[30] With this phrase, Daniel provides another link to

---

29. Rotohka, "Daniel," 1091.
30. Cf. Hartman and Di Lella, *The Book of Daniel*, 146. The meaning of this phrase has become disputed, but there remains significant support for taking it in the traditional sense (see LXX, KJV, JPS). For detailed treatments, see Kevin Chen, *The Messianic Vision of the Pentateuch* (Downers Grove: InterVarsity, 2019), 109–114; Stephen Dempster, "'At the End of the Days'

the strategic poems in the Pentateuch. The poem in Genesis 49:1–27 likewise concerns "what will happen to you [Israel] in the last days" (v. 1, author's translation). The poem in Numbers 24:15–19 is about "what this people [Israel] will do to your people [Moab] in the last days" (Num 24:14, author's translation). The poem in Deuteronomy 32:1–43 is about "the disaster that will happen to you in the last days" (Deut 31:29, author's translation). The Lord's eschatological defeat of the nations in the latter two poems (Num 24:8; 17–19; Deut 32:40–43; cf., Gen 49:10; Exod 15:6–7, 14–16) is even the focus of Nebuchadnezzar's dream, seen from the perspective of this Gentile king. The exilic setting also matches the connection between the phrase, "in the last days," and the theme of exile in Deuteronomy 4:30; 31:29.

In addition to the four appearances of the phrase, "in the last days," in the Pentateuch (Gen 49:1; Num 24:14; Deut 4:30; 31:29), this phrase occurs ten more times in the OT, all in prophetic books (including the Aramaic equivalent in Dan 2:28). Significantly, the first appearance in Isaiah 2:2 predicts, "*In the last days* the *mountain* of the LORD's temple will be established as the highest of the mountains" (author's translation). There is also a "huge mountain" in Daniel 2:35, and together these two links strongly suggest an allusion to Isaiah 2:2–4.[31] Both visions come towards the beginning of each prophetic book, and both set the course for each book's direction and message. Additional allusions to Isaiah in Daniel will also be discussed in due course.[32] The book of Daniel's use of other OT books has been recognized by commentators.[33]

Daniel begins by describing Nebuchadnezzar's dream (2:29–35), which is what the king asked of the wise men earlier (vv. 5–6, 9). Daniel again refers to God as the "revealer of mysteries" (v. 29; cf. vv. 22, 28), emphasizing that the dream is about the future (v. 29; cf. v. 28). Though none of the other wise men could do what Daniel is about to do (v. 27), he makes it clear that his

---

(בְּאַחֲרִית הַיָּמִים) – An Eschatological Technical Term? The Intersection of Context, Linguistics and Theology," in *The Unfolding of Your Words Gives Light: Studies on Biblical Hebrew in Honor of George L. Klein*, ed. Ethan Jones (University Park: Eisenbrauns, 2018), 118–141. Also, the OG translation of Daniel 2:29, 45 have two additional mentions of "in the last days."

31. Michael Shepherd calls the mountain in Daniel 2 "remarkably reminiscent" of Isaiah 2:1–5 and sees the repetition of "in the last days" as hardly coincidental. Shepherd, *Daniel in the Context of the Hebrew Bible*, 75. Lucas believes that Daniel 2:35 "echoes" Isaiah 2:2 and Micah 4:1 and that its reference to "filling the earth" likewise "echoes" Isaiah 6:3; 11:9. Compare Lucas, *Daniel*, 74.

32. Cf. Brooke Lester, *Daniel Evokes Isaiah: Allusive Characterization of Foreign Rule in the Hebrew-Aramaic Book of Daniel* (London: T&T Clark, 2015).

33. See "Biblical Allusions in the Book of Daniel," pages 123–124.

"wisdom" does not come from himself (v. 30). In this sense, the astrologers' earlier objection in verse 10 was valid.

Daniel explains that Nebuchadnezzar's dream was of "a large statue" (v. 31) or "image" (*tselem*, Aramaic). This term appears four times in verses 31–35 and repeatedly in Daniel 3 to describe the "image of gold" that Nebuchadnezzar builds (3:1). The statue in Daniel 2 is evidently an "image" of a man (vv. 32–33).[34] This contrasts with mankind itself being made in the superior "image" (*tselem*, Heb.) of God to rule and "fill the earth" in Genesis 1:26–28 (cf. Dan 2:35, "filled the whole earth"). Humanity apart from God will never rule the earth forever, but the Son of Man and the saints will (Dan 7:13–14, 27). The NIV further describes the statue as "awesome" (*dehil*, Heb.), but a similar Aramaic term (*dehilah*) is rightly translated as "terrifying," with reference to the fearsome fourth beast in Daniel 7:7, 19.

The statue has four parts: a head of "pure gold," chest and arms of silver, belly and thighs of bronze, legs of iron, and feet of iron and clay (2:32–33). The dream is not static like a photograph, however, since a rock that is cut out "not by human hands" proceeds to strike the statue on its feet (v. 34). This live-action sequence results in the destruction of the whole statue, which becomes like chaff and is blown away (cf. Ps 1:4; Isa 17:13; 41:15–16), whereas the rock becomes a large mountain that fills the earth (Dan 2:35). We might think of famously large mountains in Asia, such as Mount Everest, K2, Mount Fuji, or others. Daniel will interpret the dream shortly, but the dream itself shows that a special rock triumphs in the end, not the mighty statue.

2:36–45 DANIEL INTERPRETS NEBUCHADNEZZAR'S DREAM

Daniel's interpretation does not begin with the details of the dream but its relevance to Nebuchadnezzar. This interpretation further affects how we view earthly rulers today. Although Nebuchadnezzar is "king of kings," the God of heaven is above him and is the one who has given him such power (vv. 37–38; cf. v. 47). Nebuchadnezzar's expansive rule, which includes animals, casts him as an Adam figure (Gen 1:26, 28).[35] Both were accountable to God, as are all rulers (Rom 13:1), and both fall far short of the creation ideal, unlike the rock that will fill the earth forever (Dan 2:35, 44).

---

34. C. F. Keil and Franz Delitzsch refer to the statue's "human form." Keil and Delitzsch, *Daniel*, Commentary on the Old Testament, vol. 9, reprinted (Peabody: Hendrickson, 1996), 555.
35. C. L. Seow, *Daniel* (Louisville: Westminster John Knox, 2003), 44–45.

As for the dream, Daniel explains to Nebuchadnezzar, "You are that head of gold" (v. 38). Just as Daniel praised God in verse 21 ("he deposes kings and raises up others"), Daniel implies that Nebuchadnezzar's kingdom will eventually come to an end: "*After you*, another kingdom will arise, inferior to yours" (v. 39, ital. added). This corresponds to the silver part of the statue (v. 32). The third kingdom is represented by bronze, which will "rule over the whole earth" (v. 39). Daniel gives no further detail about the second and third kingdoms, though subsequent passages will shed further light (e.g., Dan 8:20–21). The focus of Daniel's interpretation in Daniel 2:36–45 is not the precise identification of all four kingdoms, and postponing this discussion to the end of this section will allow us to prioritize the emphasis of the biblical text itself.

Daniel's interpretation gives by far the most attention to the fourth kingdom and the rock that triumphs over it and the entire statue (vv. 40–45). Whereas he identified the head of gold as Nebuchadnezzar/Babylon (v. 38), he did not attach any significance to gold as a material, nor to silver nor bronze (v. 39). However, Daniel here implies that iron represents strength, "for iron breaks and smashes everything . . . iron breaks things to pieces" and destroys the other materials/kingdoms (v. 40). Yet because the feet are partially made of clay, this fourth kingdom "will be a divided kingdom," which is "partly strong" and "partly brittle" (vv. 41–43).

Daniel's interpretation emphasizes the "mixing" (*'arav*, Aramaic) of iron and clay (vv. 41, 43), which recalls the "mixed multitude" (*'erev*, Heb.) of Exodus 12:38 and Nehemiah 13:3, who are distinct from Israel. Ezra 9:2 uses a similar Hebrew verb (*'arav*) with reference to Israel intermarrying with foreigners (cf. Ps 106:35). Some scholars believe that the Aramaic text translated, "the people will be a mixture," in Daniel 2:43 involves intermarriage (cf. "remain united," or "cling" [*davaq*] to one another in Gen 2:24).[36] The KJV and NASB translate this phrase in 2:43 more literally and reference this mixing to "the seed of men" (cf. Gen 6:1–4). In any case, this is not a successful union. Thus, this fourth kingdom, as powerful as it is (2:40), and this statue representing human kingdoms, as impressive and intimidating as it is, have fundamental weaknesses and instability.

---

36. E.g. Goldingay, *Daniel*, 50; Collins, *Daniel*, 170. Cf. Ray McAllister, "Clay in Nebuchadnezzar's Dream and the Genesis Creation Accounts," *Journal of the Adventist Theological Society* 18 (2007): 123.

The more detailed explanation of the fourth kingdom leads to the climax of the dream and its interpretation: God will establish an everlasting kingdom that will crush all four kingdoms, as symbolized by the rock crushing the iron, bronze, clay, silver, and gold (vv. 44–45). Thus, even though iron "breaks and smashes everything" (v. 40), this rock breaks iron and is stronger than iron. We already know from verses 34–35 that this rock strikes the feet of the statue and becomes a mountain that fills the earth. Daniel's interpretation emphasizes "the rock cut out . . . but not by human hands" (v. 45; cf. v. 34). The lack of human involvement ("hand"; cf. v. 38) implies that this cutting is an exclusively divine action, which accords with the explanation that "the God of heaven" who "raises up [*qum*] kings" (v. 21) will ultimately "raise up" (*qum*) a kingdom that will "stand [*qum*] forever" (v. 44, Aramaic). In contrast, the statue representing human kingdoms was large and terrifying but only "stood" (*qum*) temporarily (v. 31).

The main point of the triumph of God's everlasting kingdom over all earthly kingdoms is clear enough, but a closer look at the language, themes, and imagery in Daniel 2:44–45 will sharpen the picture. We have already seen above that Daniel's use of the phrase "in the last days" in verse 28 (author's translation) links the dream to previous eschatological prophecies in the OT, especially Isaiah 2:2–4, with its additional link of a gigantic mountain. In particular, God "raising up" (*qum*) a kingdom that triumphs over all other earthly kingdoms and "stands" (*qum*) forever in Daniel 2:44 (Aramaic) fits the Davidic covenant exactly. Whereas Saul's kingdom was not so "established" (*kun*, Heb.) and would not "stand" (*qum*, Heb.; 1 Sam 13:13–14), the Lord promised to "raise up" (*qum*) David's seed and "establish [*kun*] his kingdom" (2 Sam 7:12). He repeats emphatically, "I will establish [*kun*] the throne of his kingdom forever" (2 Sam 7:13), and "Your house and your kingdom will endure ['*aman*] forever before me; your throne will be established [*kun*] forever" (2 Sam 7:16; cf. 1 Chr 17:11–12, 14; Amos 9:11). Daniel's interpretation is "trustworthy" ('*aman*, Aramaic; Dan 2:45), which uses a cognate of the Hebrew term translated "endure" in 2 Samuel 7:16 (cf. Deut 32:4). This prophetic message for the monarch David is even called a "vision" (2 Sam 7:17, ESV), just as the Babylonian king's dream is referred to as "visions" (Dan 2:28). Thus, both kings received visions of the everlasting kingdom.

The rock (*even*, Aramaic) in Daniel 2:34–35 further links to Messianic texts in Isaiah 28:16 ("I lay a stone [*even*, Heb.] in Zion, a tested stone [*even*], a precious cornerstone [*pinah*] for a sure foundation; the one who relies on it ['*aman*] will never be stricken with panic") and Psalm 118:22–23 ("The stone [*even*] the builders rejected has become the cornerstone [*pinah*]; the LORD has done this"). In both passages, a stone is divinely chosen to mark an important beginning of a new order, just as it is in Daniel 2:34–35, 44–45. The striking and crushing of the statue by the stone further matches the prophecies of the Messiah doing the same to his enemies (Gen 3:15; Num 24:17; Ps 2:9).

When Daniel 2 is read first in the context of the OT and only later in the context of subsequent world history, these numerous connections strongly suggest that the kingdom symbolized by the rock-turned-mountain in Daniel 2:34–35, 44–45 is both the eschatological kingdom foretold in Isaiah 2:2–4 and the Messianic kingdom that fulfills the Davidic covenant. From the perspective of the latter, the dream can even be seen as a sort of imagistic or pictorial version of the Davidic covenant contextualized for a Gentile king. Thus, whether set in relation to other Israelite kings, such as Saul (1 Sam 13:13–14), Solomon (1 Kgs 9:4; 11:11), or Ahaz (Isa 7:9), Gentile kings like Nebuchadnezzar and the kingdoms that will "arise" (*qum*) after his (Dan 2:39), or any ruler who ascends to power today, the Messianic kingdom is the only one established by God to last forever. Although there are no explicit references to the Davidic covenant in Daniel, the reference to "one like a son of man" and his everlasting kingdom (Dan 7:13–14) supports the existence of a human ruler over this kingdom and the use of the Davidic covenant as significant background for Daniel.[37] As one who "com[es] with the clouds of heaven" (Dan 7:13), this ruler is distinguished from other human beings on earth and bridges the seemingly unbridgeable gap between humanity and God (Dan 2:10–11; cf. Gen 11:4; 28:12).

As for identifying the four kingdoms, Daniel identifies the head of gold as Nebuchadnezzar (2:38). Since the rock strikes the fourth kingdom (v. 34), and the rock represents the Messiah whose kingdom is set up "in the time of those kings" (v. 44), the traditional interpretation (which accepts the possibility of predictive prophecy) identifies the fourth kingdom as Rome, the second kingdom as Medo-Persia, and the third kingdom as Greece. Yet the continuance of the Roman Empire long after the coming of Jesus seems to conflict with rock striking the feet of the statue and the whole statue being swept away (Dan 2:34–35), and therefore Sailhamer believes that the fourth

---

37. Cf. House, *Daniel*, 131; Shepherd, *Daniel in the Context of the Hebrew Bible*, 29, 75.

kingdom represents "any human government" that wants to rule apart from dependence on God.[38]

If the four kingdoms in Daniel 7 are the same as the four kingdoms in Daniel 2, then Daniel 7 provides additional information about these kingdoms, including hints about the identities of the second and third kingdoms (7:5–6). The vision of the ram and the goat in Daniel 8 seems to be about the same two kingdoms (8:3–8), which are identified as Medo-Persia and Greece (8:20–21). We should be aware that the identities of the latter three kingdoms are contested, and these issues will be revisited in the commentary on Daniel 7–8.[39] Either way, we should keep in mind that the point of Daniel 2 is not to identify the latter three kingdoms, but rather to highlight the everlasting kingdom of God as being represented by a rock that crushes the fourth kingdom, becomes a mountain, and fills the whole earth.

Another interesting way of looking at the statue in Nebuchadnezzar's dream is to see it as another Tower of Babel. Like the tower, the statue is "large" and "stood" upright (Dan 2:31). The tower's "head" (Heb.) was intended to reach the heavens (Gen 11:4). The top of the massive statue is its gold "head" (Dan 2:32, 38), representing Nebuchadnezzar ("king of kings," Dan 2:37) and Babylon. Daewoong Kim further points out the common themes of God's transcendence ("the LORD *came down* to see," Gen 11:5; "God of heaven," Dan 2:37, 44), confusion or mixing (Gen 11:7, 9; Dan 2:41, 43), and clay and stone as materials (Gen 11:3; Dan 2:33–35, 43–45).[40] For both the tower and the statue, their glory is short-lived, and their end is divine judgment that includes scattering (Gen 11:8–9; Dan 2:35). The statue's temporary "standing" is contrasted with the eternal "standing" of God's everlasting kingdom (Dan 2:31, 39, 44). The unsuccessful attempt for the tower's "head" to reach the "heavens" (Gen 11:4, Heb.) in the broader context of Genesis contrasts with

---

38. John Sailhamer, *NIV Compact Bible Commentary* (Grand Rapids: Zondervan, 1994), 399–400.
39. Based on the similarity between the fourth beast and its small horn in Daniel 7:7–8 and the goat and the small horn in Daniel 8:8–11, some argue that the fourth kingdom is Greece. For example, Lucas, *Daniel*, 76. Wendy Widder also has a helpful chart comparing various views. Widder, *Daniel: A Discourse Analysis of the Hebrew Bible*, Zondervan Exegetical Commentary on the Old Testament (Grand Rapids: Zondervan, 2023), 115–117. Collins also holds that the fourth kingdom is Greece, but for him this involves "the chronological restraints of the Book of Daniel," including the fact that the "latest gentile sovereignty acknowledged anywhere in the book is that of the 'prince of Greece' in 10:20." Collins, *Daniel*, 166. Thus, rejection of predictive prophecy can be a contributing factor for critical scholars.
40. Daewoong Kim, "Biblical Interpretation in the Book of Daniel: Literary Allusions in Daniel to Genesis and Ezekiel" (PhD diss., Rice University, 2013), 77–79.

the "head" of the "stairway" (*sullam*; cf. *tselem*, "statue/image") in Jacob's dream, which does reach the heavens (Gen 28:12).[41] There are even two languages used in the biblical text of Daniel 2, a consequence of the original confusion of languages in Genesis 11:7, 9.

As explained in the commentary on Daniel 1:1–2, "Babel" and "Babylon" are the same words in Hebrew, so the historical kingdom of Babylon already has an inner-biblical lineage traceable to the Tower of Babel. Babel and Babylon in the Bible often represent humanity united against God, whether by building a tower (and a city, Gen 11:4–5) or an earthly kingdom. As such, Babylon is especially suitable as the head of the statue, not only as the beginning of a historical sequence, but also as representative of human kingdoms generally. Accordingly, the number four here could suggest totality (cf. Dan 1:4), as it does elsewhere, especially with reference to the physical world (e.g., Dan 7:2).[42]

2:46–49 NEBUCHADNEZZAR HONORS DANIEL

Daniel's declaration of the dream and its interpretation convinces Nebuchadnezzar, who honors Daniel lavishly (vv. 46, 48) as promised (v. 6). More importantly, Nebuchadnezzar realizes the greatness of Daniel's God, whom he calls the "God of gods" (v. 47). With Daniel's help, this Gentile "king of kings" also grasps the main point of the dream, which is that there is a "Lord of kings" above him who is a "revealer of mysteries" (v. 47; cf. vv. 28, 44). These are the very things that Daniel praises God for in verses 20–23, and this knowledge has now spread to Nebuchadnezzar.

Moreover, the particular "mystery" in Daniel 2 seems to be not only the previously undisclosed dream but also its interpretation. Throughout this passage, Nebuchadnezzar wants to know "the dream" *and* "its interpretation" (vv. 5–6, 26, ESV). The wise men refer to this double request as "the thing that the king asks" (v. 11, ESV), which Daniel later seems to lump together as "the *mystery* that the king has asked" (v. 27, ESV, ital. added). Accordingly, after Daniel explains the "dream" and "its interpretation" (v. 45), Nebuchadnezzar praises God because Daniel is "able to reveal *this mystery*" (v. 47, ital. added), without differentiating between the two. Even Daniel's earlier praise of God for

---

41. For relating the tower and the stairway, see Cornelius Houtman, "What Did Jacob See in His Dream at Bethel? Some Remarks on Genesis XXVIII 10–22," *VT* 27 (1977): 350–351.
42. Cf. Goldingay, *Daniel*, 160; Michael Kuykendall, "Numerical Symbolism in the Book of Revelation: A Weakness of Modern Bible Versions," *Themelios* 47.3 (2022): 473; Richard Bauckham characterizes its use in Revelation as "the number of the world." Bauckham, *The Climax of Prophecy* (Edinburgh: T&T Clark, 1993), 31.

revealing the "mystery" (vv. 18–19) hints that he knows both the dream and its meaning (v. 21) or interpretation. Thus this "mystery" certainly includes the dream but ultimately also the triumph of the eschatological kingdom of God. This "mystery of the kingdom" is at the heart of the message of Daniel 2, the book of Daniel, and the Bible itself (cf. Matt 13:11; Mark 4:11; Luke 8:10).

Nebuchadnezzar's words and actions in verses 46–49 are significant given the glory this Gentile king gives to God in a foreign land, though subsequent chapters reveal that it should not be equated with a conversion. Indeed, the glory of the Lord is being declared in the nations (Ps 96:3), in this case by one of their kings, as it will continue to be until it fills the whole earth (Isa 6:3).

Like Joseph, Daniel is given a prominent position of rule after interpreting the king's dream (v. 48; Gen 41:39–44). He is also put in charge of the wise men. Daniel's three friends, who prayed with him for revelation, are also promoted at his request (v. 49) and share in this victory. These faithful believers have borne witness to the mystery of the kingdom of the last days and will continue to do so at great cost to themselves.

DANIEL 3

FAITHFUL UNTO DEATH

Abdullah, a young West Asian man, was zealous for his religion and part of a radical political group. After becoming disillusioned, he started searching online for information about Christianity. On Facebook, he met a pastor from his country who had since moved abroad. The pastor invited him to an online Bible study, and Abdullah made a decision to follow Christ. The pastor connected him with a local believer in Abdullah's city, who continued discipling him. However, when Abdullah's father found out about his faith, he threatened him, beat him, and shunned him by forcing him to eat alone. He was trying to get Abdullah to recant and return to his former faith.[1]

Shadrach, Meshach, and Abednego were also young men living in West Asia who faced persecution for their faith. In their case, persecution threatened their very lives. In Daniel 3, Nebuchadnezzar sets up a golden image and requires everyone to worship it or else be thrown into a fiery furnace (vv. 1–7). However, Shadrach, Meshach, and Abednego refuse to worship the image and are reported to the king (vv. 8–12). After being brought before the king, the three young men insist that they will not participate in this idolatrous worship or abandon their faith (vv. 13–18). Nebuchadnezzar becomes so angry that he heats the furnace even hotter and then has them thrown in (vv. 19–23). However, God performs a miracle so that Shadrach, Meshach, and Abednego are unharmed (vv. 24–27). Nebuchadnezzar then praises God and promotes these three men (vv. 28–30).

3: 1–7 NEBUCHADNEZZAR SETS UP A GOLDEN IMAGE

Though Nebuchadnezzar praises God and honors Daniel in the previous section (2:46–49), Nebuchadnezzar evidently has not become an exclusive worshiper of Yahweh. He had recognized Daniel's God as "God of gods and the Lord of kings and a revealer of mysteries" (2:47), but Daniel 3 begins with Nebuchadnezzar setting up "an image of gold" to be worshiped by his whole

---

[1]. This account and its continuation at the end of this chapter comes from friends of mine, who know Abdullah personally. His name has been changed and his country concealed for his sake and that of other believers living there.

kingdom (v. 1). There is a loose connection between this "image" and the "statue" or "image" (*tselem*) that he dreams about in Daniel 2, including its head of "gold" (2:31–32). Daniel had also identified Nebuchadnezzar as this head of gold (2:38), some commentators suggest that Nebuchadnezzar has this dream in mind and is seeking to be worshiped.[2] Either way, if the point of the dream was the destruction of an image representing human kingdoms (including his) and the triumph of the kingdom of God, then Nebuchadnezzar has not yet gotten the point.[3] The image that he sets up in Daniel 3 is not correspondingly destroyed, but the king's purposes behind it are still thwarted.

Seow points out that Daniel 3 describes Nebuchadnezzar as having "set up" this image nine different times (vv. 1, 2, 3 [twice], 5, 7, 12, 14, 18).[4] This literary feature reinforces the king's purpose in requiring all to worship it. Suggestively, the verb "set up" or "raise" (*qum*) was used earlier in Daniel 2, where it refers to God who "raises up" kings (v. 21) and will "raise up" an everlasting kingdom (v. 44). From this perspective, Nebuchadnezzar ironically sets himself up for failure in Daniel 3.

The text does not reveal much else about the appearance of this golden image other than its dimensions: "sixty cubits high and six cubits wide" (3:1). The book of Daniel at times seems to attach symbolic significance to numbers, whether in revelatory material or the narrative itself (e.g., four: 1:17; 2:37–40; 3:25; 7:2–3, 17; seven: 9:24–27; ten: 7:24).[5] Although six is not always a bad number in the Bible (Isa 6:2), the numbers sixty and six have negative associations in Daniel 3:1, just as 666 does in Revelation 13:18 ("the number of a man").

The image's towering height of sixty cubits (about ninety feet) recalls the "large statue" in Daniel 2:31 (cf. 4:10–11) and echoes the Tower of Babel again (see commentary on Daniel 2). Daniel 3 also has several unique connections to Genesis 10–11, such as the terms "nations," "clans/peoples," and "languages" (Gen 10:5, 20, 31–32; 11:6–7, 9; Dan 3:4, 7, 29). These texts also share an emphasis on a man-made structure and the physical setting of a

---

2. Collins, *Daniel*, 181–182.
3. House, *Daniel*, 80.
4. Seow, *Daniel*, 52. Cf. House, *Daniel*, 79–80.
5. Symbolic numbers are also found in the dreams recounted in the Joseph narrative (Gen 37:5–10; 40:9–19; 41:1–7). Compare Shaul Bar, *A Letter That Has Not Been Read: Dreams in the Hebrew Bible*, trans. Lenn Schramm (Cincinnati: Hebrew Union College, 2001), 46, 52, 56, 61; Michael Fishbane, *Biblical Interpretation in Ancient Israel* (Oxford: Clarendon, 1985), 450–451.

"plain" in Babylon/Babel (Gen 11:2, 9; Dan 3:1).[6] Both the Tower of Babel and the golden image in Daniel 3 unified people in a godless way, with the former built for the sake of a human "name" (Gen 11:4) and the latter for government-mandated idolatry.

The detailed list of "satraps, prefects, governors, advisers, treasurers, judges, magistrates and all the other provincial officials" is repeated twice in Daniel 3:2–3 and corresponds with the frequent use of lists in Daniel 2–6 (e.g., 2:5, 7, 27; 4:7; 6:7). In the case of cultic personnel (e.g., magicians, enchanters, etc.), there also appears to be a rhetorical significance to these lists being often found in the midst of "pompous speeches of the pagan king" (2:2; 4:7; 5:7, 11) and thus the subject of a "polemic against the impotent apparatus of the Babylonian cult."[7]

In Daniel 3, musical instruments are listed four times in verses 5, 7, 10, 15, which is particularly notable in such a short section of text. Coxon argues that this list, along with the list of officials in verses 2–3, is satirical given its exposure of "the mechanistic and thoughtless behavior of the pagan worshipers, of the pagan government bureaucracy in particular."[8] Avalos argues that when the music plays, these pagans mindlessly worship, like "a version of Pavlov's dog."[9] Montgomery points out that the list of instruments in this text "is very cosmopolitan" when compared with the description of temple music in Chronicles.[10] Coxon sees the lists of instruments and officials as contributing to "the intense Babylonian colour in the whole episode."[11] The frequent use of Babylonian names for Shadrach, Meshach, and Abednego in Daniel 3 contributes to this color as well.

The fact that Nebuchadnezzar summons all his officials (3:2–3) shows how important the dedication of this image was to him and also how he mixed political power and religion. His command to "nations and peoples of every language" (v. 4) to worship this image reveals the enforced unification that

---

6. Kim, "Biblical Interpretation in the Book of Daniel," 90–98.
7. Peter Coxon, "The 'List' Genre and Narrative Style in the Court Tales of Daniel," *JSOT* 35 (1986): 101.
8. Coxon, "The Narrative Style in the Court Tales of Daniel," 102. Coxon mistakenly counts five appearances of a list of musical instruments in this section. See also Hector Avalos, "The Comedic Function of the Enumerations of Officials and Instruments in Daniel 3," *CBQ* 53 (1991): 582.
9. Avalos, "Enumerations of Officials and Instruments in Daniel 3," 585.
10. Montgomery, *Daniel*, 201, followed by Collins, *Daniel*, 184.
11. Coxon, "The Narrative Style in the Court Tales of Daniel," 103. Although this quotation refers specifically to the list of musical instruments, Coxon earlier notes that the lists of secular officials in Daniel "give a genuinely Babylonian flavor to the narrative," 100.

he was trying to achieve through this state-mandated religious act. The multilingual context ("peoples of every language," vv. 4, 7) further hints that the divine judgment of linguistic confusion at the Tower of Babel (Gen 11:6–7) could be overcome. Nebuchadnezzar's actions parallel the proud Babylonian in Habakkuk 2, who "gathers to himself all the nations" (v. 5) while simultaneously going against the Lord's purpose for all nations to worship him alone (Isa 2:2–4; Hab 2:14). Nebuchadnezzar's opposition to the Lord's will places him in the line of Pharaoh (Exod 1:10; 5:2), Balak (Num 22:4–6), and others in the Bible and throughout history who have openly resisted God and his people.

The herald's command to worship the golden image as soon as the music starts playing (vv. 4–5) is backed up by the threat of death by fire, "Whoever does not fall down and worship will be immediately thrown into a blazing furnace" (v. 6). When "all the nations and peoples of every language" comply (v. 7), it seems that Nebuchadnezzar's anti-God plan is working. Rotohka explains that "Nebuchadnezzar's intention was probably to demand a public display of loyalty to the state, of the kind demanded by many totalitarian governments."[12] A well-known historical example is the cult of emperor worship in the Roman Empire. Various types of imperial cults are also part of the histories of China, Japan, and Southeast Asia.

---

12. Rotohka, "Daniel," in *South Asia Bible Commentary*, 1093.

A BIBLICAL PERSPECTIVE ON MUSIC

Music plays a significant role in the mandated worship of the golden image in Daniel 3. Whereas there is a verbal edict explaining Nebuchadnezzar's order (vv. 4–7), the actual signal that worship must begin is non-verbal: instrumental music (vv. 5, 7, 10, 15). There is no need to rely on a common language, such as Aramaic, for these worshipers made up of "nations and peoples of every language" (vv. 4, 7), since this musical "sound" transcends language and effectively communicates that worship must begin. In a similar way, classical music has been enjoyed by people throughout history and around the world, regardless of the languages they speak.

Yet the use of music to facilitate idolatry in Daniel 3 raises questions about music in general. What does the Bible teach or imply about music? Is music itself good, bad, or neutral? The first reference to music in the Bible is in Genesis 4:21, which describes Jubal as "the father of all who play stringed instruments and pipes" (cf. "lyre," "pipe" in Dan 3:5). Notably, Jubal is part of the line of Cain and a son of Lamech, who (like Cain) is characterized by violence (Gen 4:23–24) and is distinct from the chosen line of Seth (Gen 4:25–5:8).

In spite of the negative characterization of Cain's line, it is important to ask whether everything that Cain's line does in Genesis 4:17–25 should be seen in a negative light. Certainly, violence and polygamy are negative (v. 19), and man-centered city building might be (v. 17). Yet Cain's line (through Lamech's three sons) is also involved in raising livestock, playing musical instruments, and crafting metalwork (vv. 20–22). Although some have interpreted Jubal's musicianship negatively, others resist projecting broader problems about Cain's line onto every detail in this passage.[1] For instance, Grossman positively highlights "the sheer diversity of the creative genius in a single family."[2] Hamilton relatedly argues that "Genesis is making the point that through the (disobedient) line of Cain, many of the world's significant cultural discoveries emerged. This point may provide another illustration of the grace of God at work in this fallen line."[3]

Another important consideration is the great number of positive references to music in the Bible, often with regard to worshiping the Lord. According to one count, these positive usages account for 80 percent of all references to music, outnumbering the negative usages (as in Daniel 3) by four to one.[4] One classic example of a positive use is the Song of the Sea in Exodus 15:1–18, which "Moses and the Israelites" (v. 1) sing after crossing the Red Sea. The song begins, "I will sing to the LORD, for he is highly exalted. Both horse and driver he has hurled into the sea" (v. 1).[5] Miriam uses a "timbrel" in her shorter song (Exod 15:20–21). The psalms abound with the use of singing and instruments to worship God joyfully (e.g., Pss 33:1–2; 57:7–9). At the same time, psalms and songs can be used for instruction (Ps 78:1), warning (Deut 31:19), lament (2 Chr 35:25; Ps 3), and other legitimate purposes (e.g., 2 Kgs 3:15; Song of Songs).

Thus the broader context of the Bible suggests that music is a gift from God, which should be used to glorify God in various ways, though it can be misused (Job 30:9; Ps 69:12). Begbie points out that "music has been used in the exercise of power," for better or for worse.[6] The latter is exactly what is happening in Daniel 3.[7] If music can be seen under the broader umbrella of the arts, then we may also recall that the tabernacle was constructed skillfully with Spirit-led leadership (Exod 31:2–11) according to a God-given heavenly "pattern" (Exod 25:9, 40). Thus, the Renaissance artist Albrecht Dürer's comment about the arts can also be applied to music, "The arts in themselves are good. What God hath formed that is good, misuse it how ye will."[8] Likewise, music in itself is good, being one of God's good gifts, despite its misuse at times.

---

1. For the former, see Bruce Waltke, *Genesis: A Commentary* (Grand Rapids: Zondervan, 2001), 100. Jonathan Grossman cites Rashi as another example, although Grossman himself does not take this view. Grossman, *Creation: The Story of Beginnings*, trans. Sara Daniel (New Milford: Maggid, 2019), 191.
2. Grossman, *Creation: The Story of Beginnings*, 192.
3. Victor Hamilton, *The Book of Genesis: Chapters 1–17* (Grand Rapids: Eerdmans, 1990), 239.
4. Paul Munson, "A Biblical View of Music," in *The Worldview Study Bible*, ed. David Dockery and Trevin Wax (Nashville: Holman Bible Publishers, 2018), 727.
5. The literary context suggests that the song was composed in a short time frame by modern standards (Exod 14:31; 15:22). For music as "an expression of a collective experience" rather than "the work of a single individual," which seems to apply to Exodus 15:1–18, see Jeremy Begbie, *Resounding Truth: Christian Wisdom in the World of Music* (Grand Rapids: Baker, 2007), 31.
6. Begbie, *Resounding Truth*, 46.
7. Rotohka describes the common scene in India of large idols being set up during a festival and then paraded down the street on the last day with loud music. Cf. Rotohka, "Daniel," 1093.
8. William Martin Conway, ed., *Literary Remains of Albrecht Dürer* (Cambridge: Cambridge University Press, 1889), 176.

Daniel 3

3:8–12 SHADRACH, MESHACH, AND ABEDNEGO REFUSE TO WORSHIP THE IMAGE

The picture of uniform obedience to Nebuchadnezzar's command in verse 7 is quickly disrupted by the charges brought against "the Jews" in verse 8, which concern the faith-inspired civil disobedience of Shadrach, Meshach, and Abednego (v. 12). Those who report this disobedience are "astrologers" (v. 8), the group who had been called upon to interpret Nebuchadnezzar's dream earlier but were unable to do so (2:5, 10). Having been involved in a contest with Daniel in Daniel 2, the astrologers are now in intense conflict with Shadrach, Meshach, and Abednego in Daniel 3. Having lost previously, they will lose again this time, and they will keep losing throughout the book of Daniel (4:7; 5:7–8, 11).[13] The Aramaic phrase translated "denounced" (3:8) is the same one used in 6:24, where it describes the accusations against Daniel for praying in his room to God. Whereas this idiom is attested in the ANE, Coxon points out that its literal meaning, "ate their pieces," makes a possible association with a devouring animal, in accordance with the use of the Aramaic verb "eat" elsewhere (7:5, 7, 19, 23; cf. 4:33).[14] The astrologers' accusations frame Shadrach, Meshach, and Abednego's actions as a personal affront to the king (Dan 3:10–12), which was an easy sell for the Babylonian monarch (cf. v. 13).

The confrontation over worshiping the golden image also involves the racial tension of the astrologers, or "Chaldeans" (Heb.; see KJV, ESV), denouncing "the Jews" (v. 8). While the conflict in Daniel 3 is primarily about worship, racial dynamics arise because Shadrach, Meshach, and Abednego are accused as Jews who refuse to worship the golden image according to Nebuchadnezzar's mandate. From a Babylonian perspective, this conflict could easily be framed as a problem with Jewish identity, but informed readers know that what is at stake is far more, encompassing faithfulness and obedience to the one true God and hence applicable to all people. Noting the connection to verse 12, where the Babylonian astrologers speak of "some Jews whom you have set over the affairs of the province of Babylon," Collins comments, "Their motivation presumably involved resentment against the foreigners who had been

---

13. House notes, however, that previously they were "not unfriendly," as they certainly are here. House, *Daniel*, 81.
14. Coxon, "The Narrative Style in the Court Tales of Daniel," 112–113.

appointed over them."[15] Seow accordingly sees both "professional jealousy" and "xenophobia" at play.[16]

Such complex dynamics fit the context of the book of Daniel. In the opening verses of Daniel 1, Nebuchadnezzar's defeat of Jerusalem, taking temple treasures to the temple of his god, and exile of the Israelites is inseparable from the reality that the *Babylonians* triumphed over the *Israelites* and enrolled their best and brightest in Nebuchadnezzar's training program (vv. 3–4). Likewise, Daniel's subsequent refusal to "defile himself with the royal food and wine" (1:8) was both an act of obedience to God and a line in the sand that distinguished himself and his friends as Israelites who kept the dietary laws of Moses. In Daniel 2:25, Daniel was identified as "a man from among the exiles from Judah" prior to interpreting Nebuchadnezzar's dream, something that the Babylonian wise men could not do.

In Daniel 3, Shadrach, Meshach, and Abednego's refusal to worship the golden image springs from their conviction that only the one true God should be worshiped. This fundamental truth is classically stated in both the *Shema* (Deut 6:4) and the Ten Commandments. The latter forbids the worship of other gods and specifically the worship of any "image" (*pesel*, Heb.; Exod 20:3–5; Deut 5:7–9). Though we are dealing with different terms in different languages, the Ten Commandments also prohibit "bowing down" (*havah*, Heb.) and "worshiping" (*'avad*, Heb.) such images (Exod 20:5; Deut 5:9), in direct conflict with Nebuchadnezzar's mandate to "fall down" (*nefal*, Aramaic) and "worship" (*segad*, Aramaic) his golden image (e.g., Dan 3:5–7).[17] Besides the Ten Commandments, numerous OT texts forbid "bowing down" and "worshiping" any other god (e.g., Exod 23:24; Deut 4:19; Josh 23:7; 1 Kgs 9:6). Daniel 3:12 uses another term related to worship, "serve" (*pelach*), which provides both a thematic and lexical link to the ultimate reality that all will worship "one like a son of man" and the true God himself (Dan 7:13–14, 27).[18]

Accordingly, Lucas sees "the youths' primary reason for standing firm [to be] . . . their adherence to the first two commandments of the Decalogue."[19]

---

15. Collins, *Daniel*, 186. Cf. House, *Daniel*, 82.
16. Seow, *Daniel*, 54.
17. In Targum Onkelos, *segad* is frequently used to translate *havah*, including Exodus 20:5 and Deuteronomy 5:9.
18. In Targum Onkelos, *pelach* is frequently used to translate *'avad*, including Exodus 20:5 and Deuteronomy 5:9.
19. Lucas, *Daniel*, 91. An allusion to the Ten Commandments would not be surprising in light of Daniel's frequent use of earlier OT Scripture. For this, see "Biblical Allusions in the Book of Daniel," pages 123–124.

Just as it will be for Daniel later (6:5), the refusal of his three friends to worship the golden image (3:8–12) can be understood in terms of their commitment to the law of God. Their earlier refusal to defile themselves with the royal food suggests the same (1:8–13). Esther 3:8 also makes an explicit connection between Jewish identity and keeping the law of God.

3:13–18 SHADRACH, MESHACH, AND ABEDNEGO ARE BROUGHT BEFORE NEBUCHADNEZZAR

In keeping with the astrologers' framing of this incident as a personal affront to the king and his quick temper previously (2:12), Nebuchadnezzar becomes "furious with rage" and calls for Shadrach, Meshach, and Abednego to be brought before him for questioning (3:13). His initial question seeks to confirm the report of their refusal to "serve" (*pelach*) and "worship" (*segad*) his image (v. 14). Nebuchadnezzar repeats his mandate to worship the golden image when the music starts to play, or else they will be thrown "immediately" into a fiery furnace (v. 15; cf. vv. 6, 11).

This particular mode of punishment has led some scholars to search for both biblical and ANE parallels. Whereas execution specifically by a fiery furnace is unparalleled, execution by fire does occasionally occur in the Bible and the ANE.[20] Judah wanted to have Tamar burned to death (Gen 38:24). Perpetrators of certain egregious acts of sexual immorality are subject to execution by fire (Lev 20:14; 21:9). The king of Babylon burns two false prophets with fire (Jer 29:22).[21] Achan and his family are burned after they are stoned (Josh 7:24–25). The fourth beast in Daniel 7 is similarly burned after being killed (v. 11).[22] On the other hand, the "Ancient of Days" in Daniel 7 is immune to fire, since his throne is "flaming with fire" and "its wheels . . . ablaze" (v. 9), and from him flows a "river of fire" (v. 10). Indeed, the Pentateuch refers to the Lord as a "consuming fire" (Deut 4:24), who descended on Mount Sinai with fire (Exod 19:18; 24:17), spoke from fire (Deut 4:33; 5:24, 26), and at times executed judgment through fire (Lev 10:2; Num 11:1; 16:35).

Accordingly, the Lord will enable his faithful followers to overcome fire (cf. Isa 43:2), but Nebuchadnezzar is unaware of this and boastfully concludes, "what god will be able to rescue you from my hand?" (Dan 3:15). Just as

---

20. Paul-Alain Beaulieu, "The Babylonian Background of the Motif of the Fiery Furnace in Daniel 3," *JBL* 128 (2009): 277; Collins, *Daniel*, 185.
21. Tawny Holm, "The Fiery Furnace in the Book of Daniel and the Ancient Near East," *Journal of the American Oriental Society* 128 (2008): 86.
22. Beaulieu, "Fiery Furnace in Daniel 3," 278.

the astrologers claimed earlier that it was impossible to know and interpret Nebuchadnezzar's dream (Dan 2:11), Nebuchadnezzar implies in Daniel 3 that it will be impossible for Shadrach, Meshach, and Abednego's God to rescue them. This boast provides a perfect setup for the Lord's power and incomparability to be revealed again. The impossibility in Daniel 2:11 was not based on the impotence of the gods, but rather the impossibility of communicating with them. This time, Nebuchadnezzar directly challenges the power of all gods to deliver anyone from a fiery furnace and from his "hand" (3:15), lumping together the Lord with all false gods and implying his impotence in this matter as well. But as other passages of Scripture proclaim, "Surely the arm of the Lord is not too short to save" (Isa 59:1; cf. 50:2), and "salvation belongs to the Lord" (Ps 3:9, ESV). Though enemies may lift their own "hand" (Deut 32:27), "no one can deliver out of [the Lord's] hand" (Deut 32:39; Isa 43:13). As Isaiah declares, "With whom, then, will you compare God? To what image will you liken him? . . . 'To whom will you compare me? Or who is my equal?' says the Holy One" (40:18, 25).

Shadrach, Meshach, and Abednego resolve to remain faithful to the Lord, even though it may cost them their lives. We can learn much from their courageous words. First, they maintain respect for the king by addressing him as "king" (3:17–18, Heb.; NIV: "Your Majesty").[23] In some Asian contexts, we might say that they gave him "face." Second, they explain their decision clearly and bear witness to "the God we serve" and his power to save (v. 17; cf. Jonah 1:9) without muddling the main issue. In the process, they contradict Nebuchadnezzar's claim that no god is "able to rescue . . . from my hand" (v. 15). Montgomery sees their initial words in verse 16 ("we have no need to answer you in this matter," RSV) as a confession of disobedience to the king.[24] Kwong points out that their actions speak for themselves.[25] Third, they maintain faith in God under extreme pressure while at the same time accepting whatever his sovereign will might be in this particular situation, including the possibility of a horrific death. They know that God can deliver them and ultimately will deliver them (v. 17), but "even if he does not," they will be faithful to him (v. 18).

---

23. Cf. House, *Daniel*, 83. Although the NIV suggests that they also do so in verse 16, other translations do not include "king" in quoted material and read, "said to the king, 'O Nebuchadnezzar.'"
24. Montgomery, *Daniel*, 206.
25. Kwong (鄺炳釗), *Daniel*, 114.

Compared to the two situations in Daniel 1 and 2, there is considerably less "wiggle room" for the faithful in Daniel 3. In the case of avoiding defiled food, Daniel was granted a ten-day trial period for a vegetarian diet by an official and his guard (1:8–14). In the case of Nebuchadnezzar's dream, Daniel spoke with Arioch, the king's commander, and was also granted time, which he used to pray with his friends for revelation (2:14–19). In both of these cases, Daniel and his friends were able to avoid direct confrontation with the king. The threat to their physical well-being went as far as Arioch coming to gather them for execution, but this threat was quickly averted (2:13–16).[26]

In contrast, the officials in Daniel 3 are firmly on the side of Nebuchadnezzar and egg him on to enforce the decreed consequences (vv. 8–12). The stakes are also higher, since the dedication of the image is a public event attended by many officials and "peoples of every language." Neither gathering more information (2:15), asking for time (1:12–13; 2:16), or getting a second chance (3:15, 18) will be of any use. Nebuchadnezzar is demanding immediate compliance, and Shadrach, Meshach, and Abednego rightly take a stand. They demonstrate that whereas there are situations where the interests of all or most parties can be satisfied, there are others where it is impossible, and we must "obey God rather than men" (Acts 5:29, KJV). Many heroes of faith throughout history have taken similar stands, including in Asia.

3:19–27 SHADRACH, MESHACH, AND ABEDNEGO IN THE FIERY FURNACE WITH A FOURTH MAN

Nebuchadnezzar was already angry in verse 13 when he received the report of Shadrach, Meshach, and Abednego's defiance of his command, and their insistence in verses 16–18 makes him even angrier (v. 19). Not content simply to throw them into the fiery furnace, he first has it "heated seven times hotter than usual" (v. 19) – so hot in fact that it kills the soldiers who bring them to the furnace (v. 22). Tying up (*kefat*, Aramaic) Shadrach, Meshach, and Abednego (v. 20) may have been standard procedure for such execution.[27] More importantly, this binding is emphasized in the text (vv. 21, 23–24) and factors into the miracle in the subsequent context (v. 25). The details concerning the clothes that Shadrach, Meshach, and Abednego are wearing (v. 21)

---

26. Montgomery believes that this was to be "a formal execution under the proper officials and in the appointed place, hence the first purpose of the officials was to assemble the condemned." Montgomery, *Daniel*, 149–150.
27. Collins, *Daniel*, 188.

also contribute to this miracle (v. 27). As Shadrach, Meshach, and Abednego fall into the furnace, the narrative artfully prepares the reader for the rest of the story by explicitly referring to the "*three* men" (v. 23).

The Lord's miraculous protection of the three men is described from the perspective of Nebuchadnezzar (vv. 24–25), who had just boasted of his power over all gods (v. 15). Nebuchadnezzar's surprise does not simply focus on the survival of Shadrach, Meshach, and Abednego. He knows that only three men were tied up and thrown into the fire, and he exclaims, "Look! I see four men walking around in the fire, unbound and unharmed" (v. 25). The king goes on to observe, "the fourth looks like a son of the gods" (v. 25).[28] In verse 28, Nebuchadnezzar refers to this fourth man as an "angel."

Some traditional interpreters have seen this figure as the pre-incarnate Christ, whereas others, especially modern interpreters, reject this interpretation.[29] Given the frequency of angelic activity in the book of Daniel (e.g., Dan 6:22; 8:16; 9:21; 10:13, 21; 12:1), it is hard to prove that this fourth man was more than just an angel. What is clear is that his appearance is singled out by Nebuchadnezzar (Dan 3:25) and that he is visible while Shadrach, Meshach, and Abednego are in the furnace, but not before or after. More importantly, the fourth man's presence with Shadrach, Meshach, and Abednego in the fire signifies God's presence with the three men during this trial.

Another aspect of this miracle is that all four men are "unbound" (v. 25). The preceding context emphasizes how Shadrach, Meshach, and Abednego were tied up (vv. 20–21, 23–24), but now they are walking freely in the furnace with the fourth man (v. 25). Just as the fourth man is free and immune to fire, God enables the three friends to be free and immune to fire. Their being "unharmed" (*haval*, Aramaic, v. 25) accords with the fact that God's everlasting kingdom will not be "destroyed" (*haval*, 2:44; 6:26; 7:14). Likewise, "the fire had no power" (*shelet*, Aramaic) over their bodies (v. 27, KJV; see same verb for "rule" in Dan 2:38–39, 48).

---

28. For the plural "gods" instead of "G/god," see S. R. Driver, *The Book of Daniel with Introduction and Notes* (Cambridge: University Press, 1901), 44; Goldingay, *Daniel*, 67. Driver and Goldingay argue that unlike the Hebrew, *elohim*, the Aramaic parallel, *elahin*, only refers to plural "gods." On the other hand, the standard lexicon (*Hebrew and Aramaic Lexicon of the Old Testament*) sees this Aramaic term in Daniel (4:8–9, 18; 5:11, 14) as either singular or plural ("spirit of the holy god[s]"). See also Montgomery, *Daniel*, 153, along with the commentary below on Daniel 4:8–9.
29. Collins, *Daniel*, 190. Those who reject that this angel was the pre-incarnate Christ include House, *Daniel*, 85–86; Kwong, *Daniel*, 117.

Lester argues that the miracle in Daniel 3:25–27 alludes to Isaiah 43:2 ("When you pass through the waters, I will be with you . . . When you walk through the fire, you will not be burned; the flames will not set you ablaze"), which links the theme of the second exodus with the theme of deliverance from fire (see "Second Exodus in the Prophets and in Daniel," pp. 54–55).[30] Lester points out that the parallels not only include deliverance from fire, but also "walking" (*halak*, Heb. and Aramaic) in or through fire as well as the Lord's presence with his people in the midst of trial ("I will be with you," Isa 43:2; the fourth man). Additional parallels with other biblical texts include the "throwing" (*ramah*, Aramaic) of Shadrach, Meshach, and Abednego into the furnace (Dan 3:20–21, 24; cf. 6:16), just as the Egyptians were "hurled" (*ramah*, Heb.) into the Red Sea (Exod 15:1, 21). Second exodus themes are certainly appropriate in the book of Daniel, which is set during the Babylonian exile, and allusions to Isaiah can also be discerned in the preceding context (Dan 1:1–4; 2:34–35).[31] Accordingly, Van der Toorn draws a connection between the deliverance in Daniel 3 and the characterization of the exodus as deliverance from "the iron-smelting furnace" in Deuteronomy 4:20, 1 Kings 8:51, and Jeremiah 11:4.[32] In these three texts, the Lord "brought out" (*yatsa*, Heb.) his people from the furnace, and in Daniel 3:26, the three men similarly "come out" (*nefaq*, Aramaic) from a furnace.

The earlier detail about their clothes (3:21) reenters the narrative in verse 27, which states that their clothes were not burned either. Whereas verses 25–26 focus on Nebuchadnezzar's realization that the three men are "servants of the Most High God," verse 27 describes the officials' confirmation of this. Thus none of them can deny the saving power of the God of Shadrach, Meshach, and Abednego. Like Pharaoh and the Egyptians long ago (Exod 14:4, 18), these Babylonians see for themselves that the Lord is God.

3:28–30 NEBUCHADNEZZAR PRAISES GOD AND PROMOTES SHADRACH, MESHACH, AND ABEDNEGO

Nebuchadnezzar blesses the God of Israel, who sent his "angel" to "rescue" his "servants" (Dan 3:28). Previously, the Lord revealed himself as "the God

---

30. Lester, *Daniel Evokes Isaiah*, 119–121.
31. Respectively, see Jennie Grillo, "From a Far Country," 363–380; Michael Shepherd, *Daniel in the Context of the Hebrew Bible*, 75.
32. Karel Van Der Toorn, "Scholars at the Oriental Court: The Figure of Daniel Against Its Mesopotamian Background," in *The Book of Daniel: Composition and Reception*, vol. 1, ed. John Collins and Peter Flint (Leiden: Brill, 2001), 53.

of gods" and "a revealer of mysteries" to the king (Dan 2:47). Now he shows himself to be the God who can deliver from the king's hand (3:28–29; cf. vv. 15, 17). Nebuchadnezzar's words aptly summarize this chapter with implications for readers, "They trusted in him and defied the king's command and were willing to give up their lives rather than serve or worship any god except their own god" (v. 28). Earlier, the king lumped the Lord together with other impotent gods (v. 15), but now he issues a decree forbidding anyone "of any nation or language" (cf. vv. 4, 7) from speaking against this God who can save like no other (v. 29). Although Nebuchadnezzar is probably still not converted (see Daniel 4), the Lord's glory is vindicated in the eyes of the nations.[33]

In the introduction to this chapter, we met Abdullah, who faced persecution from his father for his faith in Christ. Despite these challenges, Abdullah persevered, and his life started to change, such as by quitting smoking. When his father saw the positive changes in Abdullah's life and how Abdullah held fast to his faith, his heart softened. He eventually came to accept Abdullah back into the family and to respect him as a person and a valued family member. Meanwhile, Abdullah continued to follow Jesus and grow as a believer. Persecution like this is extremely difficult and outcomes are not always perfect, but Daniel 3 stands as a timeless encouragement of God's presence with us and his all-surpassing power to deliver us according to his will, timing, and wisdom.[34]

---

33. Lucas, *Daniel*, 96. Lucas writes, "This is not a conversion to monotheism. What measure of conversion he experiences is partial."
34. For a recent example of catastrophic persecution in West Asia, see Jenkins, *The Lost History of Christianity*, 169–171.

DANIEL 4
A DREAM OF A GREAT TREE

Native to South Asia and India's national tree, banyan trees can be as tall as a hundred feet and have the remarkable characteristic of being able to spread out laterally.[1] They expand sideways because their branches grow aerial roots that descend to the ground, take root, and become new trunks. As a result, a single banyan tree can look like multiple trees in a grove. The world's largest banyan tree is the Great Banyan near Kolkata, India, which covers over 3.5 acres.[2] As a species of the fig tree, banyan leaves are large, and they provide considerable shade and support diverse animal life. A particularly invasive banyan tree has engulfed an abandoned warehouse in Tainan, Taiwan, and has become an attraction called the Anping Tree House. The longevity and regenerative ability of the banyan tree have made it a symbol of immortality in India.[3] True to form, the beloved banyan tree in the historic downtown of Lahaina, Maui, survived a major fire in August 2023 and continues to show signs of recovery at the time of writing.[4]

In Daniel 4, King Nebuchadnezzar tells of his dream of a magnificent tree. The text does not identify the species of tree, but it has mythical proportions and qualities (vv. 11–12). The chapter begins with the king's declaration of praise concerning the signs that the Most High has performed (vv. 1–3). Next, he describes how once again he has had a disturbing dream that his wise men cannot interpret. This sets the stage for Daniel to interpret another one of Nebuchadnezzar's dreams (vv. 4–18; cf. 2:1–11). Though troubled by the dream's meaning, Daniel explains that the magnificent tree represents the proud Nebuchadnezzar and that God is about to judge him by taking away his kingdom until he humbles himself (vv. 19–27). One year later, the dream

---

1. https://www.britannica.com/plant/banyan, last updated 1 Mar 2024. David Haberman, *People Trees: Worship of Trees in Northern India* (Oxford: Oxford University Press, 2013), 164–166.
2. Evita Roche, "The largest banyan tree in the world is located in India," 21 April 2022, https://www.cntraveller.in/story/kolkata-west-bengal-largest-banyan-tree-in-the-world/.
3. Haberman, *People Trees*, 165–166.
4. https://mauinow.com/2024/04/11/lahaina-banyan-tree-continues-to-show-signs-of-recovery-eight-months-after-the-maui-fires/.

is fulfilled, and Nebuchadnezzar loses his kingdom (vv. 28–33). But after he acknowledges God, his kingdom is restored (vv. 34–37).

4:1–3 NEBUCHADNEZZAR DECLARES THE WONDERS OF GOD TO HIS KINGDOM

Daniel 4 begins with Nebuchadnezzar speaking in the first person (vv. 1–18) before switching to conventional third-person narrative (vv. 19–33) and back again to first person (vv. 34–37).[5] Unlike Daniel 2 in which the king's dream is narrated straightforwardly, the dream in Daniel 4 is communicated to the reader through a message that Nebuchadnezzar sends to his kingdom after the dream and its aftermath. Several scholars see verse 1 as introducing a letter (cf. Ezra 7:11–12), with Lucas pointing out that the "royal letter" here "gives the content of the story a special authority."[6] Nebuchadnezzar's address to "nations and peoples of every language" in Daniel 4:1 repeats the terminology used in Daniel 3 (vv. 4, 7, 29), but its purpose contrasts with the king's earlier mandate to worship the golden image. Seow further notes that the phrase "in all the earth" (4:1) coordinates with the repetition of "earth" and "heaven" in this passage (vv. 10–13, 20–23).[7] He explains, "At issue in the chapter is the relationship of earthly power and heavenly power – the power of Nebuchadnezzar versus the power of God."[8] Nebuchadnezzar thought that he was a great ruler in the world, but he learns the hard way that "Heaven rules" (v. 26) because "the King of heaven" is above all (v. 37; cf. Ps 2:4–9).[9]

After wishing peace upon his subjects, the king explains his purpose to declare the "signs" and "wonders" that God has done in his life (4:2–3). The terms "signs" (*'at*, Aramaic) and "wonders" (*temah*, Aramaic) appear twice in verses 2–3 and again in Daniel 6:27, and they are reminiscent of the "signs" (*'ot*, Heb.) and "wonders" (*mofet, niflaot*, Heb.) that the Lord did in Egypt (Exod 3:20; 7:3) and at other times (Deut 34:11; Neh 9:17; Ps 78:43). But unlike Pharaoh long ago, Nebuchadnezzar praises God to his kingdom subjects. In the subsequent context of Daniel 4, "signs" and "wonders" naturally refer to Nebuchadnezzar losing and then regaining his kingdom. At the same

---

5. For additional discussion of the form of Daniel 4, see House, *Daniel*, 91–92.
6. Lucas, *Daniel*, 103. Cf. Collins, *Daniel*, 221. Goldingay calls it a "royal encyclical." Goldingay, *Daniel*, 82.
7. Seow, *Daniel*, 65.
8. Seow, *Daniel*, 65.
9. Collins explains that the grandiosity expressed by Nebuchadnezzar in verse 1 was common in the ANE. Collins, *Daniel*, 221.

time, other miraculous events such as Daniel's interpretation of the king's first dream (Daniel 2) and the deliverance of Shadrach, Meshach, and Abednego from the fiery furnace, which elicits "amazement" (Dan 3:24), could also be classified as signs and wonders. Even as the exiles in Babylon were waiting for the eschatological second exodus (see "Second Exodus in the Prophets and in Daniel," below), which will be accompanied by "wonders" (Joel 2:30–31), God is already doing signs and wonders in their midst to preserve them and remind them that a greater exodus is to come.

In verse 3, Nebuchadnezzar testifies that God's signs are "great" (*rav*, Aramaic) and his wonders "strong" (*taqif*, Aramaic). These descriptors will factor into his dream (see vv. 11, 20, 22, 30). Yet such "signs" are not merely isolated displays of God's power but demonstrate that "His kingdom is an eternal kingdom; his dominion endures from generation to generation" (v. 3). In addition to being a close parallel to Psalm 145:13, this line previews the main takeaway of Daniel 4 (vv. 34–37) and also reinforces the central theme of the book of Daniel.[10] Like the poetry in Daniel 2:20–23, the brief poem in Daniel 4:3 proclaims the eternal reign of God. The poetry in verses 10–12, 14–17, 34–35 do likewise. As mentioned in the commentary above on Daniel 2:20–23, poetry is used strategically in the book of Daniel, as it is elsewhere in several OT books.

---

10. Seow, *Daniel*, 65.

SECOND EXODUS IN THE PROPHETS AND IN DANIEL

The theme of a second exodus has been mentioned at several points in the above commentary (Dan 1:1–2; 3:25–27; 4:3) and reappears subsequently (e.g., Dan 6:10, 27; 9:2, 15–19). Second exodus (or new exodus, though this is a broader term that can encompass multiple exodus-like events) is an important way in which the prophets foretell eschatological salvation in terms of the language, themes, imagery, and plot line of the exodus from Egypt. As von Rad explains, "The specific form of the new thing which they herald is not chosen at random; the new is to be effected in a way which is more or less analogous to God's former saving work."[1] Sailhamer calls this "a kind of typological pattern of thinking."[2] Since the exodus is the paradigmatic example of historical salvation in the OT, it is only fitting that the prophets would employ it in their prophecies of eschatological salvation. As Zakovitch argues, "All the raw materials needed to construct scenarios of the future redemption are found in the tradition of the past redemption, the Exodus, sometimes amalgamated with elements borrowed from Creation traditions."[3]

The book of Isaiah is probably the clearest example of the use of the second exodus theme. In describing the restoration of Israel after the exile, Isaiah 11:11 says that the Lord will gather his people "a second time" from the nations. Isaiah 11:15–16 continues with a prediction that the Lord will dry up a body of water for his people to cross, just "as there was for Israel when they came up from Egypt." This theme is heavily emphasized in Isaiah 40–55. Among the ten examples in these chapters of what Anderson calls "exodus typology," Isaiah 48:20–21 is particularly obvious, "Leave Babylon, flee from the Babylonians! . . . say, 'The Lord has redeemed his servant Jacob.' They did not thirst when he led them through the deserts; he made water flow for them from the rock; he split the rock and water gushed out."[4] Hugenberger adds additional examples and sees the second exodus as "the controlling and sustained theme" of Isaiah 40–55, where it is "almost omnipresent."[5]

Yet Isaiah is not the only prophetic book that draws on the theme of second exodus. For example, Jeremiah says, "It will no longer be said, 'As surely as the Lord lives, who brought the Israelites up out of Egypt,' but it will be said, 'As surely as the Lord lives, who brought the Israelites up out of the land of the north and out of all the countries where he had banished them'" (16:14–15). Likewise prophesying after the division of the Israelite kingdom, Hosea foretells Israel's restoration and reunification in terms of the second exodus, "The people of Judah and the people of Israel will come together; they will appoint one leader and will come up out of the land" (1:11). Drawing especially on the drowning of the Egyptians in the Red Sea, Micah declares that one day Israel's *sins* will be conquered and hurled into the sea (7:19).[6]

The prevalence of the theme of the second exodus in the prophetic books suggests that connections to this theme in the book of Daniel are not accidental, whether through its Babylonian setting (Dan 1:1–2), the account of deliverance from fire (Dan 3:25–27; cf. Isa 43:2), references to "signs" and "wonders" (Dan 4:2–3; 6:27), or otherwise (Dan 9:2).

---

1. Gerhard von Rad, *Old Testament Theology*, trans. D. M. G. Stalker (Peabody: Prince, 2005), 2:117.
2. John Sailhamer, *The Meaning of the Pentateuch*, 331.
3. Yair Zakovitch, *"And You Shall Tell Your Son . . . ": The Concept of the Exodus in the Bible* (Jerusalem: Magnes, 1991), 56–57.
4. Bernard Anderson, "Exodus Typology in Second Isaiah," in *Israel's Prophetic Heritage: Essays in Honor of James Muilenberg*, ed. Bernard Anderson and W. Harrelson (New York: Harper, 1962), 177–195.
5. Gordon Hugenberger also lists references to the second exodus elsewhere. Hugenberger, "The Servant of the Lord in the 'Servant Songs' of Isaiah: A Second Moses Figure," in *The Lord's Anointed: Interpretation of Old Testament Messianic Texts*, ed. P. E. Satterthwaite, R. S. Hess, and G. J. Wenham (Grand Rapids: Baker, 1994), 122.
6. Kevin Chen, *Wonders from Your Law: Nexus Passages and the Promises of an Exegetical Intertextual Old Testament Theology* (Downers Grove: InterVarsity, 2024), 231–232.

4:4–18 NEBUCHADNEZZAR'S DREAM OF A MAGNIFICENT TREE

Just prior to dreaming about the tree, Nebuchadnezzar is at ease in his "house" (Aramaic) and "palace" (v. 4). The Aramaic word translated as "prosperous" (*ra'nan*) may be a loanword from Hebrew (*ra'anan*), where it often characterizes a flourishing tree (Deut 12:2; Jer 11:16), in accordance with the dream that follows (vv. 12, 21).[11] It could appear that the king is enjoying the blessedness that is reserved for the righteous, who will flourish like trees in the "house of the Lord" (Ps 92:12–14; cf. 1:3; 52:8; Jer 17:7–8), but Nebuchadnezzar is more like David, whose comfortable life in his "house"

---

11. Lucas, *Daniel*, 108; Collins, *Daniel*, 222.

led to a serious sin (2 Sam 11:1–2). Montgomery elliptically draws a parallel between Nebuchadnezzar and "another Rich Man in another story," presumably a reference to the prophet Nathan's parable in 2 Samuel 12:1–4.[12] Seow points out the negative connotations of the word translated "contented" in Daniel 4:1 (*sheleh*, Aramaic; see similar term, *shalu* ["negligence"] in 3:29; 6:4; Ezra 4:22; 6:9).[13] This analogy between David and Nebuchadnezzar may extend further, since David was walking on the "roof" of his palace when he saw Bathsheba (2 Sam 11:2), and some believe that Nebuchadnezzar was walking on his roof when he made his ill-fated boast ("he was walking on the palace of his kingdom," v. 29, Aramaic).[14]

As in Daniel 2:1–3, Nebuchadnezzar does not understand his dream and wants to have it interpreted (4:5–7). Whereas his previous dream "troubled" him (2:1; cf. 2:3), this dream "made me afraid" and "terrified [*bahal*, Aramaic] me" (4:5; cf. 2:31).[15] Thus, just as Psalm 2:5 declares, the Heavenly King "terrifies" (*bahal*, Heb.) earthly kings (see Ps 2:2) and will do so again in Daniel 5:6, 9. Similar to his first dream, Nebuchadnezzar calls his wise men to interpret the dream and they are unable to, even though this time he actually tells them what the dream was (4:5–7; cf. 2:5–11). With the Babylonian sages' impotence even more apparent, the stage is set once again for Daniel to enter the scene to interpret Nebuchadnezzar's dream (4:8–9). As in Daniel 2 (see commentary), his superiority to Babylonian wise men echoes Joseph's superiority to Egyptian wise men in Genesis 41. Moreover, the reference to Daniel's foreign name, Belteshazzar (Dan 4:18–19), connects to Joseph's foreign name (Gen 41:45), and the repeated characterization, "the spirit of the holy god[s] is in him/you" (Dan 4:8–9, 18), connects to Pharaoh's recognition that Joseph is "one in whom is the spirit of God" (Gen 41:38).[16] The name Belteshazzar was

---

12. Montgomery, *Daniel*, 225.
13. Seow, *Daniel*, 66.
14. For example, NIV, ESV, NASb; Collins, *Daniel*, 230.
15. Lucas, *Daniel*, 109.
16. Joyce Baldwin argues for the translation, "spirit of the holy gods," based on the plural adjective (conceding the possible exception in Josh 24:19), Nebuchadnezzar's use of the same term to refer to his own god in Daniel 4:8, and the usage of the term in Daniel 5:11, 14. Baldwin, *Daniel* (Downers Grove: InterVarsity, 1978), 111. However, Nebuchadnezzar has already encountered the true God multiple times at this point, describing Daniel's God as "God of gods" (2:47) and "the God of Shadrach, Meshach and Abednego" as uniquely able to save (3:29). Even if he were still a polytheist at the time he called Daniel to interpret his second dream, Nebuchadnezzar still likely recognized the distinctiveness of Daniel's God and would not as easily have attributed Daniel's ability vaguely to gods in general. Goldingay refers to Nebuchadnezzar's recognition that "God's spirit dwells [in Daniel]." Goldingay, *Daniel*, 87. See also the commentary on 5:11 and "son of the gods" in 3:25.

given to Daniel in 1:7 and is used several times in Daniel 4 (vv. 8–9, 18–19). Indeed, the Spirit-imparted wisdom of Daniel means that "no mystery is too difficult for you" (4:9), with "mystery" (*raz*, Aramaic) providing yet another link to Daniel 2 (see vv. 18–19, 27–30, 47).

Nebuchadnezzar describes the dream to Daniel (and the reader) in verses 10–17. Similar to the dream in Daniel 2, there is an initial image of something glorious (4:10–12; cf. 2:31–35), followed by an action sequence involving the destruction of that object (4:13–17; cf. 2:34–35). However, the two dreams end differently in that what the tree represents is restored (see 4:16, "till seven times pass by"), but the statue is utterly destroyed and gives way to a triumphant rock-turned-mountain (2:35).

The tree in Nebuchadnezzar's dream is both "large" and "strong" (4:11). Its height is emphasized through being "enormous" (v. 10), "its top touch[ing] the sky" (v. 11), and being "visible to the ends of the earth" (v. 11). This echoes the Tower of Babel again, whose builders of Babel tried to build "a tower that reaches to the heavens" (Gen 11:4). In the book of Daniel, three chapters in a row make allusions to this archetype of godlessness (see above commentary on Dan 2:36–45; 3:1–7).[17] Coxon makes this Babel-Babylon connection and traces it even further back to the fall of Jerusalem (Dan 1:1–2), an apparent "traumatic reversal" of the judgment at Babel (Gen 11:5–9).[18] Babylon's pride is also characterized in terms of height in Isaiah (14:13–14).

The tree's location "in the middle of the land" (Dan 4:10), in addition to having ANE parallels, also parallels the moniker, "Middle Kingdom," the literal translation of the Chinese name for China, *zhongguo* (中國).[19] But taken to an extreme, such centrality, exaltation, and even visibility to the ends of the earth conflicts with the Lord's glory and his salvation through his Servant (Isa 2:2–4; 11:10; 52:10, 13).

Besides its size, the tree in Nebuchadnezzar's dream also has beautiful leaves, bears abundant fruit, and provides shelter (Dan 4:12). The provision of food for "all" likely refers to animals only, given the subsequent mention of "wild animals," "birds," and "every creature" (v. 12). In the dream of the statue, the subjugation of "beasts of the field and the birds in the sky" to

---

17. Pointing out the similar characterization of Pharaoh in Ezekiel 31:3, 10, 14, Daewoong Kim argues that both texts draw upon Genesis 11:1–9. Kim, "Biblical Interpretation in the Book of Daniel," 127–128.
18. Peter Coxon, "The Great Tree of Daniel 4," in *A Word in Season: Essays in Honor of William McKane*, ed. James Martin and Philip Davies (Sheffield: JSOT Press, 1986), 91–92.
19. Collins describes cosmic tree imagery in the ANE as "well known." Collins, *Daniel*, 223.

Nebuchadnezzar, its "head of gold" (Dan 2:38) is another link between his two dreams. Just as before, the tree seems to be ruling over animals just as Adam was intended to in Genesis 1:26, 28.[20]

The glory of this tree is short-lived, however, for a heavenly messenger descends and calls for the tree to be cut down, its leaves and fruit to be removed, and the animals under its shelter to flee (Dan 4:13–14). Coxon sees a dependence on Ezekiel 31 where Pharaoh's downfall is likened to Assyria's and described in terms of a tall, verdant cedar that is cut down.[21] Coxon also cites Ezekiel 17 as another text in which a tree represents a king as having influenced Daniel 4.[22]

At the same time, the tree in Nebuchadnezzar's dream is not utterly destroyed because "the stump of its roots" (Aramaic) remains in the ground, though "bound with iron and bronze" (4:15a). The image of a tree being cut down but its stump and roots remaining can be found in Isaiah.[23] The Lord's humiliation of everything proud in Isaiah 2:11–18 includes "the cedars of Lebanon" and "the oaks [*allon*, Heb.; cf. *ilan*, Aramaic, Dan 4:10] of Bashan" (Isa 2:13). Accordingly, Isaiah 10:33–34 depicts the Lord cutting down tall trees with an iron tool. Whereas the cutting down of the tree in Nebuchadnezzar's dream corresponds to the Lord's judgment of the nations in Isaiah 10, the survival of its "stump" and "roots" echoes imagery used in other Isaianic texts for the salvation of Israel through the Davidic Messiah. Despite being felled like other trees, Israel's "holy seed" remains as a "stump in the land" (Isa 6:13). Just as this verse is juxtaposed with the subsequent prophecy of Immanuel (Isa 7:14), so the judgment in Isaiah 10:33–34 is immediately followed by a vision of new growth from "the stump of Jesse" and its "roots" (11:1).[24]

In Daniel 4:14–17, the point is not that Messianic salvation is coming, but that even though the tree is cut down, it has hope because its stump survives. The tree metaphor is left behind in Daniel 4:15b–17, which decrees that the one whom the tree represents live outside like an animal and lose his mind in order to demonstrate that the Most High God rules all earthly kingdoms

---

20. J. B. Doukhan, "Allusions à la création dans le livre de Daniel," in *The Book of Daniel in Light of New Findings*, ed. A. S. Van Der Woude (Leuven: Leuven University Press, 1993), 286–287.
21. Coxon, "Great Tree of Daniel 4," 102–103.
22. Coxon, "Great Tree of Daniel 4," 95–96, 101–102.
23. Cf. Collins, *Daniel*, 226; Coxon, "Great Tree of Daniel 4," 105–106.
24. J. Alec Motyer, *The Prophecy of Isaiah* (Downers Grove: InterVarsity, 1993), 120–122.

and their kings. The hint at restoration, "till seven times pass by for him" (v. 16), is clarified in the interpretation (v. 25) and fulfillment (vv. 34–36).[25] The one who ruled all the animals (v. 12) will become like an animal himself (v. 16). The Most High's sovereignty over the kings and kingdoms of the earth (v. 17) is a major theme in the book of Daniel (e.g. 2:21). His exaltation of the lowly to rule demonstrates this sovereignty, which Nebuchadnezzar himself experiences when he is restored after being humbled. Humble rule by a God-fearing king has always been the divine ideal (Deut 17:20; 1 Sam 2:6–8; 2 Sam 23:3; Zech 9:9).

The dream itself includes the explanation that its main point is God's sovereignty over all earthly kingdoms (4:17) and hints that the tree represents a human ruler (vv. 15–16), but Nebuchadnezzar is still unable to connect the dots regarding the meaning of the dream.[26] His previous dream about the golden statue was also partly about himself (Dan 2:38, "You are that head of gold"), including the implication that his kingdom will be destroyed (Dan 2:35, 44–45), but Nebuchadnezzar's pride blinds him to the "mystery" of God's kingdom (Dan 2:47; 4:9). As Seow notes, the tree represents a kingship that is oblivious "that its power is derived and its existence contingent on a heavenly will."[27] In any case, Nebuchadnezzar's blindness provides another opportunity for "Belteshazzar" (Daniel) to interpret his dream (v. 18; cf. vv. 8–9). But like David in the prophet Nathan's parable (2 Sam 12:7), Nebuchadnezzar is "that man," or, in this case, "that tree" (4:22).[28]

4:19–27 DANIEL INTERPRETS NEBUCHADNEZZAR'S DREAM OF THE TREE

Daniel is "appalled" (author's translation; see NASB) and "terrified" to hear Nebuchadnezzar's dream (v. 19). "Perplexed" in the NIV differs from other English versions and could be misleading because it suggests that Daniel does not understand the dream initially. Observing Daniel's fearful reaction, Nebuchadnezzar encourages Daniel not to be terrified by the dream (v. 19). Daniel's wish that the dream was about the king's adversaries tips off that the dream is about Nebuchadnezzar (v. 19). House believes that this response also

---

25. Andrew P. C. Kwong notes the symbolic significance of the number seven with reference to a set period of time. Kwong (鄺炳釗), *Daniel*, 137.
26. Goldingay calls the dream's meaning "obvious." Cf. Goldingay, *Daniel*, 88, 93–94.
27. Seow, *Daniel*, 70.
28. Goldingay also makes this connection to 2 Samuel 12. Goldingay, *Daniel*, 94.

shows Daniel's "concern, even his love for Nebuchadnezzar."²⁹ If so, there is a parallel to Abraham's intercession for Sodom (Gen 18:23–33) and Jeremiah's call to the exiles to seek the peace of the Gentile cities in which they live (Jer 29:7).

After describing the tree that the king saw in his dream (vv. 20–21; cf. vv. 10–12), Daniel explains, "Your Majesty, you are that tree!" (v. 22). As in verses 13 and 17, the heavenly decree is issued by "a holy one, a messenger" (v. 23), which likely refers to an angel. Daniel's retelling of this decree includes the command to "destroy it" (*haval*, Aramaic), which repeats the verb used in Daniel 2:44 to describe the greater "kingdom that will never be destroyed" and also in Daniel 3:25 to describe the four men in the furnace who were "unharmed." The passing of seven "times" (4:23; cf. vv. 16, 25, 32) likewise recalls how God "changes times" in Daniel 2:21 (cf. "change," Dan 4:16). Daniel does not explain the meaning of the "iron" and "bronze" used for binding (4:15, 23), and the Aramaic text is not clear whether these strong metals are used on the stump or on the animal.³⁰ House takes the iron and bronze to be rings that are used on the stump to preserve its shape, but Lucas takes them to refer to the restraints put on the demented king.³¹

As Daniel explains, the angelic "decree" (v. 17) is none other than the "decree" of the Most High God himself (v. 24). Nebuchadnezzar learns that the one who will lose his mind (*levav*, Aramaic) and have the mind of an "animal" (*hevah*, Aramaic) is himself (v. 16). He will live outside like an animal and eat grass like an ox until he recognizes the rule of God (vv. 25–26). He even ended up looking like an animal (v. 33). Some have seen Nebuchadnezzar's experience as an example of zooanthropy or lycanthropy, which are mental illnesses in which a person believes him/herself to be an animal or wolf, respectively.³² In the book of Daniel, the blurring of the line between human and animal/beast (*hevah*, Aramaic) also notably appears in Daniel 7, where the four "beasts" represent four human kingdoms (v. 3).³³ In both cases, this blurring represents the degradation of human beings, who have been uniquely created in the image of God and as such distinct from animals (Gen 1:26–28).

---

29. House, *Daniel*, 96.
30. Collins, *Daniel*, 226–227.
31. House, *Daniel*, 96; Lucas, *Daniel*, 112.
32. Lucas, *Daniel*, 111–112; Rotohka, "Daniel," 1095; Collins, *Daniel*, 228; Seow, *Daniel*, 70.
33. Daniel 7:4 even describes the reverse transformation of a beast being given "the mind of a human," a hint at the grace and saving power of God.

Kwong points out that for Nebuchadnezzar the transformation begins with the king's mind or "heart" (Aramaic, Dan 4:16).[34]

Whereas the temporary nature of the judgment ("till seven times pass") is suggested in verse 16, restoration is explicit in verses 25–26. Nebuchadnezzar's acknowledgment of God will result in both his personal restoration and his kingdom being restored to him (v. 26). At the same time, Daniel does not treat the impending judgment as a foregone conclusion and calls the king to repentance (v. 27). The same presupposition underlies Moses's intercession for Israel for their sin with the golden calf (Exod 32:11–13), the Ninevites' repentance in response to Jonah's preaching (Jonah 3:4–9), and other prophetic texts (e.g., Jer 18:7–10; Ezek 33:14–16). Nebuchadnezzar in particular needed to pursue righteousness and be merciful to the needy (Dan 4:27; cf. Hab 2:12). This is the same standard that is applied to Israelite kings (cf. Ps 72:1–2), demonstrating the consistency of divine law.[35]

At this point in Daniel's response, he has already explained the meaning of the dream, but his "advice" to the king (4:27) shows that the purpose of the revelation includes a call to action. Likewise, the dream in Daniel 2 was not just a curiosity to be explained nor a problem to be solved but a prediction of the triumph of the kingdom of God. Thus, what should not be lost amidst the sometimes-unusual visions in the book of Daniel are that they serve the ultimate purpose of testifying to God's kingdom and urging us to live faithfully in light of it. Similarly, the book of Revelation with its abundance of difficult visionary material is not meant to baffle us but to captivate us into obedience (Rev 1:3; cf. Luke 11:28).[36]

4:28–33 NEBUCHADNEZZAR LOSES HIS MIND AND HIS KINGDOM

Nebuchadnezzar's dream was fulfilled (v. 28), though not right away. Daniel's exhortation to repent in verse 27 may have had a short-term effect on Nebuchadnezzar, but the biblical text is silent about this.[37] In any case, twelve months later, while Nebuchadnezzar is walking on the roof of his

---

34. Kwong, *Daniel*, 136–137.
35. Cf. Seow, *Daniel*, 71.
36. In describing the purpose of Revelation, Robert Mounce says, "The work was considered to be moral instruction, not simply prediction." Mounce, *The Book of Revelation* (Grand Rapids: Eerdmans, 1997), 43.
37. John Collins seems open to this, whereas Seow is more pessimistic. Collins, *Daniel*, 230; Seow, *Daniel*, 72.

palace (see above commentary, Dan 4:4), he boasts about "Babylon the *great*, which I myself have *built* . . . by the *might* of my *power* and for the *glory* of my majesty" (4:29–30, NASB; ital. added). The terms "great" (*rav*, Aramaic) and "might" (*teqaf*, Aramaic) are cognates of the verbs that describe how the tree in the king's vision "grew large and strong" (vv. 11, 20; *revah, teqaf*, Aramaic) and how the king himself had "become great and strong" (v. 22; *revah, teqaf*, Aramaic). As Widder points out, the king had already been told in Daniel 2:37 that his "power" (*hesen*), "might" (*teqaf*), and "glory" (*yeqar*) were bestowed by the God of heaven (whose acts are truly mighty, v. 3), but he has not yet learned his lesson.[38] The king's arrogance regarding the great city he "built" (*benah*, Aramaic) is yet another link to the "city and tower" at Babel "built" by humanity (Gen 11:4). As great as ancient Babylon was (cf. Isa 13:19; 47:8, 10), only the city that God builds will endure forever (Heb 11:10). This truth had already been demonstrated earlier for Jerusalem and Solomon's temple (Dan 1:1–2; cf. Jer 7:14; 9:11).

As soon as Nebuchadnezzar made his boast, "a voice came from heaven," where the true King of kings reigns, declaring that his rule is being taken away and that he will live like an animal (vv. 31–32), just as the dream and interpretation had said (vv. 15–16, 23, 25). The "taking away" (*'adah*, Aramaic) of Nebuchadnezzar's kingdom (v. 31) is referenced again in Daniel 5:20, which accords with the broader truth of God's sovereignty over earthly kingdoms (Dan 2:21; 7:12, 26) and contrasts with the kingdom of the Son of Man (Dan 7:14). The declaration from heaven in verse 32 is identical to Daniel's interpretation in verse 25, except it omits the detail about Nebuchadnezzar being drenched with dew. Whereas Nebuchadnezzar's own account of the dream explained its purpose broadly to be so "that the living may know" (*yeda*, Aramaic; v. 17), both Daniel and the heavenly voice make a more pointed application to the king: "until/when *you* acknowledge" (*yeda*, Aramaic) the rule of the Most High God (vv. 25–26, 32). Hope is thus held out to Nebuchadnezzar *if* he humbles himself before God. The slow, difficult process of a Gentile king coming to know God fits the classic example of Pharaoh (Exod 5:2; 7:17; 8:10, 22; 14:4, 18).

Nebuchadnezzar's boast not only triggers the voice from heaven but also his punishment (v. 33). As predicted, he is driven away, eats grass like an ox, and is drenched with dew from living outside (vv. 15–16, 23, 25). Furthermore, his hair and fingernails grow long like an eagle's feathers and claws (v. 33).

---

38. Widder, *Daniel*, 229.

As Widder explains, Nebuchadnezzar in his pride "blurred the lines between divinity and humanity, and the Most High God judged him by blurring the lines between his humanity and sub-humanity."[39] The fulfillment of this shorter-range prophecy (i.e., in twelve months, v. 29) implies that the Lord's words elsewhere in Daniel about the distant future will likewise be fulfilled.

4:34–37 NEBUCHADNEZZAR RESTORED

Nebuchadnezzar's madness lasts for the divinely appointed period of "seven times" (vv. 16, 23, 25, 32), and he testifies that "at the end of that time," his mind was restored (v. 34). The act of lifting his eyes to heaven (v. 34) suggests his acknowledgment of God as required in verses 25–26, 32.[40] His praise and glorification of the Most High makes explicit his new, humble posture before God. Although Nebuchadnezzar's subjects wished for his longevity (Dan 2:4; 3:9; cf. 5:10; 6:6, 21), the king declares that it is only the Most High "who lives forever" and has "an eternal dominion" (v. 34). This is the same point that he made in verse 3b. Nebuchadnezzar declares that those who dwell on earth, presumably including himself, are nothing compared to God (v. 35; cf. Isa 40:17). His acknowledgment that God "does as he pleases" (v. 35) shows that the king has learned the intended lesson of God's sovereignty over human kingdoms (vv. 17, 25, 32).

Just as Daniel said (v. 26), Nebuchadnezzar's repentance brings about the restoration of his kingdom (v. 36). In his closing statement of praise, he calls God "the King of heaven" (v. 37). Deuteronomy 32:4 declares that the Lord's "work" is "perfect" and "his ways . . . just," and Nebuchadnezzar learns this profound truth through experience ("everything he does is right and all his ways are just," v. 37), implying that his punishment is deserved. Whereas God's power is displayed through creation and other overtly divine acts, what the king emphasizes is God's ability to humble the proud (which is also a "sign," v. 3). This seemingly impossible task is attributed to the Lord elsewhere in the OT (e.g., 2 Sam 22:28; Isa 2:11–17; Job 40:9–13).

Nebuchadnezzar's life testifies to this fact. Lucas believes that Nebuchadnezzar had been "half-converted" previously, but in Daniel 4 his conversion becomes complete.[41] House argues that he had learned of God's wisdom and ability to save his servants in Daniel 2–3 but needed to learn

---

39. Widder, *Daniel*, 229.
40. Cf. Lucas, *Daniel*, 113; Seow, *Daniel*, 72.
41. Lucas, *Daniel*, 97, 104.

"that this God rules *him*."[42] Nebuchadnezzar's story in the book of Daniel ends here, but Coxon rightly points out his "central importance because the author subsumes under him not only the entire neo-Babylonian empire but all pagan empires which precede the messianic age."[43] Indeed, he is the "head of gold" (2:38) atop the statue in the first dream, and if God can do signs and wonders in his life (4:3) so that even he acknowledges the "King of heaven" (4:37; cf. 7:4), then surely nothing is impossible.

---

42. House, *Daniel*, 93 (emphasis in original).
43. Coxon, "Great Tree of Daniel 4," 91.

DANIEL 5

THE WRITING ON THE WALL

Now also the name of a popular language learning software, the original Rosetta Stone is an ancient Egyptian stele with an inscription of the same message in three languages: Egyptian hieroglyphic, Demotic, and Ancient Greek. When this stone was discovered by Napoleon's army in 1799, no one knew how to read Egyptian hieroglyphs, but the trilingual inscription enabled researchers to use their knowledge of other languages to decode this mysterious pictorial script and unlock the history of Ancient Egypt.[1] Research into ancient scripts of dead languages still continues today.[2] One of these scripts is Kitan, which was used by the Liao dynasty that ruled northern China from approximately 907–1125.[3] The late expert, Daniel Kane, dubbed the bilingual Kitan-Chinese inscription on the so-called "stele with no inscription" (無字碑) in Xian, China, "the Rosetta Stone of Kitan studies," though the Kitan language has proven very difficult to decipher.[4]

Daniel 5 likewise involves the challenge of reading and interpreting an obscure message. Unlike the two aforementioned steles, this message is written in only one language, and once again Daniel rises to the occasion to unlock a mystery, which involves a written text this time instead of a dream. Polaski notes the importance of writing in the book of Daniel, beginning with Daniel's study of Babylonian literature (Dan 1:4; cf. 9:2) and ending with his possession of a sealed book (Dan 12:4).[5] As he further points out,

---

1. See https://www.britishmuseum.org/blog/everything-you-ever-wanted-know-about-rosetta-stone.
2. For example, the Kushan script. See https://www.scientificamerican.com/article/ancient-unknown-script-is-finally-deciphered/ (19 July 2023).
3. Valerie Hansen, "The Kitan-Liao and Jurchen-Jin," in *Routledge Handbook of Imperial Chinese History*, ed. Victor Cunrui Xiong and Kenneth Hammond (London: Routledge, 2019), 213–214; Daniel Kane, *The Kitan Language and Script* (Leiden: Brill, 2009), 3.
4. Kane made this comment during his recorded George E. Morrison lecture, "The Decipherment of Dead Languages in China: The Case of Kitan," which he delivered on 19 October 2017; http://hdl.handle.net/1885/145873.
5. Donald Polaski, "*Mene, Mene, Tekel, Parsin:* Writing and Resistance in Daniel 5 and 6," *JBL* 123 (2004): 649.

"The fate of Daniel's people (12:1) as well as that of the emperor (5:24–28) is determined by writing."[6]

Daniel 5 begins with a new Babylonian king in power, Belshazzar, who holds a feast in which he acts arrogantly towards the Lord (vv. 1–4). A disembodied hand interrupts the party, and the terrified king summons his wise men to read what it wrote on the wall (vv. 5–9). When they are unable to, the queen recommends Daniel, who is brought before Belshazzar (vv. 10–16). Daniel first reminds Belshazzar of how the Lord previously humbled Nebuchadnezzar (Daniel 4) and then confronts Belshazzar about his pride (vv. 17–23). Finally, Daniel reads and interprets the writing on the wall, and its prediction about the end of Belshazzar's reign is promptly fulfilled (vv. 24–31).

5:1–4 BELSHAZZAR'S FEAST

The book of Daniel does not mention the end of Nebuchadnezzar's reign nor Belshazzar's accession to the throne. Only Belshazzar's final acts leading to the end of his reign are recorded (cf. passing references to Belshazzar, 7:1; 8:1). This demonstrates how the historical accounts in the Bible are selective, especially in relation to each biblical author's purpose.

Nevertheless, a historical perspective on Daniel 5 raises legitimate questions about the repeated references to Nebuchadnezzar as Belshazzar's "father" (vv. 2, 11, 13, 18) and a reference to Belshazzar as Nebuchadnezzar's "son" (v. 22), since historians agree that Nebuchadnezzar died in 562 BC and was succeeded by his son, Evil-Merodach, who is mentioned in 2 Kings 25:27.[7] There were even two more kings before Babylon's last king, Nabonidus, Belshazzar's father with whom Belshazzar served as co-regent and whose reign ended in 539 BC.[8] However, the Aramaic terms for "father" and "son" (*'av, bar*) have a broad semantic range (e.g., "a son of the gods," Dan 3:25), just as the parallel terms in Hebrew can simply indicate ancestry (e.g., "God of your fathers" [Exod 3:16] and "sons of Israel" [Gen 32:33, *passim*]) or characterization (e.g., "sons of Belial," Heb., Deut 13:13; "son of death," Heb., 1 Sam 20:31).

Furthermore, although Nabonidus was not a descendant of Nebuchadnezzar, he may have married Nebuchadnezzar's daughter, which would have made Belshazzar the grandson of Nebuchadnezzar.[9] Either way,

---

6. Polaski, "Writing and Resistance," 649.
7. Collins, *Daniel*, 30.
8. House, *Daniel*, 104, 107.
9. House, *Daniel*, 107. Cf. Collins, *Daniel*, 32.

House believes the issue here is "not just one of blood relationship, but of claims to royal legitimacy or affinity," citing how Elisha calls Elijah his "father" (2 Kgs 2:12).[10]

These historical issues are important, but in the book of Daniel, Nebuchadnezzar and Belshazzar serve as bookends for its presentation of the Babylonian kingdom, even though Nabonidus was more significant historically than his son, Belshazzar and Nebuchadnezzar was not actually Babylon's first king.[11] This literary bookending can be seen not only through the repeated references to Belshazzar in relation to his "father" Nebuchadnezzar in Daniel 5 and but also through the content of verses 1–4.

Just as "King Nebuchadnezzar made" (*'avad*, Aramaic) an image of gold and summoned his officials to attend its dedication (3:1–2), so "King Belshazzar made" (*'avad*; "gave" in NIV) a feast for a thousand of his nobles (5:1; cf. ESV).[12] More importantly, the book of Daniel opens with Nebuchadnezzar taking "vessels" (*keli*, Heb.) from the temple in Jerusalem and putting them in the temple of his own god (1:2), and now his "son," Belshazzar, commands that these "vessels" (*ma'n*, Aramaic) of gold and silver be brought out so that his guests may drink wine with them (5:2) – like father, like son. Nebuchadnezzar's plundering of the temple already symbolically represented his triumph over the God of Israel, but now Belshazzar takes it to another level by desecrating these vessels while praising his own gods (vv. 3–4).[13] This time, royal arrogance is of a particularly sacrilegious and probably drunken kind. After an initial reference to the feast (v. 1), verses 1–4 repeatedly refer to drinking and wine (*shetah, hamar*, Aramaic). Widder points out that Belshazzar even drinks "in front of" his guests (v. 1, ESV), who are all described with reference to the focal point, the proud king himself ("his nobles," "his wives," "his concubines," vv. 2–3).[14]

The listing of materials used to make these gods in verse 4 ("gold, silver, bronze, iron, wood, and stone") highlights their impotence as created things (cf. Deut 29:16; Isa 44:9–20) and recalls the destruction of the same four metals in Nebuchadnezzar's first dream (2:35, 45). Both the human kingdoms

---

10. House, *Daniel*, 107–108.
11. Collins explains that Nabopolassar, Nebuchadnezzar's father, "had inaugurated the dynasty in Babylon in 626 B.C.E." Collins, *Daniel*, 29. Lucas also defends the title of "king" (*melek*, Aramaic) used for Belshazzar in Daniel 5:1, arguing that it has a relatively wide meaning in Aramaic and can fairly be applied to Belshazzar. Lucas, *Daniel*, 126.
12. Widder, *Daniel*, 251, 254.
13. For the "unparalleled theological crisis" and "profound theological problem" resulting from the events of Daniel 1:1–2, see Seow, *Daniel*, 22.
14. Widder, *Daniel*, 255.

represented by these metals and the false gods made out of them are impotent before the God of heaven. Among other things, Nebuchadnezzar's first dream foretold the end of the Babylonian empire (2:39), and this part of the dream is about to be fulfilled. Sometimes world leaders today also do things that are quite insulting to God, but whether God brings immediate judgment as in Belshazzar's case or not, we can be sure that God will bring about justice at the appointed time (Deut 32:35).

5:5–9 THE WRITING ON THE WALL

While Belshazzar and his guests are drinking, mocking the God of heaven, and praising their own gods, the fingers of a hand suddenly appear and begin writing on the wall (v. 5). Seow draws a parallel between the supernatural "fingers" here and "the finger of God" as representing the power of God in writing the law at Sinai (Exod 31:18; Deut 9:10), sending the plague of gnats against Egypt (Exod 8:19), and casting out demons through Jesus's ministry (Luke 11:20).[15] Psalm 8:4 further describes the heavens as "the work of your fingers." Among these parallels, the closest to Daniel 5 is probably the divine writing at Sinai.[16] At the same time, the work of this supernatural "hand" (*yad*, Aramaic) in Daniel 5 (vv. 5, 24) is a reminder of the omnipotent "hand" of God (v. 23; 4:35), which surpasses all other "hands" (2:34, 45; 3:17; 6:28).[17]

The specific location "near the lampstand" suggests that the hand and the writing are in a visible and prominent spot, and Belshazzar indeed "watched the hand as it wrote" (5:5).[18] Furthermore, there is something ironic about Belshazzar desecrating the vessels taken from the "temple" (*hekal*, Aramaic) in Jerusalem (vv. 2–3) and the message being written on a wall in his "palace/temple" (*hekal*) near another "lampstand" (v. 5).[19] Just as judgment suddenly came upon Nebuchadnezzar as he boasted on the roof of his "palace/temple" (4:29–31), so judgment suddenly comes upon Belshazzar as he boasts in his "palace/temple" (5:5). It seems that the Lord is avenging his temple and bringing judgment upon Babylon and its "temple[s]."

---

15. Seow, *Daniel*, 79.
16. Kwong also points out the theme of judgment common to Exodus 8:19 and Daniel 5:5. Kwong (鄺炳釗), *Daniel*, 161.
17. Lucas, *Daniel*, 139.
18. House, *Daniel*, 109.
19. Michael Hilton connects these two lampstands. Cf. Hilton, "Babel Reversed – Daniel Chapter 5," *JSOT* 66 (1995): 101–102.

Upon seeing the hand and the writing, Belshazzar's cavalier attitude instantly changes to one of overwhelming fear (v. 6). Although Nebuchadnezzar was also "frightened/terrified" (4:5; *bahal*, Aramaic) by a dream, Belshazzar's face also turns pale, and he becomes weak-kneed. His feast and show of power are exposed for the sham that they are as the Lord humiliates him in front of his guests. Several commentators see the description of Belshazzar's terror as having comical elements ("his legs became weak and his knees were knocking").[20] The phrase translated "his legs became weak" can be translated more literally as "the joints/knots [*qetar*, Aramaic] of his loin were loosened [*sherah*, Aramaic]." Wolters notes the connection to Daniel's ability to "solve difficult problems" or "loosen knots" (*sherah qetar*, Aramaic) in verses 12, 16 and further believes that Belshazzar wet his pants in fear (v. 6), which is ironically alluded to later (vv. 12, 16).[21]

Just as Nebuchadnezzar had done before (2:2, 12; 4:6), Belshazzar calls in his "wise men" to dispel his confusion (5:7). Reinforcing this connection, "enchanters," "astrologers," and "diviners" were also involved previously (2:10, 27; 4:7).[22] The reward of purple clothing, a golden necklace, and the rank of third in command in the kingdom (5:7) is ultimately given to Daniel (v. 29), which broadly parallels Joseph's reward of linen clothing, a golden necklace, and being made second-in-command for interpreting Pharaoh's dreams (Gen 41:42–43).[23] This adds yet another link between Daniel and Joseph to those already pointed out in the above commentary (Dan 2:1–3; 4:4–18). The analogy between Daniel and Joseph is thus repeated and sustained in these chapters of Daniel.[24] The promise of being made "third" in the kingdom (5:7) could be explained by the co-regency of Belshazzar and Nabonidus, the queen's role

---

20. Collins, *Daniel*, 246–247; Seow, *Daniel*, 79.
21. Al Wolters, "Untying the King's Knots: Physiology and Wordplay in Daniel 5," *JBL* 110 (1991): 117–122. Cf. Danna Nolan Fewell, *Circle of Sovereignty: A Story of Stories in Daniel 1–6* (Sheffield: Almond Press, 1988). She writes, "either his legs give way or he loses control of certain bodily functions," 120. She further refers to "a puddle at [Belshazzar's] feet," 122.
22. Cf. Coxon, "The Narrative Style in the Court Tales of Daniel," 100–101.
23. Cf. Seow, *Daniel*, 79.
24. Cf. Tim Meadowcroft, "Metaphor, Narrative, Interpretation, and Reader in Daniel 2–5," *Narrative* 8 (2008). Meadowcroft remarks that Daniel is "a figure probably reflecting the same wisdom tradition as the Joseph Cycle. Each chapter in Daniel 2–5 entails a central metaphor, and the tension of the narrative centers on the search for an understanding of that metaphor, as initially perceived by the Babylonian king and subsequently interpreted by the Jewish sage," 257.

as second-in-command, or the Aramaic expression for "third highest ruler" simply referring to a high official.[25]

True to form, the wise men are of no help (v. 7) and again "afford an ample target for a monotheistic polemic against the impotent apparatus of the Babylonian cult."[26] Whereas in Daniel 2 the wise men did not even know what the dream was (see 2:4–7) and in Daniel 4 they knew the dream but could not interpret it (see 4:7), in Daniel 5 their problem is rooted in being unable to "read" (*qera*, Aramaic; vv. 7–8). If they can't even read the writing, they obviously can't provide an "interpretation" either (*peshar*, Aramaic; vv. 7–8). In this sense, their situation is similar to the wise men of Daniel 2, who had no chance of interpreting Nebuchadnezzar's first dream because they didn't even know what it was.[27] While Nebuchadnezzar at least knew what his dreams were, Belshazzar "has no knowledge of either the inscription's content or its meaning – he must ask for both."[28]

Reading and interpreting divine words will also be important in Daniel 9, in connection with Jeremiah's prophecy of the seventy years (9:2, 22). Thus the end of Belshazzar's kingdom and the Babylonian empire, the restoration of Jerusalem, and the salvation of the righteous (12:1) all depend on the written word. The importance of reading (*qara*, Heb.) divine words is also found in Deuteronomy 17:18–20, Isaiah 29:11–12, and Habakkuk 2:2. This emphasis on the written word in the book of Daniel is particularly significant in light of its many visions and dreams. Ultimately, the book of Daniel is a *book*, and we would do well to study its visions and dreams in the context of this book and of the rest of Scripture (see "Dreams and Visions," pp. 19–21).

Since the inscription on the wall was in Aramaic (5:25–28) and the wise men knew Aramaic (2:4), why couldn't they read the message, even if they are not able to interpret it? The biblical text does not answer this question, but this has not prevented some interpreters from proposing fascinating, though speculative, solutions.[29] For example, the Talmud (Sanhedrin 22a) gives several possibilities: the inscription was in an unfamiliar script, the writing was encoded using *atbash* (i.e., any appearance of the first letter of the alphabet would be substituted for the last letter, the second with the second-to-last,

---

25. Cf. Seow, who takes the "queen" (v. 10) as a "queen mother." Seow, *Daniel*, 79–80.
26. Coxon, "The Narrative Style in the Court Tales of Daniel," 111.
27. Cf. Meadowcroft, "Metaphor, Narrative, Interpretation, and Reader in Daniel 2–5," 262–263.
28. Polaski, "Writing and Resistance," 653.
29. Wolters, "The Riddle of the Scales," *Hebrew Union College Annual* 62 (1991): 157–158.

etc.), the words of the message were not written from right to left as usual but from top to bottom, the words were written with the letters in reverse order, or the words were written with the first two letters of each word reversed.[30] More conservatively, Goldingay reminds us that this Aramaic message would have been written with consonants only and that reading such an unpointed text "is partly dependent on actually understanding it."[31] He also observes that even Daniel's interpretation in verses 25–28 involves reading the words in one way but interpreting them in another (i.e., wordplay).[32]

Belshazzar was already "frightened" (*bahal*) when he saw the hand writing on the wall (vv. 5–6), but his wise men's inability to read or interpret the writing makes him "even more terrified" (*bahal*, Aramaic; v. 9; see 4:5, 19).[33] He takes the writing seriously, but there seems to be no hope of understanding the message. Even the "nobles," who had also been drinking from the temple vessels and mocking God (5:3–4), are disturbed (v. 9). The queen's words in verse 10 are a response to the dismay that these nobles voice along with the king. God and his word have thus stopped them in their blasphemous tracks and set the stage for Daniel to enter the scene.

5:10–16 DANIEL COMES BEFORE BELSHAZZAR

Belshazzar's "wives" and "concubines" were described in 5:2–3 as drinking from the temple vessels, but verses 10–12 feature the counsel of the "queen." Since she "came into the banquet hall" after hearing the voices of the king and the nobles, it seems that she was not present and hence not among the "wives" mentioned in verses 2–3.[34] Many commentators take this "queen" to be the queen mother rather than the queen consort. Montgomery points out her "masterful appearance on the scene" as befitting a queen mother, and Collins observes that "her memory goes back farther than that of the king."[35] Both scholars cite an ANE parallel as evidence that the term "queen" can be used

---

30. https://www.sefaria.org/Sanhedrin.22a.10?lang=bi. See *Belshazzar's Feast* by Rembrandt. For analysis of Rembrandt's use of Aramaic in this painting, see Mirjam Alexander-Knotter, "Rembrandt's Hebrew," *Jahrbuch der Berliner Museen* 51 (2009): 30–31.
31. Goldingay, *Daniel*, 109.
32. Goldingay, *Daniel*, 109.
33. Goldingay believes that the Aramaic expression in verse 9 further means that the king's "face grew *more* pale" than in verse 6. Goldingay, *Daniel*, 101.
34. Widder, *Daniel*, 266.
35. Montgomery, *Daniel*, 258; Collins, *Daniel*, 248.

in this way.³⁶ This seems reasonable if the king's mother outlived his father, the previous king, which would mean that she had been a queen in the proper sense and retained the title.³⁷

In any case, the queen tries to calm Belshazzar (v. 10). After a particularly ironic customary greeting ("May the king live forever!") in view of the king's imminent death (v. 30), she attempts to quell his fear (v. 10) in language that directly recalls verses 6 and 9 (*bahal*, *ziv*, *shanah*, Aramaic). Like Pharaoh's cupbearer in Genesis 41:9–13, she informs Belshazzar that there is someone who has the special ability to help (Dan 5:11). Like Joseph's track record of interpreting dreams (Gen 41:11–13), Daniel's "wisdom" has already been proven through his distinguished service to Nebuchadnezzar (Dan 5:11). The presence of "the spirit of the holy god[s] in him" recalls Nebuchadnezzar's characterization of Daniel (4:8–9, 18). Montgomery interprets the ambiguous Aramaic term for "god[s]" in Daniel 5:11 as a singular "God," based on lexical evidence, which also applies to the same phrase in Daniel 4:8–9, 18 and "son of the god[s]" in Daniel 3:25.³⁸ Pharaoh likewise described Joseph as one in whom is "the spirit of God" (Gen 41:38), which adds to the extended analogy between Joseph and Daniel in the book of Daniel and suggests the author is drawing out the work of the same Spirit in both men.³⁹

The queen's counsel is based on Daniel's reputation for divine "insight," "wisdom," and "intelligence" (Dan 5:11). Her words remind readers of how God has worked through Daniel thus far: giving him wisdom on multiple occasions (1:17; 2:23), being made chief of the wise men after interpreting Nebuchadnezzar's first dream (2:48), and being recognized as having the Spirit of God (4:8–9, 18).⁴⁰ This one who has also been called "Belteshazzar" (1:7; 2:26; 4:9) interpreted Nebuchadnezzar's dreams in the past, and the queen is confident that he can also solve the mystery of the writing on the wall (5:12; cf. 2:22, 28–30).

---

36. The source is Arrian's *Anabasis of Alexander* 2.12, written in Greek. This text is in the public domain.
37. Collins points out the ancient interpretation that this "queen" was Belshazzar's grandmother (Josephus) or mother (Origen, as cited by Jerome). Collins, *Daniel*, 248.
38. Montgomery, *Daniel*, 153, 258.
39. Although the Hebrew phrase *ruach elohim* in Genesis 41:38 could also be interpreted as "spirit of the gods," Pharaoh uses *elohim* to refer to a singular God in the very next verse (Gen 41:39), and *ruach elohim* consistently means "the Spirit of God" in the Pentateuch (Gen 1:2; Exod 31:3; 35:31; Num 24:2).
40. Joseph also had a track record of success (that is, in both Potiphar's house and prison), though he also suffered repeated injustices.

Daniel 5

When Daniel enters, Belshazzar confirms his identity as an Israelite exile (5:13), drawing Daniel's foreignness into the foreground again (cf. 1:3–6; 2:25). This time, his status as "one of the exiles my father the king brought from Judah" (5:13) associates him with the fall of Jerusalem and the temple vessels that Belshazzar has just desecrated (5:2–3; 1:1–2).[41] Already humbled by the writing on the wall (vv. 5–9), Belshazzar now has to rely on a captive whose God he has just insulted. The king, whose power seemed unchecked at the beginning of Daniel 5 is thus again exposed for the sham that he is. Belshazzar recognizes Daniel's reputation (vv. 14, 16; cf. vv. 11–12), explains the impotence of Babylonian wise men (v. 15; cf. v. 8), and promises Daniel a reward if he can read and interpret the writing (v. 16; cf. v. 7).

5:17–23 DANIEL REBUKES BELSHAZZAR FOR HIS PRIDE

Daniel's response to the king in verses 17–28 can be divided into two parts: Daniel's rebuke of the king (vv. 17–23) and his interpretation of the writing on the wall (vv. 24–28). Rather than immediately reading and interpreting the writing, Daniel first addresses the core issue of Belshazzar's arrogance, the reason for the inscription in the first place. The connection to Nebuchadnezzar's experience in Daniel 4 will become even more explicit below, but the rebuke of a king's pride provides an important link between Daniel 4 and 5. In both texts, a proud Babylonian monarch receives a divine revelation that baffles him but whose application is quite simple: humble yourself before the Most High (see 4:27, 37).

Daniel begins his speech by declining the reward from Belshazzar (v. 17), which shows that he is not motivated by money.[42] This is like the apostle Paul, who at times refused financial support so as not to "hinder the gospel of Christ" (1 Cor 9:12). Although it is not wrong to receive financial support in many circumstances (1 Cor 9:9–10), both Daniel and Paul remind us that we are servants of God, not money (Matt 6:24). Though Daniel is later rewarded as promised (v. 29), his delivery of an unwelcome message shows that he is not influenced by a desire for gain.[43] After Daniel declares that he will "read the writing" (v. 18), he leaves Belshazzar in suspense momentarily and speaks

---

41. Fewell rightly notes, "Daniel, being an exile, falls into the same category as do the temple vessels. They were brought from Judah by Nebuchadnezzar, the king, the father." Fewell, *Circle of Sovereignty*, 124. At the same time, I am unconvinced of her argument that Belshazzar is trying to best Nebuchadnezzar and is putting down Daniel.
42. Kwong also cites Abram's refusal of the king of Sodom's goods. Cf. Kwong, *Daniel*, 165–166.
43. Lucas, *Daniel*, 132.

first to the bigger issue of the king's pride by recalling in detail what happened to Nebuchadnezzar in Daniel 4. Lucas explains, "There can be little doubt that the author of Dan. 5 wrote it, and intended it to be read, with ch. 4 in mind."[44] He points out the references to Nebuchadnezzar in Daniel 5:2, 11 and the "extended comparison and contrast" between Nebuchadnezzar and Belshazzar in verses 18–23.[45] Nebuchadnezzar thus looms over this chapter in multiple ways – as the one who took the temple vessels in the first place (v. 2), as Belshazzar's "father" (vv. 2, 11), and as the one to whom Belshazzar unfavorably compares (v. 22).

Daniel's recounting of Nebuchadnezzar's experiences in Daniel 4 does not directly mention the dream of the tree but only what happened to him and what he learned. At the same time, Daniel's opening remarks about Nebuchadnezzar in Daniel 5:18–19 also allude to Daniel 2–3. Just as Daniel declared in Daniel 2:37, God "gave" (*yehav*, Aramaic) the "kingdom" (Heb.; *malku*, Aramaic) and "glory" (*yeqar*, Aramaic) to Nebuchadnezzar (5:18; cf. 4:22, 36). This comment by itself already informs Belshazzar that there is a God in heaven who is sovereign over all earthly kings, including him. Nebuchadnezzar's "high position" (*revu*, Aramaic; 5:19) echoes the height of the tree (4:22), and his power over "peoples, nations, and languages" (5:19, ESV) reminds readers of the command to these same groups to worship Nebuchadnezzar's golden image (3:4, 7). Hilton notes the irony of lordship over "languages" in Daniel 5 in view of the linguistic confusion at Babel (Gen 11:6–9), describing Babel as "the city where misunderstanding started" and commenting, "Here of all places it should be realized that God alone is master of all languages!"[46] Thus, just as the analogy between Daniel and Joseph appears multiple times (Daniel 2, 4, 5), so the analogy between Babylon and the Tower of Babel appears multiple times in Daniel 1–5 (see above commentary). Taken together, these entwined narratives remind readers that the Lord works among nations, even the most wicked ones, through faithful, wise, and long-suffering exiles.

Nebuchadnezzar was feared (5:19), just as the statue in his first dream was fearsome (2:31, ESV), and on more than one occasion, he dictated who would be killed (2:12; 3:6, 15) or who would be promoted (2:48–49; 3:30). Yet Nebuchadnezzar needed to learn that his power over life and death as well

---

44. Lucas, *Daniel*, 137.
45. Lucas, *Daniel*, 137.
46. Hilton, "Babel Reversed," 106. Angukali Rotohka points out the divine punishment of confusion in Genesis 11:7–9, Daniel 4:25, and Daniel 5. Cf. Rotohka, "Daniel," 1098.

as to exalt or humiliate (5:19) were relative to the Most High's absolute power (4:14; cf. Deut 32:39; 1 Sam 2:6–7). Despite appearances, Nebuchadnezzar could not really do whatever he "wanted" (*tseva*, Aramaic; Dan 5:19), since only the Most High can do as he "pleases" (*tseva*, Aramaic; 4:35), including giving kingdoms to whomever he "wishes" (*tseva*, Aramaic; 4:17, 25, 32; 5:21).

Daniel's description of Nebuchadnezzar's pride and fall in Daniel 5:20–21 concisely summarizes key events from Daniel 4. Just as Daniel 4:30–31 says, the king became arrogant, and God "stripped" (or "took away"; '*adah*, Aramaic) the kingdom from him (cf. 2:21). The Aramaic terms for "arrogant" (*rum*) and "hardened" (or "strong"; *teqaf*) in Daniel 5:20 are also used to describe the tree and Nebuchadnezzar in Daniel 4 (vv. 10–11, 20, 22, 30). The pride of his "heart" in Daniel 5:21 (*levav*, Aramaic; cf. Dan 4:16) contradicts the standard for kings in Deuteronomy 17:20 (*rum, levav*, Heb.), while also recalling the hardness of Pharaoh's heart (e.g., Exod 7:13, 22).[47] Thus, the one who exalted and humiliated others (5:19) was himself "brought down" from his "throne" (v. 20, ESV), even thinking and living like an animal (v. 21; cf. 4:25, 32–33).

Having finished retelling the story of Nebuchadnezzar's humiliation, Daniel redirects the focus back to Belshazzar by saying, "But you, Belshazzar" (v. 22).[48] Belshazzar was guilty because he did not "humble [his] heart" (*shefal, levav*, Aramaic), even though he "knew" what had happened to Nebuchadnezzar (v. 22, ESV; cf. Jer 3:7–8, 11; Ezek 23:11). He "exalted [him]self" (*rum*, Aramaic; cf. Dan 5:20), desecrated temple vessels, and glorified idols rather than the One whose "hand" sustains his very life and knows all his ways (v. 23; cf. vv. 1–4).

5:24–31 DANIEL READS AND INTERPRETS THE WRITING ON THE WALL, AND ITS MESSAGE IS FULFILLED THAT NIGHT

As in Daniel 5:4–5, the impotence of lifeless idols contrasts with the power of the living God demonstrated through the hand that writes on the wall (vv. 23–24). The timing of the writing already suggested that it was a divine response to Belshazzar's offensive acts (cf. v. 5; Gen 22:13–14), and Daniel clarifies that the hand was "sent" from God (v. 24). At long last, Daniel relieves the suspense of the narrative by reading the inscription: *mene, mene, tekel, parsin* (v. 25). As mentioned in the above commentary (vv. 7–8), the obscurity

---

47. Collins points out a parallel with the way the Targums describe the hardening of Pharaoh's heart. Collins, *Daniel*, 250.
48. Lucas observes how "you" in verses 18, 23 ('*ant*, Aramaic) "divides Daniel's indictment into two parts." Lucas, *Daniel*, 132. The same word in verse 13 opens Belshazzar's address to Daniel.

of this message is partially due to the need to supply vowels to a consonantal text. Many commentators believe that these words refer to units of weight: *mene* = minah, *tekel* = shekel, *parsin* = half-mina.[49] Yet even adding vowels does not make plain what these words mean together as a message.

Thankfully, Daniel explains the meaning, with the help of wordplay. The Aramaic word *mene* plays on the verb *menah* ("count/number") to convey that "God has *numbered* the days of your reign and brought it to an end" (v. 26, ital. added). Incidentally, if the second and third letters of *mene* are reversed (*nun*, *aleph*), the result is the consonants for the word "vessel," which is used in verses 2–3 to describe the temple objects that Belshazzar violated.[50] The Aramaic word *tekel* is a cognate of the verb "weigh" to represent Belshazzar being "weighed" and "found wanting" (v. 27). Wolters sees coherence between the measures of weight in the message itself and the "weighing" of Belshazzar, who does not measure up to the standard of God's justice.[51] The Aramaic word *parsin* plays on the verb *peras* ("divide") and also the noun *paras* ("Persia"; v. 28, "Your kingdom is divided and given to the Medes and Persians").

Despite the challenges in reading and interpreting the writing on the wall, the bottom line is clear enough: the God whose temple vessels have been desecrated has power over Belshazzar's "kingdom" (vv. 26, 28). As great as Belshazzar thinks he is (v. 23), he is lacking in God's eyes (v. 27). His time has come, and so has that of the Babylonian kingdom, just as Nebuchadnezzar's first dream predicted (Dan 2:39). The "Most High," not any earthly king, is "sovereign over all the kingdoms on earth" as emphasized in verse 21 as well as 4:17, 25, 32.

Daniel receives the promised reward (v. 29), though being the "third highest ruler in the kingdom" will shortly become useless when Belshazzar is slain that night and the kingdom taken over by the Medes (vv. 30–31).[52] Thus this promise by Belshazzar is as empty as his showing off to his guests earlier. Babel/Babylon falls again, in conjunction with linguistic confusion no less. Yet at the same time, Daniel dispels linguistic confusion and thus reverses Babel

---

49. For example, Wolters, "Riddle of the Scales," 160; Polaski, "Writing and Resistance," 657. They follow M. Clermont-Ganneau, "Mene, Tekel, Peres, and the Feast of Belshazzar," trans. Robert Rogers, *Hebraica* 3 (1887): 87–102.
50. The theme of holiness may also relate to the other two terms. "Shekel" naturally has a broad usage but note the phrase "sanctuary shekel" in Exodus 30:13 and elsewhere. Likewise, the Hebrew verb *paras* ("divide") appears in Leviticus 11 and Deuteronomy 14 in relation to unclean animals and the theme of holiness (Lev 11:44–47; Deut 14:2).
51. Wolters, "Riddle of the Scales," 163–164.
52. Hilton, "Babel Reversed," 109.

so that the word of God can be understood.[53] As Hilton points out, Daniel had to speak Aramaic, a post-Babel language, in order to communicate with Belshazzar and interpret the writing.[54] In the same way, the word of God has been written for humanity, but those who have had little exposure to it often need someone to read and interpret it for them. Later in Daniel 9, Daniel himself needs help interpreting Jeremiah's all-important prophecy of seventy years. Scripture is thus written once and for all but requires wisdom to be understood (5:11–12, 14; 9:22).

---

53. Cf. Hilton, "Babel Reversed," 107.
54. Hilton, "Babel Reversed," 110.

DANIEL 6
A LAW WHICH CANNOT BE CHANGED

As the first emperor of the Ming Dynasty (1368–1644), Zhu Yuanzhang (朱元璋) initiated many reforms, which were guided by one of the most important legal codes in Chinese history, *The Great Ming Code* (*da ming lü/* 大明律).[1] This code begins with a preface and a more general first chapter, and the next six chapters list penalties for various crimes.[2] For example, failure to accurately maintain household registration will be punished by being beaten with a heavy stick eighty times.[3] Even more serious are the "Ten Abominations," which are "crimes that endanger the fundamental hierarchical order" (that is, heaven, earth, gods, spirits, rulers, officials, family elders, or teachers), receive severe punishment, such as death by slicing (*lingchi/* 凌遲, or "death by a thousand cuts").[4]

Although the general principles of the first chapter of *The Great Ming Code* call for a consideration of the circumstances of a crime, "the penalties prescribed in the *Code* are all fixed. Once crimes and conditions are determined, there will be no room for a judge's discretion and no alternative remedies to select."[5] This code served "as the fundamental law of the dynasty," for later Ming emperors and officials followed the command of their first emperor: "the established *Code* should not be changed."[6]

In Daniel 6, Daniel's promotion by King Darius incites the jealousy of other officials, who futilely attempt to find fault with him (vv. 1–5). Seeing no other way to take Daniel down other than his obedience to God, they convince

---

1. Jiang Yonglin, *The Great Ming Code/Da Ming lü* (Seattle: University of Washington Press, 2005), xxxiii.
2. Yonglin, *Great Ming Code*, lv.
3. Yonglin, *Great Ming Code*, lvi–lvii.
4. Yonglin, *Great Ming Code*, lxvi.
5. Yonglin, *Great Ming Code*, lvii–lviii.
6. Yonglin even argues, contrary to convention, that "the early Ming ruling elite headed by Zhu Yuanzhang did not see law merely as a tool for behavioral control . . . . [but] as a concrete embodiment of the cosmic order," based on "heavenly principle" (*tianli*) and "human sentiment" (*renqing*). Yonglin, *The Mandate of Heaven and The Great Ming Code* (Seattle: University of Washington Press, 2011), 4. Yonglin continues, "If the ruler violated the cosmic order, Heaven would send down a warning and might eventually revoke the emperor's mandate to rule" (5; cf. 13). Yonglin, *Great Ming Code*, lxxxviii.

the king to issue an unchangeable decree forbidding prayer to anyone except himself for thirty days (vv. 6–9). When Daniel is caught praying to the Lord, he is reported to Darius, who despite his concern for Daniel cannot change the law (vv. 10–15). So Daniel is thrown into the lion's den, but God sends an angel to protect him (vv. 16–24). Then Darius issues another decree for all his subjects to honor the God of Daniel (vv. 25–28).

6:1–5 DANIEL PROMOTED BY KING DARIUS

Daniel 5 ended with the Babylonian kingdom falling to the Medes and Persians (v. 28) with Darius the Mede as the new king (v. 31). Critical scholars often cast doubt upon the historicity of Darius the Mede. Collins, for example, points out that there is no extra-biblical evidence confirming his existence.[7] On the other hand, conservative scholars have offered various solutions regarding the historicity of Darius the Mede, such as equating him with Cyrus or proposing that there are references to him in independent ancient sources.[8] Although extra-biblical support is important, we should also remember that it is unrealistic to expect external verification for every historical detail recorded in Scripture.

Daniel 6 begins with Darius appointing one hundred and twenty "satraps" to help govern his kingdom (v. 1). These provincial officials were mentioned earlier in Daniel 3:2–3, 27.[9] Three administrators, including Daniel, are set over all the satraps (v. 2). Through his "excellent spirit," Daniel distinguishes himself as the best of these three administrators, so much so that the king wants "to set him over the whole kingdom" (v. 3, ESV). The king's idea parallels Joseph's actual rule "over all the land of Egypt" in Genesis 41:40–44 (ESV).[10]

Perhaps Darius heard of Daniel's reputation in the midst of the transfer of power, but in any case, Daniel's continued success and influence were notable (cf. Dan 1:21). The Babylonian empire was gone, but by the grace of God, he still holds a position of influence in the new regime (cf. 5:29).[11] His longevity

---

7. Collins, *Daniel*, 30.
8. Respectively, see Donald J. Wiseman, *Notes on Some Problems in Daniel* (London: Tyndale Press, 1965), 12–16; Steven Anderson and Rodger Young, "The Remembrance of Daniel's Darius the Mede in Berossus and Harpocration," *BibSac* 173 (2016): 315–323. Cf. House, *Daniel*, 117.
9. Regarding satraps, see Goldingay, *Daniel*, 127.
10. Cf. Seow, *Daniel*, 52 and House, *Daniel*, 89.
11. From a broader historical perspective, House points out that Cyrus, who led the conquest of Babylon, kept many local leaders in place for the sake of continuity and stability. House, *Daniel*, 116, 118. Even so, the biblical text does not draw attention to this and still shows Daniel's longevity.

Daniel 6

bears witness to his membership in the "kingdom that will never be destroyed" (2:44). Likewise, believers can be assured of God's faithfulness to us, even in the midst of political upheaval.

The satraps and the other two administrators, however, become jealous and try to find fault with Daniel's work in order to bring him down (6:4). It is useless though because he is "trustworthy" (*aman*, Aramaic). Daniel truly loved the Lord and was faithful in the day-to-day work that King Darius appointed him to do. This is consistent with how earlier Daniel learned "the language and literature of the Babylonians" (1:4) and experienced God's blessing (1:17). Similarly, Paul commands the Thessalonians to "work with your hands . . . so that your daily life may win the respect of outsiders" (1 Thess 4:11–12). Throughout the book, Daniel is described as being faithful in his work and also faithful to God (cf. 6:23).

The only way that Daniel's enemies can trap him is if it "has something to do with the law of his God" (6:5). Daniel was devoted to God's word and even the administrators and satraps knew this. Whereas obedience to Scripture is basically implied in his earlier refusal to defile himself with the royal food (1:8) and in his three friends' refusal to worship the golden image (3:12–18), here Daniel's commitment to "the law of his God" is explicit (6:5). Later, in Daniel 9:2, he will be seen studying the Scriptures. At the same time, the term "law" (*dat*, Aramaic) sets up a contest between the law of God and "the law [*dat*] of the Medes and Persians" (6:8, 12, 15).[12]

While Daniel 6 is a continuation of the narrative in Daniel 5, scholars have also long recognized numerous parallels between the deliverance narratives in Daniel 6 and Daniel 3.[13] In both cases, the faithful are targeted by jealous enemies (3:8–12; 6:4–9), contradict an idolatrous decree (3:12, 16–18; 6:10–11), are sentenced to death (3:19–23; 6:16), and are miraculously delivered by God through an angel (3:24–28; 6:22), resulting in a Gentile ruler praising God publicly (3:28–29; 6:25–27). Of course, there are also differences between the two chapters, such as the king's role in devising the decree and his attitude toward the faithful (3:1–2, 10–15, 19; 6:5–9, 12–20). Nevertheless, there is a strong connection between Daniel 3 and Daniel 6, and chapter-level parallels in Daniel 2–7 help constitute the structure of the entire book (see "The Structure of Daniel," below).

---

12. Carol Newsom, *Daniel*, Old Testament Library (Louisville: Westminster John Knox, 2014), 194.
13. Newsom, *Daniel*, 189–190.

THE STRUCTURE OF DANIEL

As shown above, the deliverance of Daniel from the lion's den in Daniel 6 has extensive links to the deliverance of Shadrach, Meshach, and Abednego from the fiery furnace in Daniel 3. In addition, the commentary to Daniel 4–5 reveals how these two chapters also have many parallels, such as the humbling of a Babylonian king, the references to Nebuchadnezzar and Belshazzar in Daniel 5 as "father" and "son" (vv. 2, 11, 13, 18, 22), and verbal links (e.g., "spirit of the holy god[s]," "heart"). Furthermore, Daniel 2 and Daniel 7 both focus on an eschatological "vision"/"dream" of four earthly kingdoms, which are followed by the everlasting kingdom of God. Taken together, Daniel 2–7 exhibits a concentric or ring structure, in which Daniel 2 and Daniel 7 match, Daniel 3 and Daniel 6 match, and Daniel 4 and Daniel 5 match. Furthermore, this chiastic structure of Daniel 2–7 aligns with the bilingual profile of the book as a whole, in which Daniel 2–7 is written in Aramaic and Daniel 1 and Daniel 8–12 in Hebrew. Lucas describes Daniel 2–7 as "a distinct unit within the book," noting its emphasis on the themes of God's sovereignty over human kingdoms in history, the suffering of the faithful, and God's ability to humble proud kings.[1]

On the other hand, many commentators instead divide the book into two halves, with Daniel 1–6 being comprised of stories (or "court tales") and Daniel 7–12 of Daniel's visions. This proposed structure does not treat the linguistic shifts between Hebrew and Aramaic as decisive in the structure of the book, and besides grouping Daniel 1 with the subsequent chapters, emphasizes that Daniel 7 is a vision of Daniel that as such belongs with his other visions in Daniel 8–12. For example, Collins argues that this "contrast in genre" is "obvious" and sees Daniel 7 as being closer to Daniel 8–12 than to Daniel 2–6.[2] While recognizing the connections that Daniel 7 has to Daniel 2 and 4, he thinks that Daniel 7 is distinct because of Daniel's role as a dreamer and the lack of narrative context in the chapter, which accords with the visions of Daniel 8–12.[3]

Granting that the vision in Daniel 7 is Daniel's and lacks a narrative framework, its use of Aramaic and the main theme of four earthly kingdoms still stands as a very strong connection to Daniel 2. Indeed, Albertz rejects the basis for structuring Daniel as two halves and emphasizes that for Daniel 2–7, "we can clearly identify a main goal, the realization of God's kingdom against the mighty foreign empires of the world, which links each chapter like a chain."[4] He further points out that the supposed distinction between non-apocalyptic content in

> Daniel 1–6 and apocalyptic content in Daniel 7–12 does not hold for the apocalyptic material in Daniel 2:31–45 (cf. "in the last days," v. 28; author's translation).[5] Thus I prefer to see the structure of Daniel as a trifold division: Daniel 1, Daniel 2–7, and Daniel 8–12, while recognizing the "pivotal place" that Daniel 7 occupies as a transition to Daniel 8–12.[6]

---

1. Lucas, *Daniel*, 68–69.
2. Collins, *Daniel*, 29.
3. Collins, *Daniel*, 29.
4. Rainer Albertz, "The Social Setting of the Aramaic and Hebrew Book of Daniel," in *The Book of Daniel: Composition and Reception*, vol. 1, ed. John Collins and Peter Flint (Leiden: Brill, 2001), 175.
5. Albertz, "Social Setting of the Aramaic and Hebrew Book of Daniel," 176–177.
6. Lucas, *Daniel*, 194.

6:6–9 JEALOUS OFFICIALS CONVINCE KING DARIUS TO FORBID PRAYER TO ANYONE EXCEPT HIMSELF

Whereas in Daniel 3 the faithful also have jealous enemies (3:8–12), the command to worship the golden image originated from Nebuchadnezzar, who had set up the image himself (3:1–2). In Daniel 6, Darius is tricked by his officials into issuing a decree that they have devised to trap Daniel. Lucas sees "the element of conspiracy" to be of "major importance" in Daniel 6.[14]

The administrators and satraps begin their address to the king with a customary greeting, "May King Darius live forever!" (v. 6). Daniel himself uses a version of this greeting in verse 21, but the reality is that human kings do not live forever. Nebuchadnezzar and Belshazzar also received this greeting (2:4; 3:9; 5:10) but both had died, increasing the irony. Only God and his kingdom will last forever (2:44; 6:26).

The Aramaic verb *regash* translated as "went as a group" in Daniel 6:6 also appears in verses 11 and 15. The cognate Hebrew verb is used in Psalm 2, which speaks of the nations "conspiring" or "raging" (*ragash*) as they gather together to plot against the Lord and his king (vv. 1–2), a situation which generally parallels the conspiracy against Daniel. Based on the broader usage

---

14. Lucas, *Daniel*, 145.

of the Aramaic verb *regash*, Collins believes that it has "overtones of tumult."[15] Just as rebellion against the Lord and his king is futile in Psalm 2, so rebellion against the Lord and his servant Daniel is futile in Daniel 6. In both cases, enemies are crushed and humiliated (Ps 2:4, 9; Dan 6:24), and the kingdom of God triumphs gloriously (Ps 2:6–8; Dan 6:26–27). Yet unlike the earthly kings in Psalm 2:2, King Darius becomes wise (cf. Ps 2:10) and honors the Lord (Dan 6:26–27). The word "son" in Psalm 2:12 ("kiss the son") uses the Aramaic (*bar*), which is very unusual.[16] Sailhamer links this "son" (*bar*) to "one like a son [*bar*] of man" in Daniel 7:13 as well as his crushing of earthly kingdoms in Psalm 2:9 to Daniel 2:44.[17] It appears that the raging and crushing of enemies in Daniel 6 fits into this matrix of connections to Psalm 2.

The listing of officials ("administrators, prefects, satraps, advisers and governors") in Daniel 6:7, along with the claim of unanimous agreement, gives their counsel greater weight before the king. Because Daniel is one of the "administrators" (v. 2) and of the unlikelihood of such widespread unanimity (even if Daniel were excluded), House argues that this claim is a lie.[18] Ironically, their advice is ostensibly based on the king's greatness when they are manipulating him with ease.[19] Shortly, the king also will not be able to do as he wishes because he is bound by the law of the Medes and Persians (vv. 14–16). Newsom notes that the temporary prohibition against praying to anyone else for the next thirty days is not "an attempt to change the nature of the kingdom permanently" and "can only be understood as an act of flattery toward the king."[20] Darius's acceptance of their proposal suggests that he is vain and gullible.

The punishment of being thrown into a lions' den means certain death (v. 7; cf. v. 24). Being "thrown" (*ramah*, Aramaic) to one's death in Daniel 6:7, 12, 16 parallels being "thrown" into the fiery furnace in Daniel 3:6, 11, 15, 20–21, 24. The accusations of Daniel's enemies as described later in Daniel

---

15. Collins engages scholars who interpret *regash* to mean "gathering." Collins, *Daniel*, 266. Cf. JPS ("came tumultuously") and NRSV ("conspired and came").
16. Wilson explains that Aramaisms do appear in other biblical Hebrew texts but claims that *bar* never does. Gerald Wilson, *Psalms – Volume 1*, NIV Application Commentary (Grand Rapids: Zondervan, 2002), 113. Even if Wilson may have overlooked *bar* in Proverbs 31:2, such an Aramaism is still rare. Furthermore, as Wilson rightly points out, the Hebrew word for "son" (*ben*) is used in Psalm 2:7.
17. John Sailhamer, *The Meaning of the Pentateuch*, 507.
18. House, *Daniel*, 119. Cf. Newsom, *Daniel*, 194.
19. Cf. Lucas, *Daniel*, 149.
20. Newsom, *Daniel*, 195.

6:24 can be translated literally as, "ate their pieces," which sets up a parallel between them and fierce lions.[21] In Psalms 7:2; 10:9; 17:12; 22:13, 21, the wicked are likewise compared to lions. In Daniel 4:16, Nebuchadnezzar was "given the mind of an animal," and he is represented by a lion in the vision in Daniel 7:4, further supporting the metaphorical use of animals to represent human beings in the book of Daniel. Elsewhere in the OT, God himself is represented by a lion (Hos 11:10), as is the Messianic king (Gen 49:9). As Daniel 6:17, 23–24 shows, the lions' "den" is evidently "a pit that could be closed with a stone."[22]

The officials' plot not only takes advantage of the docile Darius but also uses the force of law to achieve their own selfish ends (v. 7). In this case, it is even a law that "cannot be altered – in accordance with the law of the Medes and Persians, which cannot be repealed" (v. 8). This is a clear example of an unjust law that is both idolatrous and devised for the purpose of entrapping an innocent person. In general, Christians are to obey the law and be known as law-abiding citizens (Rom 13:1–7), but there are cases when human laws conflict with the higher law of God as revealed in the Bible. The prophet Isaiah spoke against this: "Woe to those who make unjust laws, to those who issue oppressive decrees" (Isa 10:1). Gandhi's statement, "An unjust law is itself a species of violence," is also apt here.[23]

Once King Darius "inscribed the writing" (Dan 6:9, Aramaic), "Daniel's fate seems to be sealed," just like Belshazzar's fate was sealed by the writing on the wall in Daniel 5:24–25.[24] However, there is a categorical difference between the King of heaven who wrote the writing on the wall and the human king Darius, the law of the Medes and Persians notwithstanding. Polaski notes the theme of writing in Daniel 5–6 and argues that this emphasis strategically precedes the apocalyptic visions of Daniel 7–12.[25]

Daniel was in conflict with a king's order earlier (1:8–10) and on another occasion was ordered to be executed along with other wise men (2:12–13),

---

21. Cf. Coxon, "The Narrative Style in the Court Tales of Daniel," 112–113; Newsom, *Daniel*, 195.
22. Collins, *Daniel*, 267.
23. Mahatma Gandhi, *Gandhi on Non-Violence: Selected Texts from Mohandas K. Gandhi's Non-Violence in Peace and War* (New York: New Directions, 1965), 71. For Gandhi's interest in Daniel and Daniel 6, see Ed Noort, "Gandhi and the World of the Hebrew Bible: The Case of Daniel as Satyagrahi," *Religions* 13 (2022): 1–18.
24. Coxon, "The Narrative Style in the Court Tales of Daniel," 111.
25. Polaski, "Writing and Resistance," 650.

Despite Darius's desire to save Daniel, he is bound by "the law of the Medes and Persians" (vv. 12, 15). Though Darius issued the law, he cannot change it and is subject to it. So much for his supposed greatness that was the premise of the edict to begin with (v. 7). Only he can be prayed to for thirty days, but "he cannot bring about the one thing that he wants to happen."[35] Meanwhile, Daniel is committed to another law, the law of God, which also does not change. As Psalm 119:89 says, "Your word, LORD, is eternal; it stands firm in the heavens." Daniel's actions testify that divine law is even higher than the law of the Medes and Persians. Christians are also bound first and foremost to God's law, even as we are to follow earthly laws as a general rule.

Thus, there are two unchangeable laws that are in conflict. Yet we may ask whether Darius's decree truly cannot be "altered" (*shenah*, Aramaic) or "repealed" (*'adah*, Aramaic) in an absolute sense (Dan 6:8, 12, 15). Certainly, Darius's edict did not change and was enforced on Daniel, with the king even using his royal signet ring to make clear that "Daniel's situation might not be *changed*" (*shenah*, Aramaic; v. 17). On the other hand, Daniel 5 has just described a regime change from Babylon to the Medes and Persians. Even if this particular prohibition did last for the prescribed thirty days, "the law of the Medes and Persians" could only be in effect for as long as the *kingdom* of the Medes and Persians is in power. The same is true for the *Great Ming Code* mentioned in the introduction and any other law code on earth. In fact, Nebuchadnezzar's dream about the statue and its meaning of the triumph of the kingdom of God over all earthly kingdoms already implies the eventual demise of the kingdom of Medo-Persia (2:44), especially if the silver part of the statue represents this kingdom (2:32; 8:3–4, 20).

Furthermore, the Aramaic terms used for "alter" (*shenah*) and "repeal/change" (*'adah*) in Daniel 6:8, 12, 15 are strategically used elsewhere to testify to this central theme of the unchanging kingdom of God in contrast with the changing kingdoms of earth. Like Daniel 6:8, Daniel 2:21 uses both terms in a key poem, declaring that God "changes [*shenah*] times and seasons; he deposes [*'adah*] kings and raises up others." Nebuchadnezzar's kingdom "passed away" (*'adah*, Aramaic) from him for a period of time when God judged him for his pride (4:31; 5:20). In contrast, the kingdom of the son of man "will not pass away" (*'adah*, 7:14). Related to the theme of earthly law, Shadrach, Meshach, and Abednego are even said to have "set aside" or "changed" (*shenah*,

---

35. Lucas, *Daniel*, 151.

Aramaic) Nebuchadnezzar's command (3:28).[36] The law that Darius "set up" (*qum*, Aramaic; vv. 7–8, 15) also contrasts with the kingdom that God "sets up," which crushes all earthly kingdoms and "will itself endure forever" (2:44).

6:16–24 DANIEL IN THE LION'S DEN

Despite his best efforts, Darius has no choice but to have Daniel thrown into the lion's den (v. 16). The king's parting words show his continued concern for Daniel and reaffirm Daniel's reputation as a faithful servant of God: "May your God, whom you serve continually, rescue [*sheziv*, Aramaic] you!" (v. 16; cf. vv. 5, 14). This statement also highlights Darius's inability to "rescue" (*sheziv*, Aramaic) or "save" (*netsal*, Aramaic) in verse 14, while setting up the main point of the passage that God is able to "rescue" (*sheziv*, Aramaic; v. 20) and indeed "rescues" and "saves" (*sheziv, netsal*, Aramaic; v. 27). The Lord's power to save was also a major theme in the parallel deliverance passage of Daniel 3 (see "The Structure of Daniel," pp. 82–83). Darius's hope that God will save Daniel (6:16) contrasts with Nebuchadnezzar's boast that no god could "rescue" from his hand (3:15; cf. vv. 17, 28).[37]

The placing of the stone over the opening of the den and especially the king's seal ensures that "Daniel's situation might not be changed" (v. 17). Though the deed was done, Darius continues to be distressed, to the point that he cannot sleep (v. 18; cf. v. 14). At dawn, he goes to the lion's den (v. 19) and cries out with a glimmer of hope, "Has your God, whom you serve continually, been able to rescue you from the lions?" (v. 20)[38] This question repeats Darius's earlier sentiment in verse 16 about Daniel's faithfulness to God and the possibility of God's saving power.

Darius also refers to Daniel's God as "the living God" (v. 20), which Seow observes is used to refer to "the God of Israel as the true God (Jer. 10:10; 23:36) or as the God who manifests power in the face of threats posed by

---

36. Cf. Goldingay, *Daniel*, 67.
37. House, *Daniel*, 122. Based on the Aramaic form of the verb "rescue" (with a *nun*-suffix), Louis Hartman and Alexander Di Lella argue that its usage here is not a jussive (contrary to NIV, "May your God . . . rescue you"). Instead, they translate verse 16 as, "It is the God whom you serve so constantly who must come to your rescue." Hartman and Di Lella, *The Book of Daniel*, 195. Goldingay agrees and suggests other possible modal senses, such as "could" or "might." Goldingay, *Daniel*, 121. Goldingay also says that the (imperfect) verb form "leaves open whether God must, will, may, or can rescue Daniel," 132. On the other hand, Widder seems to argue for a jussive based on context. Widder, *Daniel*, 324.
38. Seow observes that Darius "does not simply presume the worst," for he considers "the possibility of Daniel's survival." Seow, *Daniel*, 93.

foreign nations against Israel (Deut. 5:26; Josh. 3:10; 1 Sam. 17:26; 2 Kgs. 19:4)."[39] Collins remarks, "The living God stands in contrast to the idols of the Gentiles."[40] Kwong further notes the parallel to Nebuchadnezzar's confession in Daniel 4:34, where the king praises "him who lives forever."[41] Thus, Seow believes that Darius's use of "living God" is "tantamount to a confession, however tentative that may be."[42] Darius had not been able to save Daniel, but the "living God" could, and did.[43]

The fact that Daniel answers at all shows that he has survived being in the lion's den (v. 20). Ever since he was thrown in and the den sealed off (vv. 16–17), the narrative was silent about what was happening inside and focused instead on Darius's distress (vv. 18–20).[44] Daniel's gracious address to the king ("May the king live forever," v. 21) shows that he harbors no bitterness, even though Darius had unwittingly endangered his life (vv. 6–9). House comments, "Unlike his opponents, who used the phrase before lying to the king in 6:6, Daniel speaks for his benefit."[45] His kind word is consistent with biblical teaching about gracious speech (e.g., Prov 12:25; Col 4:6).

Daniel proceeds to declare that God has delivered him by miraculously shutting the mouths of the lions (6:22). Darius's question about whether God is "able to rescue" (v. 20) is thus answered resoundingly in the affirmative. As with the salvation of Shadrach, Meshach, and Abednego in the fiery furnace, God "sent his angel" to protect his own (v. 22; Dan 3:28). Yet once again, God's people were not spared from danger but first "thrown" (*ramah*, Aramaic; v. 16; Dan 3:21) to their deaths before being delivered. Passages such as Daniel 7:21, 25 further show that whereas God is certainly able to save his people from suffering and sometimes does, in other situations he calls us to endure, just as Jesus did (1 Pet 2:21).[46]

---

39. Seow, *Daniel*, 93. Those who hold a more conservative view of Scripture do not need to follow Seow in taking these words as having been "put in the mouth of a foreign king" or characterize them, as Collins does, as "premature" and possibly "redactional." Collins, *Daniel*, 270.
40. Collins, *Daniel*, 270.
41. Kwong (鄺炳釗), *Daniel*, 187.
42. Seow, *Daniel*, 93.
43. Lucas, *Daniel*, 152. Rotohka refers to "the king's knowledge of the Lord." Cf. Rotohka, Daniel," 1099.
44. Newsom argues that the effect is to "increase suspense." Newsom, *Daniel*, 198.
45. House, *Daniel*, 123.
46. Cf. Philip Jenkins, *The Lost History of Christianity*, 97–100; 139–143.

Daniel explains that his survival is also God's declaration of his innocence (v. 22).[47] He had done no real harm to Darius (v. 22), even though he did not keep the edict. The king has Daniel lifted out of the den, and the biblical text provides the important comment, "no wound was found on him, because he had trusted ['aman, Aramaic] in his God" (v. 23; cf. v. 4 regarding his faithfulness ['aman] in his work).[48] Although there are more obvious links between Daniel and Joseph (see commentary), Daniel's being thrown into a den (or "pit") and being brought up from there broadly parallels Joseph's experiences of the same (Gen 37:20, 22, 24, 28; 40:15; 41:14).[49] Justice is served when Darius has Daniel's accusers thrown to the lions, who crush them immediately (6:24; cf. Pss 7:15–16; 141:10).[50]

6:25–28 KING DARIUS HONORS THE LORD

Darius's message to "all the peoples, nations, and languages that dwell in all the earth," including the greeting of "may your peace abound" (v. 25, author's translation), recalls Nebuchadnezzar's greeting in Daniel 4:1.[51] Both kings proceed to glorify God for his eternal kingdom and ability to do "signs" and "wonders" (4:2–3; 6:26–27; cf. 2:44; 7:14). In both contexts, Nebuchadnezzar and Darius emphasize the Lord's unmatched saving power and set forth a new "decree" that gives glory to God (3:29; 6:26–27), unlike an earlier "decree" that did not (3:10; 6:14). Widder sees Darius's decree as "a tapestry of themes from earlier chapters, woven together to display God's sole claim to sovereignty" and as such providing a fitting conclusion to the narratives of Daniel 1–6.[52]

At the beginning of Daniel 6, Darius issued an order that no prayer should be offered to anyone but himself for thirty days (vv. 7–9), but here at the end, he declares that "in every part of my kingdom people must fear and reverence

---

47. Newsom, *Daniel*, 199–200; Collins, *Daniel*, 271.
48. Cf. Widder, *Daniel*, 331.
49. The Aramaic term *gov* ("den") appears in verses 7, 12, 16–17, 19–20, 23–24.
50. Collins sees the execution of wives and children as following "the ancient custom of corporate responsibility." Collins, *Daniel*, 271. Newsom views this differently as an expression of the king's wrath. Newsom, *Daniel*, 201. For an Israelite parallel, see the case of Achan's family in Joshua 7:24–26, which is discussed in David Howard, *Joshua*. New American Commentary (Nashville: B&H, 1998), 180–187, 198.
51. These two sections of texts are identical, but the syntax differs in that only the final wish for peace is direct speech in Daniel 6:26, whereas all of Daniel 4:1 is direct speech, spoken in the first person. Widder further observes that Darius offers his praise to God without needing to be humbled like Nebuchadnezzar. Widder, *Daniel*, 335. Widder also sees Darius's "writing" in verse 25 as continuing the theme of writing in verses 8–10. Cf. Polaski, "Writing and Resistance," 665–667.
52. Widder, *Daniel*, 335.

the God of Daniel" (v. 26).[53] Once again, Darius calls Daniel's God "the living God" (v. 26; cf. v. 20). Only he "endures forever" (v. 26), whereas Darius's prohibition against prayer will expire shortly. As for Daniel, he continues to prosper by the grace of God (v. 28; cf. 1:21). Like David (1 Sam 17:37), the Lord had "rescued Daniel from the hand of the lion[s]" (Dan 6:27, Aramaic). Lions are among the mightiest of animals, but the Lord is also like a lion and is the mightiest of all (Hos 11:10; cf. Gen 49:9). David had also been delivered from a "bear" (1 Sam 17:37), and both of these fierce animals will appear in Daniel 7.

---

53. Polaski writes, "Darius's new edict does not so much cancel the prior edict as overwhelm it." Polaski, "Writing and Resistance," 667.

DANIEL 7

THE REIGN OF "ONE LIKE A SON OF MAN"

In the summers of 2001–2002, I had the opportunity to be part of a traveling, international Christian soccer team that played at various sites in central Thailand.[1] I had never been to Thailand before, and there were many new things about Thai culture for me to learn. One such thing is that Thailand is a constitutional monarchy with a king who is greatly adored and revered. Portraits of the king are prominently displayed in public places across the country.[2] Thailand also has a strict *lèse-majesté* that prohibits defaming the monarch and punishes violators with imprisonment.[3] Yet sometimes the veneration of the king in Thailand goes beyond what a cultural outsider might expect for a human ruler. Indeed, Ünaldi describes how Thailand's previous king, King Bhumibol, participated in a "royal Brahmin ceremony" in Bangkok that was believed to infuse him with cosmic power.[4] Ünaldi refers to King Bhumibol as a "demigod" and sees "Brahman notions of divine kingship" at play.[5] Belief in divine kingship or the divine right of kings can also be found in many other cultures, such as China (e.g., *tianming*/ 天命), early modern Europe, and ancient Mesopotamia, among others.[6]

Daniel 7 likewise features "one like a son of man" (v. 13), who is given rule over the earth and is worshiped by all (v. 14). As the commentary below will explain, the identity of this "one like a son of man" is controversial but

---
1. This ministry of OMF Thailand is still ongoing.
2. Amy Sawitta Lefevre, "For Thailand, a portrait is crucial for preparations of succession," 20 April 2016, https://www.reuters.com/article/lifestyle/for-thailand-a-portrait-is-crucial-to-preparations-for-succession-idUSKCN0XI002/.
3. See https://canberra.thaiembassy.org/monarchy-of-thailand/; "Lese-majeste explained: How Thailand forbids insult of its royalty," BBC News, 6 October 2017, https://www.bbc.com/news/world-asia-29628191.
4. Serhat Ünaldi, *Working Towards the Monarchy: The Politics of Space in Downtown Bangkok* (Honolulu: University of Hawai'i Press, 2016), 29–35.
5. Ünaldi, *Working Towards the Monarchy*, 32, 43. See the discussion of recent "hyper-royalism," 41.
6. For Mesopotamia, see Barry Wood, *Invented History, Fabricated Power* (London: Anthem Press, 2020), 19–26.

also crucial to the meaning of Daniel 7 and the whole book of Daniel. Daniel 7 divides into two halves: Daniel's vision (vv. 1–14) and the interpretation of this vision (vv. 15–29). The first half begins with the setting for the vision (v. 1), proceeds to focus on four beasts (vv. 2–8), and then describes the Ancient of Days and the "one like a son of man" (vv. 9–14). The interpretation of the vision in the second half focuses on the fourth beast and its defeat by the Ancient of Days (vv. 15–29).

7:1 THE SETTING FOR DANIEL'S VISION: BELSHAZZAR'S FIRST YEAR

As verse 1 makes plain, the setting for Daniel's vision in Daniel 7 is "the first year of Belshazzar king of Babylon." Since Belshazzar's death was narrated in Daniel 5:30, Daniel 7 self-evidently disrupts the chronological ordering of the preceding chapters. Daniel certainly received this vision before he was thrown into the lion's den under Darius the Mede in Daniel 6 and likely also before Belshazzar's feast in Daniel 5, since this feast took place at the end of Belshazzar's reign.[7]

This chronological disjuncture, though generally fitting the timing of subsequent visions (cf. Dan 8:1; 9:1; 10:1), is exceptional within the Aramaic section of Daniel (Daniel 2–7). At the same time, Daniel's vision of the four beasts has clear parallels to Nebuchadnezzar's dream of the statue in Daniel 2 (see "The Structure of Daniel," pp. 82–83). Thus, Daniel 7 can be seen as both a strategic conclusion to Daniel 2–7 and a transition to the visions of Daniel 8–12. Accordingly, Seow describes Daniel 7 as being "often regarded as the most important chapter of the book."[8] It foregrounds and develops the vision of Daniel 2 and orients the visions of Daniel 8–12. In particular, Nebuchadnezzar's vision of "the last days" (2:28, Aramaic) and Daniel's vision of "one like a son of man" (7:13) serve as both an inclusio for Daniel 2–7 and an overarching framework for the visions of Daniel 8–12. This combination of "the last days" and the Messiah is also a major feature in the structure and theology of the Pentateuch (Gen 49:1, 8–12; Num 24:14–19).[9]

Commentators have pointed out that whereas earlier Daniel interprets the dreams of others (e.g., Nebuchadnezzar), now Daniel himself has a "dream"

---

7. Jordan Scheetz points out that "the third year of King Belshazzar's reign" in Daniel 8:1 would also precede the feast in Daniel 5:1. Jordan Scheetz, *The Concept of Canonical Intertextuality and the Book of Daniel* (Eugene: Pickwick, 2011), 51.
8. Seow, *Daniel*, 99.
9. John Sailhamer, *The Pentateuch as Narrative*, 36, 235–236, 408–409.

and "visions" (v. 1).[10] Furthermore, Daniel is unable to interpret his vision and needs someone to explain it to him (vv. 15–20). Similarly, Joseph both interpreted the dreams of others (Gen 40:1–41:32) and also had his own dreams (Gen 37:5–11). Daniel's writing down of "the substance of his dream" (v. 1) converts the largely visual experience he had to a text that can be shared with others (cf. Hab 2:2).[11] Indeed, every vision in Scripture comes to us in the form of texts and so understanding them is ultimately a question of exegeting the text.

7:2–8 DANIEL'S VISION PART 1: THE FOUR BEASTS

Daniel's vision was given at night as he is lying in bed (cf. 2:1, 19) and begins with "the four winds of heaven churning up the great sea" (v. 2). The number four was implicit in the material composition of the statue in Daniel 2 and is explicit in Daniel 7 (vv. 2–3, 6, 17; cf. 3:25). "Wind" (*ruach*, Aramaic) also played a role in blowing away the broken statue in Daniel 2 (v. 35; cf. "spirit" of God in 4:8–9, 18; 5:11, 14).

"Four winds" appear in several other passages of Scripture (cf. 8:8; 11:4). In 1 Chronicles 9:24 and Ezekiel 42:20, the Hebrew phrase refers to "four sides" (i.e., north, south, east, west). Similarly, the same phrase is translated "four spirits" (*ruach*, Heb.) in Zechariah 6:5, corresponding to four chariots that go throughout the earth (vv. 1–3, 7). Thus, the number four "probably signifies totality."[12] In Zechariah 6:5 as well as Jeremiah 49:36, the "four spirits/winds" are also subject to the sovereign will of God. Thus, the image of the "great sea" being stirred up by "four winds" in Daniel 7:2 suggests a tumult of global significance, though still ruled by the power of God.[13] Isaiah 17:12 similarly links enemy nations with tumultuous waters: "Woe to the many nations that rage – they rage like the raging sea! Woe to the peoples who roar – they roar like the roaring of great waters!" (17:12).

Hartman and Di Lella see Daniel 7:2 as echoing Genesis 1:2: "The Spirit of God was hovering over the waters."[14] An extended allusion to Genesis 1 is evident through the varied beasts in Daniel 7:3–8 (cf. Gen 1:20–25) as well

---

10. John Collins, *Daniel*, Hermeneia, 29, 277.
11. The phrase, "interpretation of these things" (Dan 7:16), can also be understood as "interpretation of these *words*," parallel to "the interpretation of the word" (Dan 5:26, Aramaic).
12. Newsom, *Daniel*, 221.
13. Although "great sea" refers to the Mediterranean Sea elsewhere in the OT, Collins argues that the inland nature of Babylon and Medo-Persia implies that the "great sea" here does not refer to the Mediterranean but is symbolic. Collins, *Daniel*, 295.
14. Hartman and Di Lella, *The Book of Daniel*, 211. Cf. Newsom, *Daniel*, 221.

as the climactic delegation of authority to "one like a son of man" (7:13–14; cf. Gen 1:26–28).[15]

The next scene in the vision describes "four great beasts, each different from the others," coming up from the windblown sea (7:3; cf. v. 2). Later, the meaning of this coming up from the sea is explained as "ris[ing] from the *earth*" (v. 17). Widder understands the "four" beasts to be an indication of totality, this time "refer[ing] to the totality of human kingdoms . . . [which] transcends its closest historical referents and encompasses all of human history."[16] Rising from the sea also suggests that the beasts are sea creatures, perhaps even sea monsters akin to those in Genesis 1:21, Psalm 74:13–14, Isaiah 27:1, and elsewhere in Scripture.[17] Yet as these texts make clear, even such fearsome beasts are created by God, subject to his rule, and ultimately will be defeated by God.

At the same time, the appearances of the four beasts that come out of the sea look nothing like the serpentine sea monsters described in Isaiah 27:1 and elsewhere. On the contrary, the first three are land animals (lion, bear, leopard), and all four are unnatural in varying degrees, as the lion has eagle's wings, the bear is raised up on one side, the leopard has four wings and four heads, and the fearsome fourth beast has iron teeth and ten horns (vv. 4–8). Day traces the "fundamental derivation" and "fundamental basis" of these four beasts to Hosea 13:7–8, where the Lord successively compares himself to a lion, a leopard, a bear, and a fourth unspecified "wild animal" with reference to divine judgment against Israel.[18] Whereas Day believes that the author of Daniel 7 has filled out the picture of the "unnamed wild beast" using his own imagination, Kratz points out that "the imagery [of all four beasts] actually derives from chapter 4, and that most of the formulations were borrowed from chapters 1–6."[19] He explains that whereas Nebuchadnezzar temporarily

---

15. Cf. Andre Lacocque, "Allusions to Creation in Daniel 7," in *The Book of Daniel: Composition and Reception*, ed. John Collins and Peter Flint, vol. 1 (Leiden: Brill, 2001), 114–131, though this article mostly focuses on allusions to Canaanite creation mythology.
16. Widder, *Daniel*, 258.
17. Cf. Collins, *Daniel*, 288–289, 295. In his view, "The tradition is ultimately of Canaanite origin, but the symbolism of the sea is familiar from the Hebrew Bible and does not itself require direct acquaintance with Canaanite sources." Collins, *Daniel*, 289.
18. John Day, *God's Conflict with the Dragon and the Sea: Echoes of a Canaanite Myth in the Old Testament*, reprinted (Eugene: Wipf & Stock, 2020), 156–157. He still sees secondary Canaanite influences.
19. Reinhard Kratz, "The Visions of Daniel," in *The Book of Daniel: Composition and Reception*, ed. John Collins and Peter Flint, vol. 1 (Leiden: Brill, 2001), 91–113. This approach differs from those that seek parallels to ANE mythology. Furthermore, if this and other visions were from God, then the ultimate source of these additional details is God himself.

became a beast in Daniel 4, "the empires in Daniel 7 assume a lasting beastly form."[20] Seow likewise believes that Daniel 7 alludes to earlier chapters and concludes, "one cannot interpret Daniel 7 without the background of the first half of the book."[21] He also argues that the hybrid nature of some of the beasts implies uncleanness (cf. Leviticus 11; 19:19).[22]

The first beast, the lion with eagle's wings, has its wings removed before being made to stand up like a man and given "the heart of a man" (v. 4, Aramaic). This corresponds to Daniel 4, when Nebuchadnezzar was given "the heart of a beast" (v. 16, Aramaic; cf. 5:21) and "his hair grew like the feathers of an eagle" (4:33) before his "sanity was restored" (4:34). Daniel 7:4 thus depicts this restoration by reversing the imagery of a man becoming an animal (cf. 4:33).[23] This link to Daniel 4 suggests that the beasts in Daniel 7 refer to debased human kingdoms. At the same time, the humanization of the lion is a reminder of Nebuchadnezzar's restoration and the grace and power of God. In Daniel 2, the first part of the statue (the head of gold) referred to Nebuchadnezzar (v. 38), preparing the reader for the two visions to track with one another. The prominence of Babylon in both Daniel 2 and 7 links the four kingdoms to the archetype of humanity united in rebellion at the Tower of Babel/Babylon (Gen 11:1–9) and helps explain the symbolic use of Babylon in Revelation (14:8; 16:19; 17:5; 18:2, 10, 21).

The second beast "looked like a bear" raised up on one of its sides with three ribs in its mouth (v. 5). As Montgomery notes, the bear "is chosen as ranking next to the lion in size and fierceness" (cf. Hos 13:7–8; Amos 5:19; Prov 28:15). The command for it to "eat your fill of flesh" suggests that it will enjoy power for a period of time.[24] Daniel 5:28–31 already described the fall of the Babylonian kingdom to the Medes and Persians (see discussion of chronology in commentary on 7:1). In Belshazzar's third year (see Dan 8:1), Daniel has another vision that includes a ram with two horns, one longer than the other (8:3), which may parallel the bear's imbalance and asymmetry in being raised up on one side (7:5). Daniel 8:20 explains that this two-horned ram "represents the kings of Media and Persia," which suggests that the bear

---

20. Kratz, "Visions of Daniel," 96.
21. Seow, *Daniel*, 99.
22. Seow, *Daniel*, 102. Cf. Goldingay, *Daniel*, 161.
23. Seow, *Daniel*, 103.
24. Kratz suggests that this "is perhaps an allusion to the lions' den in Daniel 6." Kratz, "Visions of Daniel," 96 note 41.

in Daniel 7 does also.[25] In any case, Daniel 7 itself does not identify the bear nor give strong hints at its identity. Collins resists interpreting the "three ribs" in the bear's mouth too specifically, taking it instead "as a vivid and realistic picture of the animal eating its prey."[26]

The third beast "looked like a leopard" and has four wings and four heads (7:6). Its being "given *authority to rule*" (v. 6, *shaltan*, Aramaic; ital. added) recalls the brief characterization of the third part of the statue in Nebuchadnezzar's dream, "which shall rule [*shelat*, Aramaic] over all the earth" (2:39).[27] If "four" wings and "four" heads suggest totality, then this accords with the bronze part of the statue's rule over "all" the earth (2:39). The goat in Daniel 8 originally has a single large horn (v. 5) but in its place grow four horns "toward the four winds of heaven" (v. 8). Its association with the number four and traversal of "the whole earth" (8:5) fit the third kingdom as described in Daniel 2:39; 7:6. As Daniel 8:21 explains, this goat is Greece, which suggests the same for the leopard in Daniel 7:6.

In any case, Daniel 7 does not focus on the second and third beasts but on the fourth (vv. 7–8, 11, 19–26). Although still a "beast" (vv. 7, 11, 19), it is not compared to any animal (vv. 4–6), as it is "different from all the former beasts" (v. 7). Daniel's description does not begin with physical features but rather that it is "*terrifying* and frightening and very *powerful*" (v. 7; *dehil*, *taqif*, Aramaic; ital. added). The statue in Nebuchadnezzar's dream was also "terrifying" (2:31; *dehil*, Aramaic), and its fourth section was "strong [*taqif*] as iron" (2:40; cf. 4:11, 20).

Accordingly, the first physical feature mentioned is the fourth beast's "large *iron* teeth" (v. 7). Like the iron part of the statue (2:40), these teeth are used to "crush/break" things (*daqaq*, Aramaic), echoing what the lions did to their victims in Daniel 6:24. The fourth beast also "trampled underfoot whatever was left" and had ten horns (v. 7). Citing Zechariah 2:1–4, Collins explains that "horns symbolize power," such that the ten horns here "represent great strength and violent power."[28] The little horn that arises later has even greater power because three horns are "uprooted before it" (v. 8). Its human eyes may suggest intelligence, and this horn is especially characterized by arrogant speech (vv. 8, 11), which recalls the serpent in the Garden of Eden (Gen 3:1,

---

25. Cf. Rashi.
26. Collins, *Daniel*, 298.
27. Cf. Kratz, "Visions of Daniel," 96.
28. Collins, *Daniel*, 299.

4–5).²⁹ The overwhelming power of the fourth beast, its ability to "crush" and trample underfoot, and its association with a horn have broad parallels with the Messianic kingdom (cf. Gen 3:15; Dan 2:34–35, 44–45; Ps 132:17), but its pride and the subsequent context show that this beast is the opposite of that kingdom.

7:9–14 DANIEL'S VISION PART 2: THE ANCIENT OF DAYS AND "ONE LIKE A SON OF MAN"

Though the fourth beast is terrifying (vv. 7–8), the majesty of God is even more so, in accordance with the elevated poetic form of verses 9–10.³⁰ The establishment of "thrones" makes plain that we are no longer dealing with beasts and temporary earthly kingdoms but the eternal heavenly King. Kratz further believes that the title, "Ancient of Days," "corresponds to the 'end of days' of 2:28 and presents him as the Lord of time" (cf. 2:21).³¹ His appearance is nothing like an unnatural animal but instead displays his purity, holiness, and divine power (i.e., white clothes, hair like wool, burning throne and wheels, vv. 9–10). Other divine appearances in the OT are also accompanied by fire (e.g., Exod 19:18; Deut 4:24; 5:4–5; Ps 97:3), and the immunity of the Ancient of Days to fire recalls the protection that he bestowed upon Shadrach, Meshach, and Abednego in Daniel 3:25–27.

The book of Ezekiel's opening vision also involves fire (Ezek 1:4, 13, 27) and wheels (Ezek 1:15–21), and Collins believes that the wheeled throne described in Daniel 7:9 derives from Ezekiel 1.³² Although the beasts and "son of man" function differently in the two visions, Kim shows numerous allusions to Ezekiel 1–3 in Daniel 7 (e.g., wind [Ezek 1:4], four beasts [Ezek 1:5–14], eyes [Ezek 1:18], throne [Ezek 1:26], exalted human king [Ezek 1:26–28], cloud [Ezek 1:28], son of man [Ezek 2:1]).³³

The "thousands upon thousands" and "ten thousand times ten thousand" that surround the Ancient of Days in Daniel 7:10 further demonstrate his glory and parallel Deuteronomy 33:2. The seating of the court in verse 10 means that judgment is about to take place, and the books also serve this purpose (cf. 12:1; Exod 32:32–33). Once again, it is God's written word, not man's, that

---

29. For human intelligence, compare Keil and Delitzsch, *Daniel*, 642.
30. Seow, *Daniel*, 106. Cf. Collins, *Daniel*, 299.
31. Kratz, "Visions of Daniel," 97.
32. Collins, *Daniel*, 302.
33. Kim, "Biblical Interpretation in the Book of Daniel," 191–213.

bears absolute authority (cf. Dan 5:24–31; 9:2).[34] Even in the presence of God and his judgment, the little horn continues speaking arrogantly (v. 11; cf. v. 8). Yet the fourth beast of which it is a part is killed and "its body destroyed and thrown into the blazing fire" (v. 11; cf. 3:6). Though powerful and different from the other beasts (v. 7), this fourth beast and the earthly kingdom it represents ultimately comes to an end. This is a comfort to believers that no matter how mighty an oppressive human kingdom may be, it will ultimately come under God's judgment and pass away.

Similarly, the dominion of the other beasts had "passed away" (*'adah*, Aramaic; v. 12), unlike the kingdom of the son of man (v. 14). As for the three other beasts being "allowed to live for a period of time" after losing their authority (v. 12), some have sought historical evidence for the continued existence of Babylon, Media, and Persia, but Collins thinks that "the point is to distinguish the fourth beast from its predecessors" by emphasizing the severity of the judgment on the fourth beast.[35]

Poetic form is fittingly used again in verses 13–14 (cf. vv. 9–10) to describe the entrance of "one like a son of man." Now that the fourth beast has been killed and the little horn silenced, the way has been cleared for the everlasting kingdom of this representative of humanity. Given the parallel relationship between Daniel 2 and 7, the son of man's correspondence to the "rock" in Daniel 2:34–35, 45 suggests a Messianic interpretation. Both come after four earthly kingdoms and are central to the establishment of an eschatological, everlasting divine kingdom (2:34–35, 44–45; 7:13–14). This Messianic interpretation will be confirmed below.[36]

Longman observes the contrast between the reign of "horrifying hybrid animals" and God's reign through a human being, consistent with humanity's creation in God's image in Genesis 1:27.[37] God originally intended for humanity to rule the animals and all the earth (Gen 1:26, 28), and "one like a son of man" finally is. Messianism in Daniel 7:13–14 is thus "the eschatological fulfillment of man's humanity; it consists of eradicating evil and ruling over

---

34. Cf. Donald Polaski, "*Mene, Mene, Tekel, Parsin:* Writing and Resistance in Daniel 5 and 6," *JBL* 123 (2004): 649–669.
35. Collins, *Daniel*, 304. Cf. Lucas, *Daniel*, 183.
36. Even opponents of this view recognize that the earliest interpretations of Daniel 7:13–14 are Messianic (e.g. 1 Enoch 48; 2 Esdras 13). See Lucas, *Daniel*, 185; Montgomery, *Daniel*, 320–321. For NT interpretation of this text, see Michael Shepherd, "Daniel 7:13 and the New Testament Son of Man," *WTJ* 68 (2006): 99–111.
37. Tremper Longman III, *Daniel*, NIV Application Commentary (Grand Rapids: Zondervan, 1999), 186.

the whole of creation."³⁸ Psalm 8:4–8 also describes a "son of man/Adam" (i.e., not Adam himself) who rules the earth and all the animals, a text interpreted Messianically in Hebrews 2:6–8.³⁹ Lacocque further makes a connection between Daniel 7 and the seed of the woman, observing, "The Beast is overcome by the Human; Gen 3:15 is fulfilled. For, while the victory is God's, it is equally Man's as well."⁴⁰ Postell adds further that "Daniel's victory over the wild lions" in Daniel 6 has prepared the way literarily "for the Messiah's victory over the four wild beasts" in Daniel 7.⁴¹

Widder observes the contrast between the four beasts coming out of the sea and the "one like a son of man" coming with the clouds (Dan 7:13), which indicates his origin from "the heavenly sphere."⁴² Consistent with this, Daniel 2:34, 45 characterizes the triumphant rock as cut out "not by human hands." Some Messianic prophecies suggest this same heavenly origin (Ps 72:6; Isa 53:1; Mic 5:2). Thus, whereas human rulers can become bestial (Dan 7:3–8) and in some cases be restored (7:4), this "one like a son of man" is a special human and rules according to the divine will.⁴³ He is "led" to the Ancient of Days and "given" rule (vv. 13–14; note the passive verbs) which parallels the Messianic figure in Psalm 2:6, who is appointed king in Zion, and in Psalm 110:1, who waits for the Lord to make his enemies his footstool.

As Widder further explains, "In the Old Testament, YHWH is the one who rides the clouds" (Isa 19:1; Ps 104:3), such that there are two divine figures in Daniel 7:13–14: the Ancient of Days and "one like a son of man."⁴⁴ The latter's reception of "worship" (*pelach*, Aramaic) confirms his divinity. In the book of Daniel, this verb was repeatedly used of Shadrach, Meshach, and Abednego's refusal to worship the golden image (3:12, 14, 17–18, 28)

---

38. Lacocque, "Allusions to Creation in Daniel 7," 130. Though for Lacocque, Messianism "becomes" this eschatological fulfillment, and he sees "Messianic expectation" as being "reinterpreted" here. For Messianic eradication of evil, see Chen, *Messianic Vision of the Pentateuch*, 55–58.
39. The literary context also mentions the eradication of evil in Hebrew 2:14 (i.e., the defeat of Satan).
40. However, Lacocque interprets "the one like a son of man" as the saints. Lacocque, "Allusions to Creation in Daniel 7," 129.
41. Seth Postell, "Does the Book of Psalms Present a Divine Messiah?" in *Reading the Psalms Theologically*, ed. David Howard Jr. and Andrew Schmutzer (Bellingham: Lexham, 2023), 108.
42. Widder, *Daniel*, 378.
43. Unlike the rule of the son of man, "The nature of their rule is bestial." Lacocque, "Allusions to Creation in Daniel 7," 127. Furthermore, humanity "implies humaneness" and "contrasts with the bestiality of pagan empires." Lacocque, "Allusions to Creation in Daniel 7," 130.
44. Widder, *Daniel*, 379.

and also to characterize Daniel's worship of the true God (6:16, 20).[45] Yet the whole point of all these passages is that only the one true God should be worshiped – not Nebuchadnezzar's golden image, nor any other god. This is what it means to be faithful to the "law" of God (Dan 6:5). How then can it be *wrong* for "all the peoples, nations, and languages" (ESV) to worship the golden image in Daniel 3:7, but *right* for "all peoples, nations, and languages" (ESV) to worship the son of man in Daniel 7:14? As Postell explains, "The answer must be that the one like a son of man in Daniel represents a divine figure," namely a "fully human and divine Messiah," who is presented as such by the author of the book of Daniel.[46] Furthermore, interpreting the son of man in Daniel 7:13–14 as Israel (as some do) is untenable, given this figure's reception of the worship of the nations.[47] Elsewhere, I have argued similarly that the nations' worship of a human king, who must therefore also be divine, can be found even earlier in Genesis 27:29 ("May nations serve you and peoples bow down to you").[48] Daniel 7:1–14 is thus a specifically Messianic vision, with verses 13–14 at its literary and theological center.[49] Given the importance of Daniel 7 to the book of Daniel (see above), the Messiah is therefore central to the book of Daniel itself.[50]

In any case, the "everlasting dominion" and "kingdom . . . that will never be destroyed" in Daniel 7:14 emphasizes the same eschatological hope that is woven throughout the previous chapters of Daniel (2:44; 4:3, 34; 6:26). Yet here clearly the kingdom belongs not only to God but also to a human being, the son of man. As House explains, "the Davidic messiah is the only one to whom God gives the world's kingdoms permanently in the Old Testament."[51] As pointed out in the commentary on Daniel 2:44–45, the language and themes of God "sett[ing] up a kingdom" that will "endure forever" and this

---

45. Widder explains that the Aramaic verb generally can refer to "service or worship given to humans or to gods," but in the biblical Aramaic corpus, the recipient is almost always divine. Widder, *Daniel*, 380, note 67. Yet the one exception that Widder cites, Daniel 7:27, can be understood as fitting the rule if "his" and "him" are taken as referring to the "Most High" instead of the saints.
46. Postell argues that the book of Psalms does the same. Postell, "Does the Book of Psalms Present a Divine Messiah?," 109.
47. Postell argues that "the nations worshiping the people of Israel" is "unthinkable." Postell, "Does the Book of Psalms Present a Divine Messiah?," 109.
48. Chen, *Messianic Vision of the Pentateuch*, 96–97; Chen, *Wonders from Your Law*, 258–259.
49. Sailhamer, *NIV Compact Bible Commentary*, 404.
50. Lucas offers a contrary perspective, arguing that the "weakness [of a Messianic interpretation] is that the book of Daniel seems devoid of any messianic hope as usually understood." Lucas, *Daniel*, 185. Note, however, that this reasoning is circular.
51. House, *Daniel*, 131.

prediction being "trustworthy" parallels the language and themes of 2 Samuel 7:12–16. Even though David is not mentioned in Daniel 7, and the Messiah is presented as a son of man (i.e., Adam), the Edenic promise of a "seed" of the woman (Gen 3:15) is continuous with the promise of a royal "seed" to David (2 Sam 7:12–16). Thus, both Daniel 2:44–45 and Daniel 7:13–14 hint at the Davidic covenant in their own ways, while the former also adds elements of Isaianic stone and mountain imagery (Isa 2:2; 28:16; cf. Ps 118:22), and the latter incorporates worship imagery (cf. Gen 27:29; Ps 72:11). Furthermore, just as Daniel 7:2–14 alludes to creation in Genesis 1, so the stone passages in Daniel 2 allude to Genesis 3:15 ("he will crush your head") through the stone that "strikes" and "breaks/crushes" the statue, including its golden head (Dan 2:34–35, 44–45).

7:15–28 THE INTERPRETATION OF DANIEL'S VISION

Daniel's distress after this vision (v. 15) parallels Nebuchadnezzar's reactions to his two dreams in Daniel 2:1 and 4:5. Whereas Nebuchadnezzar had Daniel to help interpret, Daniel turns to "one of those standing there" (v. 16). Widder explains that this probably refers to "one of the attendants at the throne of the Ancient of Days."[52] Collins points out the "role of the interpreting angel" in Zechariah 1:9, 14, 19 which "becomes a distinctive feature of apocalyptic visions."[53] Daniel's request for the "meaning" (*yatsiv*, Aramaic) of his vision, and the angelic attendant's giving of the "interpretation" (v. 16) continues the aforementioned role reversal (cf. 2:36, 45; 4:24; 5:17, 26).

The heavenly interpreter's response is simple and to the point: the "four great beasts are four kings that will rise from the earth" (v. 17; cf. "sea" in vv. 2–3), but the saints will possess the kingdom forever and ever (v. 18). Rather than satisfying our curiosity about every detail, the angel leaves the four kings/kingdoms unidentified. He summarily explains what the beasts represent and then focuses on the end result, which is that the saints will receive God's everlasting kingdom, as proclaimed in Daniel 2:44; 4:3, 34; 6:26; 7:14. This is the main point and hopeful takeaway of Daniel's vision.

To be sure, this commentary discusses how the description of the first beast in verse 4 suggests a connection to Nebuchadnezzar and how Daniel 8 sheds light on the second and third beasts in verses 5–6. Furthermore, the angel's apparent silence concerning the son of man does not mean that this

---

52. Widder, *Daniel*, 380.
53. Collins, *Daniel*, 311.

figure symbolizes the saints nor that he is unimportant.[54] As shown above, the language, themes, and imagery in verses 13–14 suggest a Messianic interpretation. The focus on the saints in verses 18 and 27 fits Daniel's concern for the saints' suffering in verse 21. Furthermore, as Numbers 24:17–19 and other texts show, it is the Messiah who decisively wins the victory, and his people participate in his triumph.

Nevertheless, Daniel still wants "to know the meaning of the fourth beast," including its ten horns and little horn (vv. 19–20). The angelic interpreter had not explained these details in verses 17–18. Seow sees Daniel as "an empathetic visionary," who shares the terror of the vision.[55] The fourth beast is described as "different" from the other beasts, "terrifying," possessing "iron teeth," and having "crushed and devoured its victims and trampled underfoot whatever was left" (vv. 7, 19).[56] Its surpassing power and "crushing" of enemies are similar to the stone that destroys the great statue in Daniel 2:34–35, 44–45, but in reality the fourth beast with "iron" teeth corresponds more with the iron part of the statue, which also has power to "crush" (2:40). Likewise, its power to "trample underfoot" (7:7, 19) seems to echo the divine warrior in Isaiah 63:3 and victorious Israel in Micah 5:8, but its incessant boasting shows that the resemblance is only superficial (Dan 7:8, 11, 20).

The account of the fourth beast in verses 7–11 concluded with the destruction of this beast and presumably its little horn, but verse 21 is a flashback to when the little horn was "waging war against the holy people and defeating them."[57] Perhaps the apparent triumph of the wicked over the righteous contributed to Daniel being "troubled in spirit" in verse 15, similar to the experiences of the psalmist in Psalm 73 and the prophet Habakkuk (Hab 1:2–4).

---

54. Newsom calls interpreting the son of man "as a symbolic representation of Israel perhaps the most natural," which "became the consensus position of critical scholarship from the end of the nineteenth century until the last quarter of the twentieth century." Newsom, *Daniel*, 235. For example, Montgomery argues that the saints' possession of the kingdom in verses 18, 27 "are intentional replicas" of verse 14. Montgomery, *Daniel*, 319. Collins interprets the "holy ones" in verse 18 not as "saints" (NIV) but as "angelic beings" (cf. 4:13, 17, 23) and the son of man as the angel Michael, "the leader of the heavenly host." Collins, *Daniel*, 318. Interestingly, Seow sees the "holy ones" as referring to both "angelic beings" and "God's faithful people on earth," that is, "the holy ones who serve God in heaven" and "the holy ones who serve God on earth." Seow, *Daniel*, 110.
55. Seow, *Daniel*, 109.
56. Its "bronze claws" are only mentioned in verse 19, not in verse 7. Collins notes this as the only difference between the two descriptions of the fourth beast. Collins, *Daniel*, 319.
57. Newsom, *Daniel*, 238.

Nevertheless, the painful waiting ends when the Ancient of Days comes and judges in favor of his people (v. 22), just as Deuteronomy 32:35–36 predicts. The war lasts "*until* [*'ad*, Aramaic] the Ancient of Days came" (Dan 7:22), or equivalently, "*until* [*'ad*, Aramaic] the beast was slain" (v. 11). The same waiting period is also found in the Messianic text, Psalm 110:1: "Sit at my right hand *until* [*'ad*, Heb.] I make your enemies a footstool for your feet" (ital. added). Moreover, the theme of longstanding war that finally comes to an end fits smoothly with Genesis 3:15, "I will put enmity between you [the serpent] and the woman and between your offspring and hers," which will end when "he will crush your head, and you will strike his heel." Likewise, war against the saints ends when "the Ancient of Days came and pronounced judgment in favor of the holy people of the Most High, and the time came when they possessed the kingdom" (v. 22; cf. vv. 18, 27).

Daniel's desire to know more about the fourth beast (vv. 19–20) is granted by the angel's interpretation in verses 23–27. Building upon his earlier interpretation and the vision itself (vv. 7, 17, 19, 23), the angel explains that the "ten horns are ten kings who will come from this kingdom" and that the little horn is yet "another king" who will defeat three kings/horns (v. 24). The angel clarifies that this king's boasts (vv. 8, 11, 20) are in fact blasphemies "against the Most High" and reiterates his harm towards God's people (v. 25; cf. v. 21). The heavenly attendant further characterizes this king as wanting to exercise sovereignty over "set times" (*zeman*, Aramaic) and the "laws" of God (v. 25). However, it is "God, not human rulers," who "changes times and seasons" (Dan 2:21).[58] The above commentary on Daniel 6 also explained how only divine "law" (*dat*, Aramaic) truly cannot be changed. As Daniel already saw earlier in his vision (7:10–11, 22), God will pass judgment in favor of the saints, who will possess the kingdom, whereas the little horn will be destroyed (vv. 26–27). However, Daniel is still distressed after receiving this additional interpretation (v. 28), most likely because of the fourth beast and its affliction of the saints (vv. 21, 25).

In conjunction with the fourth part of the statue in Daniel 2, commentators have long debated the identity of the fourth kingdom, with the traditional interpretation being Rome but many modern interpreters taking it to be Greece, with the little horn as Antiochus IV Epiphanes in the second century

---

58. Seow, *Daniel*, 112.

BC.[59] While recognizing the difficulty of these biblical texts, the Messianic stone's crushing of the statue's feet of iron and clay links the fourth kingdom to Rome (Dan 2:34), and the defeat of the fourth beast in connection with the coming of the son of man seems to confirm this (Dan 7:11–14). At the same time, the little horn's delayed arrival (vv. 7–8, 24), blasphemies (vv. 8, 11, 20), and war against the saints (vv. 21, 25) suggests a Satanic figure, perhaps even an eschatological one (2 Thess 2:3; 1 John 2:18). Thus, even if the fourth kingdom is Rome, it is so in an open-ended way, as this would accord with both the representative nature of *four* kingdoms and their descent from Babylon/Babel, which is a paradigmatic example of rebellious humanity.[60]

Either way, what must not be lost is the emphasis of the vision itself as well as the interpretation: ultimately the son of man will rule the everlasting kingdom (v. 14) and the saints will possess it (vv. 18, 22, 27). As Rotohka explains, "Christians living under difficult regimes that do not allow religious freedom know that the powers of the world are always at war with God, and their evil seems indestructible. But no matter how evil the human regimes, they too shall pass."[61]

---

59. Widder, *Daniel*, 386–388. For more detailed discussion within the framework of Greece as the fourth empire, see Collins, *Daniel*, 320–322; Newsom, *Daniel*, 238–241; Lucas, *Daniel*, 188–194.
60. "The fourth empire is Rome" and "its final state has not yet been fulfilled." Sailhamer, *NIV Compact Bible Commentary*, 408. On the other hand, Shepherd believes that the fourth beast "most likely . . . does not represent a historical kingdom." Shepherd, *Daniel in the Context of the Hebrew Bible*, 89.
61. Rotohka, "Daniel," 1102.

DANIEL 8

DANIEL'S VISION OF A RAM AND A GOAT

I was born in 1979, the year of the sheep (or goat; Chinese: 羊), according to the Chinese zodiac. Like the animal, people born in this year supposedly tend to be shy and gentle (among other things) and as such are better suited for certain careers as well as most compatible with those born in the year of the horse, rabbit, or pig. In today's globalized culture, more and more people are aware of their Chinese zodiac animal, even if they may not pay much attention to its traditional interpretation.

As in Daniel 7, Daniel has a vision in Daniel 8 that revolves around various animals and their significance. Whereas his previous vision includes a lion, a bear, a leopard, and a fourth particularly terrifying animal (7:4–8), this vision centers on a ram and a goat. Coincidentally, these two animals align with my birth year in the Chinese zodiac (ram = 公綿羊; goat = 公山羊). Yet these two animals in Daniel 8 are anything but gentle. Scholars have debated a connection to Teucer's matching of the Babylonian astrological zodiac to nations, but this correlation postdates the book of Daniel and does not align smoothly with Daniel 8.[1] Thus, in order to understand the significance of the ram and the goat in Daniel's vision, we will need to study Daniel 8 itself. This chapter consists of the setting of the vision (vv. 1–2), the vision itself (vv. 3–12), a brief angelic conversation about the timing of the vision's fulfillment (vv. 13–14), and Gabriel's interpretation of the vision (vv. 15–27).

8:1–2 THE SETTING FOR DANIEL'S VISION: BELSHAZZAR'S THIRD YEAR

Whereas Daniel 2:4b–7:28 is written in Aramaic, Daniel 8 switches back to Hebrew, which was used earlier in Daniel 1:1–2:4a (see "The Structure of Daniel," pp. 82–83). Hebrew will be used for the rest of the book, and Daniel 8 thus begins the main Hebrew section of Daniel (chapters 8–12). At the same time, the content of Daniel 8 relates to the content of Daniel 7, which shows a close connection to the preceding literary context in Aramaic.

---

1. Newsom, *Daniel*, 261; Collins, *Daniel*, Hermeneia, 330.

This connection is immediately apparent through the timing of the present vision, which takes place in "the third year of King Belshazzar's reign" (8:1). The previous vision took place in "the first year of Belshazzar" (7:1). Daniel 8:1 even explicitly links the two visions, describing the present one as coming "after the one that had already appeared to me," in reference to Daniel 7.[2] Both the vision in Daniel 8 and its interpretation will reinforce this connection. Widder further sees Belshazzar as "the book's prototype for a blasphemous, arrogant king who shakes his fist at Israel's God."[3] Such figures regularly appear in Daniel's visions in chapters 7–12.

Besides the historical setting in Babylon during Belshazzar's reign, there is also the visionary setting described in Daniel 8:2. Like Ezekiel 8:1–3 and 40:1–2, Daniel has a vision in which he is transported to another place. He sees himself not in Babylon but approximately two hundred miles east "in the citadel of Susa in the province of Elam . . . beside the Ulai Canal" (v. 2).[4] Nebuchadnezzar had taken control of Elam, but Susa later became "the main capital of the Persian Empire" (cf. Neh 1:1; Esth 1:2).[5] Collins explains, "The location of the vision in Susa, while still in the reign of a Babylonian king, is a clue from the author that the vision concerns the Persian Empire."[6] This becomes explicit in verse 20, and Babylon plays no part in this vision. The first of the four kingdoms in Daniel 2 and 7, whose might was on repeated display in Daniel 1–4, is now out of the picture, a reminder that all earthly kingdoms will pass away (2:34–35, 44–45; 7:27).

8:3–12 THE VISION OF A RAM AND A GOAT

Daniel had seen himself next to the Ulai "Canal" (v. 2; *'uval*, Heb.), and his vision continues with a ram standing by "the canal" (v. 3; *'uval*, Heb.). The animal has two long horns, one longer than the other (v. 3). Abnormal animals are thus part of both visions in Daniel 7–8. Since Gabriel identifies this "two-horned ram" with "the kings of Media and Persia" in verse 20, it is natural to identify the two horns with these two kingdoms, with the more powerful Persia as the longer horn.[7] The "Medes and Persians" are likewise mentioned together in Daniel 5:28; 6:8, 12, 15 (cf. Esth 1:3, 14, 18–19;

---

2. Collins, *Daniel*, 329.
3. Widder, *Daniel*, 411.
4. Regarding the distance between these two places, see Lucas, *Daniel*, 212.
5. Lucas, *Daniel*, 212.
6. Collins, *Daniel*, 329.
7. Newsom, *Daniel*, 260–261.

10:2). Incidentally, representing Media and Persia as one kingdom (a single animal with two horns) supports treating them as one kingdom instead of two, as some scholars do in the four-kingdom schema of Daniel 2 and Daniel 7.[8] The ram in Daniel's vision charges to the west, north, and south, and it overpowers other animals (8:4). The fact that none "could stand against it" nor "rescue from its power," and that it did "as it pleased" and "became great" (v. 4), emphasizes the overwhelming might of this creature and foreshadows the power of other kingdoms to come (vv. 7–11, 25; 11:3, 16, 36–37).[9] Yet Newsom points out, "The book of Daniel repeatedly contrasts the power of the king with the power of the sage . . . [T]hough kings can wield the power of violence [in Daniel 1–6], the sage wields the power of God-given knowledge. And so it is here."[10]

As Daniel ponders this ram, he sees a male goat with one "prominent" horn "crossing the whole earth without touching the ground" (v. 5). House sees such travel as indicative of great speed.[11] With "great rage," the goat charges the ram and shatters its two horns (vv. 6–7).

Whereas at the height of the ram's power, "no animal could stand against it" (v. 4), the tables have turned, and now the ram is "powerless to stand against [the goat]" (v. 7). In other words, the seeming omnipotence of an earthly kingdom is temporary and an illusion.[12] Likewise, the most powerful nations of the world today will not always be so, whether because the King of heaven humbles them in the course of history (2:21) or because the perfect rule of the son of man has begun (7:14). From a human perspective, "none could rescue" from the "power" of the ram or the goat in their respective heydays (vv. 4, 7), but such power is ultimately the possession of God alone (Deut 32:39).

The goat becomes "very great," but its large horn is broken off and replaced by four other horns (v. 8). As in Daniel 7:2, "the four winds of heaven" suggests totality and in this case, the spread of the goat's rule in all directions (8:8). Once again, human kingdoms are shown to be short-lived (cf. v. 7). Since verse 21 identifies the goat with Greece and its large horn as its "first king," this horn has been widely understood as Alexander the Great.[13] He

---

8. Collins notes how this contrasts with how he himself interprets the four kingdoms in these two chapters. Cf. Collins, *Daniel*, 330.
9. Widder, *Daniel*, 413.
10. Newsom, *Daniel*, 261.
11. House, *Daniel*, 139.
12. Cf. Newsom, *Daniel*, 262.
13. Collins, *Daniel*, 331.

came from the "west" (v. 5) and defeated the Persians several times between 334–331 BC to establish his empire.[14] Alexander's sudden death by fever in 323 BC and the division of his kingdom between his four generals (Ptolemy Lagus, Philip Aridaeus, Antigonus, and Seleucus Nicator) fit the visionary imagery of verse 8.[15] Given Daniel's reception of this vision during "the third year of King Belshazzar's reign" (v. 1; ca. 547–546 BC), Daniel 8 once again demonstrates God's detailed knowledge of and sovereignty over the future.[16]

The next scene in Daniel's vision concerns a so-called "little horn" (v. 9; KJV, ESV), which proceeds from one of the four horns. Its similarities to the little horn in Daniel 7:8, 11, 20–21, 24–25 have led many to equate the two. Lucas lists the following parallels between the two horns: arising in a later stage of a powerful empire, starting small and becoming great, blasphemy and arrogance, persecution of the saints for a period of time, and opposition to and destruction by God.[17] However, Lucas also notes "differences in detail" between the two horns: one grows in the midst of ten horns (7:8), while the other grows out of one of four horns (8:9); the former defeats three of the ten horns (7:8), while the latter does not directly affect the other horns (8:9); the former is more focused on persecution (7:21), whereas the latter focuses on the desecration of worship (8:11–13); the former has power for three and a half "times" (7:25), whereas the latter has power for "2,300 evenings and mornings" (8:14).[18] Citing the "near unanimity" among scholars that the little horn in Daniel 8 represents Antiochus IV Epiphanes, Lucas concludes that the similarities to the horn in Daniel 7 "suggest that the referent is the same here," with the differences being "complementary views resulting from differences in

---

14. Lucas, *Daniel*, 214; Newsom, *Daniel*, 262.
15. Lucas, *Daniel*, 214; Collins, *Daniel*, 331.
16. For this date, see House, *Daniel*, 138. Critical scholars do not believe in predictive prophecy. For example, Collins argues that "The dating of this chapter to the reign of Belshazzar is clearly fictional. The angel's interpretation points already to the Hellenistic age in its identification of the king of Greece . . . Daniel 8 was probably written shortly after [the desecration of the temple ca. 167 BC and a few months after Daniel 7 was written]." Collins, *Daniel*, 343. Collins points out additional considerations, such as what he perceives to be greater historical accuracy and precision in passages that concern the Hellenistic age (esp. Antiochus IV Epiphanes) and its relevance for a Maccabean era audience. Collins, *Daniel*, 25–26, 29, 33. In response, conservative commentators have offered solutions to supposed historical inaccuracies in Daniel, and precise predictions of the distant future still reinforce the faith of God's people (see also Daniel 11).
17. Lucas, *Daniel*, 214.
18. Lucas, *Daniel*, 214.

focus in the two visions."[19] Likewise, Collins and Newsom take the respective little horns in Daniel 7 and Daniel 8 as Antiochus IV Epiphanes.[20]

It is important to note that the interpretation of the "little horn" in Daniel 8 is often intertwined with the interpretation of the little horn in Daniel 7. In turn, this relationship depends on the identification of the four kingdoms in Daniel 7 (and Daniel 2). For the aforementioned scholars, the fourth kingdom in Daniel 7 is Greece. On the other hand, this commentary has argued that the fourth kingdom is Rome (in an open-ended sense and in connection with the Messianic rock/son of man), whereas Greece is the third kingdom. In such a scheme, the respective little horns in Daniel 7 and 8 are not necessarily the same horn, despite their similarities, since they do not arise from the same kingdom. Keil takes this view, arguing that the horn in Daniel 7 "will go much further" in its arrogance (e.g., speaking against God, changing divine law) and sees the relationship between the two horns as that of type and antitype.[21] Shepherd points out that ancient Greek translations of Daniel 8:9 read "strong horn" rather than "little horn," weakening the connection between the little horn of Daniel 7 and the not-little but "strong horn" of Daniel 8.[22] I incline towards distinguishing between these two horns, while still holding that the horn in Daniel 8 is Antiochus IV Epiphanes. Another interpretation that identifies Rome as the fourth kingdom argues that the so-called little horn in Daniel 8 is not necessarily descended from Greece and so could be the same as the (non-Greek) little horn from Daniel 7.[23]

In any case, the horn's movement "toward the Beautiful Land" (8:9; cf. 11:16, 41) is preparatory for its abolishment of "daily sacrifice" to the Lord and desecration of the sanctuary (vv. 11–12). Its power and pride are shown through its exaltation to the "host of the heavens," throwing some of them down and trampling them, and comparability to "the commander of the army [of the LORD]" (*sar hatsava*, Heb.; vv. 10–11). The arrogance of the horn in these verses contrasts with Joshua, who bows down to "the commander of the army of the LORD" (*sar tseva adonai*, Heb.) in Joshua 5:14.

---

19. Lucas, *Daniel*, 214–215.
20. Collins, *Daniel*, 321, 333–334; Newsom, *Daniel*, 225, 263.
21. Keil, *Daniel*, 663–664.
22. Shepherd, *Daniel in the Context of the Hebrew Bible*, 94.
23. Sailhamer argues that "not with his power" in verse 22 (ESV) means that the kingdoms of the four horns do not all necessarily derive their authority and power from Greece. Sailhamer, *NIV Compact Bible Commentary*, 408–410.

The reference to "host of the heavens" and "starry host" (v. 10) introduces a cosmic element to this earthly conflict. Such a move also appears in the poetic celebration of Deborah's victory over Sisera in Judges 5:20, which reads, "From the heavens the stars fought, from their courses they fought against Sisera." Whereas this verse could be understood figuratively, Daniel 10:13, 20 describes actual conflict in the heavenly realm between an unnamed angel and both "the prince of Persia" and "the prince of Greece" (cf. 12:1). In other words, war on earth can mirror war in the angelic realm in the book of Daniel.[24] Similarly, Paul writes in Ephesians 6:12, "Our struggle is not against flesh and blood, but against the rulers, against the authorities, against the powers of this dark world and against the spiritual forces of evil in the heavenly realms" (cf. 2 Cor 10:4–5). Commentators have also observed parallels between the horn's ascent to the heavens in Daniel 8:10–11 and the king of Babylon in Isaiah 14:12–15, who is a "morning star" that ascends to heaven even "above the stars of heaven" but falls from its height. In Daniel 8:10, the horn is depicted at "that moment of its most brazen success, yet on the eve of its inevitable downfall."[25]

Like Nebuchadnezzar in Daniel 1:1–2, who attacked Jerusalem and laid waste to the temple, this horn moves against the land of Israel, halts the worship of the Lord, and humiliates the sanctuary of the Lord (8:9, 11–12). Such opposition to the worship of the Lord further recalls Nebuchadnezzar's golden image in Daniel 3 and Darius's prohibition against prayer to anyone but himself in Daniel 6. As seen above, this "horn" in 8:9–12 has similarities to the "little horn" in 7:8 who is yet to come, and it thus has parallels to both past and future kings. Indeed, it is not surprising for anti-God kings in different eras to resemble one another in certain ways (1 John 2:18).[26] Yet unlike Daniel 3 and 6, there is no indication that God's people will be delivered in Daniel 8, only that they are "given over" to this king (v. 12). Accordingly, Newsom

---

24. This may in turn relate to the debate over the term "saint/holy one" in Daniel 7:18, 21–22, 25, 27. The same term clearly refers to angels in Daniel 4:13, 17, 23, which contributes to Collins interpreting it likewise in Daniel 7. Collins, *Daniel*, 312–318. On the other hand, Seow sees the term as encompassing both "angelic beings" and "God's faithful people on earth," that is, "the holy ones who serve God in heaven" and "the holy ones who serve God on earth." Seow, *Daniel*, 110. Given the possession of the kingdom by the "people" of God in Daniel 7:27, it seems natural to take the term in Daniel 7:18, 22 as referring to "saints" rather than angels possessing the kingdom. Likewise, verse 25 more likely refers to the suffering of the saints rather than that of angels. Nevertheless, the war between the little horn and "holy ones" in verse 21 could involve both saints and angels. Cf. Lucas, *Daniel*, 191–193.
25. Lester, *Daniel Evokes Isaiah*, 84.
26. Rotohka lists Roman emperors Caligula, Vespasian, and Nero as well as Hitler, Stalin, and Mao from more recent history. Rotohka, "Daniel," 1103.

observes that compared to Daniel 7, Daniel 8 focuses on the godless actions of earthly kingdoms, has no parallel to the vision of the Ancient of Days and "one like a son of man" in Daniel 7, and only briefly mentions the fall of the so-called "little horn" at the end of the interpretation of the vision in Daniel 8:25.[27] She characterizes the "emotional tone" of Daniel 8 as "more somber" than Daniel 7.[28]

8:13–14 THE VISION TO BE FULFILLED IN 2,300 EVENINGS AND MORNINGS

With the vision proper concluded in verse 12, Daniel overhears a conversation between two "holy one[s]" concerning the timing of the climactic part of the vision (vv. 13–14). The two angels are concerned neither with the ram nor the goat as a whole (which would include its long horn followed by its four horns), but only the last scene of the vision, in which its last horn takes away the Lord's "daily sacrifice," brings "rebellion," defiles the "sanctuary," and "tramples" the "host" (vv. 10–13).[29] Whereas the earlier part of the vision focused on the rise and fall of empires without reference to God, his people, or the land of Israel (vv. 3–8), the goat's last horn is directly opposed to all these (vv. 9–12). Just as one angel asks another a question in verse 13, an angel also asks a question (albeit of the Lord) in Zechariah 1:12. Perhaps it is not accidental that 1 Peter 1:12 describes angels as "long[ing] to look into these things" (in reference to prophecy and the gospel). The angel's concern for the Lord's glory and the suffering of his people in Daniel 8:13 mirrors Daniel's similar concern in Daniel 7:19–22.

All of this presupposes Israel's return to the land and the reestablishment of the temple, which the books of Ezra and Nehemiah record. Since Daniel received this vision in "the third year of King Belshazzar's reign" (v. 1) and permission to return and build the temple was not given until the reign of Cyrus (2 Chr 36:22–23; Ezra 1:1–4), all these developments are still yet to come. Furthermore, this return to the land and rebuilding of the temple, whether seen from the perspective of Daniel 8:9–12 or Ezra-Nehemiah (cf. Isa 44:28; 45:13), are decoupled from the coming of the Messiah, the institution of the new covenant, and other eschatological realities. The Second Temple thus was

---

27. Newsom, *Daniel*, 256.
28. Newsom, *Daniel*, 256.
29. Goldingay sees it differently, "The seer only catches the end of their conversation." Goldingay, *Daniel*, 211.

not the eschatological temple, as it would be defiled just as Solomon's temple was defiled earlier. (We might ask, how many times will this happen then?) On a related subject, the prophecy of the Messiah's birth in Bethlehem (Mic 5:2) also assumes a return to the land.

This decoupling is important because many eschatological prophecies predict Israel's return to the land as one aspect of eschatological salvation (e.g., Deut 30:1–13; Jer 29:10–14; Ezek 36:24–30). The logical conclusion seems to be that the return to the land and a new temple are part of eschatological salvation, but only as they are accompanied by other aspects of this same deliverance. Indeed, passages such as Deuteronomy 18:15–18, Isaiah 11:10–11, and Hosea 1:11; 3:5 suggest that this return to the land will be led by the Messiah, and Zechariah 6:12–13 suggests that the new temple will be built by him. Accordingly, the returnees in Nehemiah 9:36–37 recognize that they are "slaves" in their own land and in "great distress," suggesting that they need another exodus and that the problem of exile has not yet been resolved.[30] Long before, Moses's refusal to lead Israel to the land without the presence of the Lord (Exod 33:15–16) reveals that possessing the land is not the end by itself, but rather "life in the land *with God*."[31]

Collins points out that the question that begins with "How long?" in Daniel 8:13 is a "traditional refrain in penitential literature," including the Psalms (e.g., Ps 13:1) and the Prophets (e.g., Isa 6:11; Hab 1:2).[32] Kwong paraphrases the angel's question as, "How long will the chosen people suffer persecution and the temple be defiled?"[33] The answer is a bit mysterious: "2,300 evenings and mornings" (v. 14). Many commentators interpret this to mean 1,150 days, since the "daily sacrifice" (vv. 11–13) is offered twice a day, once in the morning and once in the evening (Exod 29:38–39; Num 28:3–4).[34]

Collins characterizes this duration as "slightly less than the three and a half years of 7:25" and attempts a harmonization within his framework of equating the little horn of Daniel 7 with the so-called "little horn" of Daniel 8.[35] However, if these two horns are distinct (which is my inclination), then there is no need to correlate 1,150 days with "time, times and half a time"

---

30. Cf. Goldingay, *Daniel*, 212; J. Gordon McConville, "Ezra-Nehemiah and the Fulfillment of Prophecy," *VT* 36 (1986): 205–224.
31. L. Michael Morales, *Who Shall Ascend the Mountain of the Lord? A Biblical Theology of Leviticus* (Downers Grove: InterVarsity, 2015), 91–92 (emphasis original).
32. Collins, *Daniel*, 335.
33. Kwong (廓炳釗), *Daniel*, 243.
34. Lucas, *Daniel*, 218.
35. Collins, *Daniel*, 336.

in Daniel 7:25. Either way, the horn in Daniel 8 is still linked to the Greek kingdom and naturally interpreted as Antiochus IV Epiphanes, and 1,150 days could refer to the period in which a pagan altar was set up in the temple and sacrifices to the Lord were halted (1 Macc 1:44–54; 4:52–53).[36] Lucas points out that the temple was desecrated for only three years and eight days.[37] House sees 1,150 days as well as "time, times and half a time" (7:25; cf. 12:7) as representing "a reasonably brief period, not an exact number."[38]

8:15–27 GABRIEL'S INTERPRETATION OF THE VISION

After the brief exchange concerning the "2,300 evenings and mornings" (vv. 13–14), Daniel's visionary experience continues, and he seeks "understanding" (*binah*, v. 15, Heb.), as he did in Daniel 7:16, 19 (cf. 8:5). There is an angelic interpreter "standing" nearby to assist (8:15, NASB), just as there was in Daniel 7:16. Whether or not Newsom is right that the angelic speaker in Daniel 8:16 is probably the same as the one in 8:13, the text makes it clear that the interpreting angel is Gabriel (v. 16).[39] Collins points out that the name "Gabriel" (*gavriel*, Heb.) plays on the Hebrew word for "man" (*gever*, Heb.) in verse 15.[40] Gabriel means "man of God" or, as Collins prefers, "God is my hero/warrior."[41] Thus, Daniel sees Gabriel in verse 15 and then hears a voice instructing Gabriel to help Daniel "understand" (*bin*, Heb., vv. 16–17; cf. vv. 15, 27; 9:2, 22; 10:1).

When Gabriel approaches, Daniel is terrified and falls facedown (v. 17). Gabriel's address of Daniel as "son of man" is reminiscent of the Lord's identical address of Ezekiel (Ezek 2:1, 3, 6, *passim*). Like Ezekiel in Ezekiel 2:2, Daniel is also raised up on his feet (Dan 8:18).

As Gabriel explains, Daniel's vision is about "the time of an end" (v. 17, Heb.), "the end of wrath," and "the appointed time of an end" (v. 19, Heb.).[42] Two of these phrases are my literal translations that intentionally use "*an* end"

---

36. Collins accounts for the difference with three and a half years by suggesting that Daniel 8 was written slightly later so that some of the time had elapsed. Collins, *Daniel*, 336.
37. Lucas, *Daniel*, 218.
38. House, *Daniel*, 142. House, like others, interprets this horn as Antiochus IV Epiphanes. House, *Daniel*, 144–145.
39. Newsom, *Daniel*, 268. Lucas believes that "the voice of a man" in verse 16 (ESV) is the voice of God, citing the divine "voice" in Ezekiel 1:28 as a parallel. Lucas, *Daniel*, 219.
40. Collins, *Daniel*, 336.
41. Collins, *Daniel*, 336.
42. Regarding "the end of wrath," Lucas draws a parallel to Zechariah 1:12 in which the exile was divine punishment ("wrath") for Israel's sin but "the 'ongoing' wrath [Zech 1:15] is not

to avoid eschatological connotations of "*the* end," as many English versions translate in verses 17 and 19 (i.e., "the time of *the* end," "the appointed time of *the* end," NIV, ESV). While *qets* can refer to *the* end (Dan 12:13; Hab 2:3), it is not always the case. Although the presence or absence of the Hebrew definite article ("the") is a factor, it is not decisive, and context must be considered.[43] For Daniel 8:17–19, an important contextual factor is that the vision concerns the kingdoms of Persia and Greece (vv. 20–21), which means that both the fourth kingdom and the everlasting kingdom of "one like a son of man" (7:13–14) are still to come. Neither the vision nor its interpretation mentions God's everlasting kingdom, which will be set up in "the last days" in Daniel 2:28 (Heb.). Therefore, the time reference here must concern a prior period, even if from Daniel's perspective it still "concerns the distant future" (8:26).[44] As Shepherd explains, "Gabriel's interpretation of the vision concludes with the appointed end of the horn (8:25b)."[45]

Gabriel explains that the ram with two horns represents Media and Persia and that the goat represents Greece, with the large horn representing its first king (vv. 20–21; cf. vv. 3–8). As mentioned above, this large horn most likely refers to Alexander the Great, and the four horns refer to the four kings who inherited parts of his kingdom (v. 22; cf. v. 8).

The rest of Gabriel's interpretation (vv. 23–26) focuses on the goat's so-called "little horn" and complements the vision account in verses 9–12. In accordance with the original vision, this king arises after the four horns (v. 23, "at the latter end of their kingdom," ESV; cf. vv. 8–9). Gabriel further describes this timing as "when the transgressors have reached their limit" (v. 23, ESV), similar to how the sin of the Amorites reaches its God-ordained limit in Genesis 15:16.[46] He characterizes the king as "fierce-looking" (v. 23; cf. Deut 28:50), which generally fits Daniel's vision in verses 9–12 but adds the new elements of his cleverness ("understands riddles," v. 23; "cunning," v. 25) and

---

seen as a continuing, deserved punishment for Israel's sins, but rather as the harsh treatment of Israel by the nations." Lucas, *Daniel*, 219–220. Cf. Collins, *Daniel*, 338–339; Newsom, *Daniel*, 269–270.

43. See Ezekiel 7:2–3, 6; Amos 8:2, which have "the end" (*qets*, Heb.; with the definite article) but refer to a non-eschatological "end" for Israel. The same Hebrew phrase as in Daniel 8:17 ("the time of an end") is used in an eschatological context in Daniel 11:35, 40; 12:4, 9.

44. Cf. Keil, *Daniel*, 700. In this context, Keil repeatedly states that the vision "relates to" the end without having the end as its subject. Keil, *Daniel*, 698–700. Goldingay further argues that the restoration of the sanctuary (v. 14) presupposes additional human history on earth. Goldingay, *Daniel*, 216.

45. Shepherd, *Daniel in the Context of the Hebrew Bible*, 95. Cf. Lucas, *Daniel*, 220.

46. Collins, *Daniel*, 339; Newsom, *Daniel*, 270.

deception ("deceit," v. 25). Thus, just as the beastly nature, intelligence, and arrogant speech of the little horn in Daniel 7 recall the serpent in the Garden of Eden, so the horn's cunning and deceit in Daniel 8 recall the craftiness of this serpent (Gen 3:1–5). Though the wisdom of this king superficially resembles that of Solomon and the Messianic king (Isa 11:2–3), his persecution of the "holy people" (v. 24; cf. v. 12) shows that he is their enemy.

Collins links the "Prince of princes" in verse 25 to "the commander [or 'prince'] of the army of the Lord" in verse 11 and identifies the common referent to be God himself.[47] The evil king's opposition to the Lord was described in verses 10–12 in terms of his ascent to the heavens, trampling of the heavenly host, attempt to be like God, and opposition to the worship of the Lord and his people. Yet Gabriel declares, "He will be destroyed, but not by human power [or, 'hand']" (v. 25). In other words, "truth" may be "thrown to the ground" for a time (v. 12; cf. Hab 1:4) by this arrogant, violent king, but God knows and will bring him down in the end. The suffering of God's people is intense and real, but God still reigns and promises that our suffering will not last forever and will not be in vain. Antiochus IV Epiphanes would die in an untimely manner, but Collins points out that "the point here is ideological or theological. Epiphanes' downfall will come because of his effrontery to God and by divine power."[48] Indeed, the phrase, "not by human hand" (v. 25, Heb.), recalls the stone in Daniel 2:34, 45, which was cut out "not by human hands" but by God's power.[49]

Gabriel concludes his interpretation in verse 26 by citing the "evenings and mornings" that were the subject of the angelic dialogue in verses 13–14, before his interpretation began in verse 17. As noted above, "2,300 evenings and mornings" (v. 14) refers to the divinely delimited period of time that the sanctuary will be defiled and the people of God will suffer under the arrogant horn (v. 13). Widder points out that in verse 26, Gabriel does not refer to the vision as "the vision of the smaller horn" (or something similar; cf. v. 13) but rather "the vision of the evenings and the mornings."[50] In other words, Gabriel's conclusion is "a final reminder in a chapter full of reminders that, while the evil would be unimaginable, it was on a leash."[51] His last words here emphasize this broader context for suffering, which is intended to encourage

---

47. Collins, *Daniel*, 333, 341. Cf. Newsom, *Daniel*, 264, 272.
48. Collins, *Daniel*, 341.
49. Cf. Lucas, *Daniel*, 221.
50. Widder, *Daniel*, 432.
51. Widder, *Daniel*, 432.

saints in a future time as well as Daniel himself (v. 26). The sealing of the vision can be understood in terms of it "concern[ing] the distant future" from Daniel's perspective and hence its precise fulfillment being hidden from him.[52] For today's readers, who can look back on its historical fulfillment, the vision is now unsealed and recorded in Scripture for our edification.[53]

Daniel, however, is exhausted and distraught by the vision (v. 27). As noted above, the vision in Daniel 8 is more somber than the vision in Daniel 7. Newsom argues that Daniel's ability to get up to do "the king's business" after a few days "underscores the sharpening divide between the two contexts of Daniel's consciousness, one having to do with his role as adviser to the king" (cf. v. 1; 5:11), and the other "his relation to a distant future at the end of the reign of Gentile kings."[54] Despite Gabriel's attempt to help (vv. 16–17), Daniel still does not "understand." Perhaps the darkness and evil he saw were too overwhelming. In the next chapter, however, Daniel will gain understanding through the Scriptures (9:2) and Gabriel's help in interpreting them (9:22).

---

52. Kwong, *Daniel*, 250.
53. Cf. Newsom, *Daniel*, 273.
54. Newsom, *Daniel*, 273.

DANIEL 9
SEVENTY YEARS AND SEVENTY SEVENS

Civil service examinations were a significant part of late imperial China as the main way that government officials were trained and recruited. The subject of these examinations was the Confucian classics and approved commentaries, and this system produced elites who would uphold the state's version of Confucian orthodoxy.[1] As Elman explains, "A classical education became the sine qua non [an essential condition] for social and political prestige in national and local affairs," with such education being "the correct measure of their [i.e., Chinese gentry's] moral and social worth."[2] There were different levels of examinations to weed out most examinees, so that those who passed the highest level (one in six thousand during the Qing dynasty) represented the most outstanding ability among those who had devoted themselves to the study of these authoritative texts.[3]

Miyazaki describes how boys as young as three years old started their learning at home and undertook formal education at age seven if their families could afford it. If they completed this education at age fifteen, they would have memorized the Confucian classics (Four Books and Five Classics/四書五經), consisting of 431,286 characters.[4] Such a formidable task gave rise to poems providing encouragements to study, such as "A boy who wants to become a somebody [/] Devotes himself to the classics, faces the window, and reads."[5]

Whereas Daniel 7–8 focused on Daniel's two visions during the reign of Belshazzar, Daniel 9:2 begins with him studying "books" (Heb.). Collins

---

1. Hang Lin, "Examination Essays, Paratext, and Confucian Orthodoxy: Negotiating the Public and Private in Knowledge Authority in Early Seventeenth-Century China," in *Early Modern Privacy: Sources and Approaches*, ed. Michaël Green, Lars Cyril Nørgaard, Mette Birkedal Bruun (Leiden: Brill, 2022), 297, 299–300. Cf. Benjamin Elman, *A Cultural History of Civil Examinations in Late Imperial China* (Berkeley: University of California Press, 2000), 134–136.
2. Elman, *Civil Examinations in Late Imperial China*, 128.
3. For pass rates, see Elman, *Civil Examinations in Late Imperial China*, 141. Cf. Ichisada Miyazaki, *China's Examination Hell: The Civil Service Examinations of Imperial China*, trans. Conrad Schirokauer (New Haven: Yale University, 1981), 121–122.
4. Miyazaki, *China's Examination Hell*, 14–16.
5. Cited in Miyazaki, *China's Examination Hell*, 17. This line comes from the well-known poem, 勸學詩 ("Encouragement to Study"). Other English translations exist (original: 男兒欲遂平生志，六經勤向窗前讀).

understands these works to be "the books of the Prophets."[6] Daniel 9:11, 13 further refers to "the Law of Moses," implying Daniel's knowledge of this text also. The vision of the ram and the goat in Daniel 8 had left Daniel confused (v. 27), but like believers today, he has Scripture to which to turn.[7] Indeed, Daniel 6:5 characterized Daniel as being devoted to "the law of his God," which evidently guided both his daily conduct and his outlook on the future. Coincidentally, this same passage also describes Daniel praying toward open windows (6:10), parallel to the poetic line cited above.

In Daniel 9:2, Daniel studies the book of Jeremiah and its prophecy of the seventy-year desolation of Jerusalem. His study of Scripture shows that the visions in the book of Daniel do not exist in a vacuum but within the framework of the written word of God.[8] Collins points out that unlike the rest of the book of Daniel, "another biblical text serves explicitly as point of departure for the revelation."[9] Daniel's devotion to Scripture sets an example for us to do likewise. If other authoritative texts, whether the Confucian classics or others, have been studied intensely, how much more should we study the Bible, the only text that bears divinely imparted, absolute authority.

Daniel 9 begins with Daniel's study of the book of Jeremiah (vv. 1–2) and continues with his prayer of confession (vv. 3–19). In the middle of Daniel's prayer, Gabriel arrives as before (cf. 8:16) to give him additional understanding about the fulfillment of Jeremiah's prophecy of the seventy years through a period of seventy "sevens" (vv. 20–27).

9:1–2 DANIEL STUDIES JEREMIAH'S PROPHECY OF THE SEVENTY-YEAR DESOLATION

The setting for Daniel 9 is "the first year of Darius son of Xerxes," a Mede (v. 1).[10] The Babylonian setting of Daniel 7–8 as represented by the reign of Belshazzar (Dan 7:1; 8:1) has thus passed. Those two chapters had "turned back the clock," in the sense that Belshazzar's death, the fall of the Babylonian empire, and the Medo-Persian takeover were narrated previously in Daniel

---

6. Collins takes "books" to refer "presumably to the books of the Prophets," without implying canonization at that time. Collins, *Daniel*, Hermeneia, 348.
7. Obviously, Daniel's Scriptures did not include the NT or OT books that had not yet been completed.
8. To reinforce this point, this commentary has shown that the contents of these visions (e.g. Daniel 2; 4; 7) often allude to extant Old Testament texts.
9. Collins, *Daniel*, 347.
10. Regarding Xerxes, see Widder, *Daniel*, 456.

Daniel 9

5:30–31. A Medo-Persian setting characterized Daniel 6, just as it does in Daniel 9.

The reference to Darius, who was "a Mede by descent" (9:1), recalls "Darius the Mede," who "took over the kingdom" in Daniel 5:31. As discussed in the commentary on Daniel 6, there has been controversy concerning the existence and identity of this king, but I hold to the historicity of Darius the Mede. Returning to Daniel 9:1, Widder explains, "The first year of Darius, regardless of Darius's exact identity, corresponds with the fall of Babylon in 539 BCE."[11] This is also around the time of Cyrus's edict in his "first year" that permitted the rebuilding of the temple (2 Chr 36:22–23; Ezra 1:1–4; cf. Dan 9:25).[12] Thus, it is a critical moment both in world history and in God's salvation plan. Moreover, if Daniel was exiled in 605 BC (see commentary, 1:1–7), he has been an exile for over sixty years. There was another group of exiles in 597 BC (2 Kgs 24:14) and yet another group when Jerusalem fell in 587/586 BC. With respect to the setting of Daniel 9 in the first year of Darius (539 BC), almost fifty years have passed since the fall of Jerusalem.

The significance of these chronological details arises in relation to Jeremiah's prophecies of the seventy-year "desolation" (*horbah*, Heb.) of Jerusalem. Jeremiah 25:11 says that the land will be a "desolate [*horbah*] wasteland" for "seventy years," during which Judah and surrounding nations will serve Babylon. Jeremiah 25:12 adds that after this time God will judge Babylon, which itself will be made "desolate forever." Jeremiah 29:10 likewise mentions "seventy years" in connection with a period of Babylonian dominance but further predicts Israel's restoration and return to the land. House explains that Daniel "wondered if this was also a time of renewal for his people."[13] Were the seventy years almost over?

Whether or not the exiles would return home soon has obvious personal importance to Daniel, all the more because other elements of this restoration as foretold in Jeremiah 29:10–14 characterize eschatological salvation. For example, "You will seek me and find me, for you will search for me with all

---

11. Widder, *Daniel*, 457. On page 456, notes 10, 12, she mentions the theory that Darius and Cyrus are the same person (her view), as well as the theory that Darius "was an official/general appointed over Babylon by Cyrus." For ancient evidence in support of dating the fall of the Babylonian empire to 539 BC, see Newsom who cites the Babylonian Chronicle (the most reliable source), the Cyrus Cylinder, Herodotus, Xenophon, and Berossus (who is cited by Josephus). Newsom, *Daniel*, 163.
12. Michael Shepherd takes the edict as also being given in 539 BC. Shepherd, *Daniel in the Context of the Hebrew Bible*, 95. Newsom prefers 538 BC. Newsom, *Daniel*, 504.
13. House, *Daniel*, 149.

your heart" in Jeremiah 29:13 (Heb.) alludes to Deuteronomy 4:29–30, which describes the exiles' wholehearted pursuit of God "in the last days" (Heb.).[14] Moreover, the good plans that the Lord has for his people in Jeremiah 29:11 are for their blessed "end" (*aharit*, Heb.) and "hope" (cf. Jer 31:17; Num 23:10). The Hebrew word translated "end" in Jeremiah 29:11 is part of the aforementioned phrase, "in the last days," which also appears in Jeremiah 23:20; 30:24; 48:47; 49:39 (Heb.). The promise to "restore your fortunes" in Jeremiah 29:14 (ESV; "bring you back from captivity," NIV) is repeated in the subsequent context of Jeremiah (30:3, 18; 31:23; 32:44; 33:7, 11, 26), and all of these texts are likely rooted in Deuteronomy 30:3, itself linked to the circumcision of the heart in Deuteronomy 30:6. In Daniel 9:24, Gabriel mentions "an end to sin," "atone[ment] for wickedness," and "everlasting righteousness," which seems to confirm the eschatological significance of the seventy years for the "holy city." Indeed, Daniel's love for the holy city was already evident in 6:10 through his daily prayers for Jerusalem. The ultimate restoration of Jerusalem/Zion is a central concern of the prophets (e.g., Isa 1:27; Jer 3:17; Ezek 40:1–2; Zech 1:16–17).

House points out that Daniel 8:13 also mentioned the "desolation" of a future temple in Jerusalem during the Greek era.[15] Since Daniel is living under Medo-Persian rule, this implies that the eschatological blessings that are to come at the end of the seventy years still await a future time. Indeed, the four-kingdom scheme in Daniel 2 and 7, with the everlasting kingdom of God coming after the fourth kingdom, implies the same.

---

14. Chen, *Wonders from Your Law*, xxv.
15. House explains that this desolation not only involves destruction but also the fact that Jerusalem does not fulfill its intended purpose. House, *Daniel*, 151.

BIBLICAL ALLUSIONS IN THE BOOK OF DANIEL

The book of Daniel's relationship to other OT books can be seen not only through Daniel reading Jeremiah's prophecy in Daniel 9:2 but also through numerous allusions to extant biblical material. As noted in the commentary, Daniel 9 also has allusions to the Pentateuch, 1 Kings, and Isaiah. Other parts of the book of Daniel likewise contain biblical allusions to Genesis (e.g., creation, Tower of Babel, Joseph), Isaiah (e.g., large mountain, passing through fire), Ezekiel (e.g., trees representing kings), and other books (see commentary). These and many other OT books were already written during the postexilic time in which the book of Daniel was written. An entire book has been written on the book of Daniel's allusions to Isaiah, and a dissertation supervised by Matthias Henze has explored its allusions to Genesis and Ezekiel.[1]

Henze himself characterizes the book of Daniel as "something of a *locus classicus* of inner-biblical exegesis."[2] He further connects this phenomenon of "inner-biblical interpretation" to Daniel's ability to interpret divine mysteries (e.g., 2:16–19, 24; 4:9). Commenting on "the unusually large amount of traditional material" in Daniel, Bentzen even calls the author of Daniel "a scholar who studied the old prophets and explained them with the help of his knowledge of older traditions."[3] Doukhan further points out the importance of allusion to the theology of Daniel and apocalyptic literature generally.[4] Thus, despite the presence of some obscure and esoteric elements in Daniel, especially in the second half of the book, it is actually firmly rooted in the thought world of the OT.

Working within the framework of apocalyptic literature as a genre, Collins explains that "virtually all apocalypses draw heavily on some traditional material . . . . apocalyptic language is symbolic and allusive."[5] Along with other scholars, he sees biblical allusion as playing an important role in Daniel.[6] At the same time, he believes that apocalyptic literature also has mythological allusions (e.g., Canaanite, Ugaritic), though this is debated by others.[7] In any case, the presence of numerous biblical allusions in Daniel along with their importance to the book implies that Daniel should not be studied in isolation from the rest of the OT, though it can and should be studied as a book in its own right.

---

1. Lester, *Daniel Evokes Isaiah*. Kim, "Biblical Interpretation in the Book of Daniel." See also the table of representative allusions and discussion in Daniel Block, "Preaching Old Testament Apocalyptic to a New Testament Church," *Calvin Theological Journal* 41 (2006): 30–32.

2. Matthias Henze, "The Use of Scripture in Daniel," 278–279.
3. Aage Bentzen, *Daniel*, 2nd ed. (Tübingen: Mohr Siebeck, 1952), 5.
4. Doukhan, "Allusions," 285.
5. John Collins, "Apocalyptic Genre and Mythic Allusions in Daniel," *JSOT* (1981): 93.
6. John Collins, *Daniel: With an Introduction to Apocalyptic Literature* (Grand Rapids: Eerdmans, 1984), 100; Collins, *The Apocalyptic Imagination: An Introduction to Jewish Apocalyptic Literature*, 2nd ed. (Grand Rapids: Eerdmans, 1998), 18.
7. Collins, *Apocalyptic Imagination*, 18–19; John Collins, *Apocalypse, Prophecy, and Pseudepigraphy: On Jewish Apocalyptic Literature* (Grand Rapids: Eerdmans, 2015), 67.

9:3–19 DANIEL RESPONDS TO GOD'S WORD WITH A PRAYER OF CONFESSION

The "understanding" that Daniel gains from Scripture regarding prophecy (v. 2) is not merely for the sake of satisfying intellectual curiosity but leads him to prayer (v. 3). Surely there is something to be imitated here in our own study of prophecy, the book of Daniel, and Scripture in general. Daniel's "seeking" (*baqash*, Heb.) the Lord intensely (v. 3) tracks with Deuteronomy 4:29 and Jeremiah 29:13, which describe how the Lord will answer exiles who "seek" (*baqash*) him "with all your heart." Since Jeremiah 29:10 is one of the two prophecies of the seventy years in Jeremiah, it seems that the exile Daniel has noticed the emphasis on earnest prayer in the surrounding context (Jer 29:12–13) and applied it to himself in hopes that the Lord will hear his prayer and restore his people to the land (Jer 29:14; Dan 9:15–19).[16] Kwong notes that Daniel's "fasting," "sackcloth," and "ashes" specifically suggest repentance (cf. Neh 9:1; Jonah 3:5–6).[17] Such penitential prayer is especially appropriate given that Israel was sent into exile because of their sin (Deut 4:25–27), for which they must repent (Deut 4:30; 30:2). Since Jeremiah also makes this connection (e.g., 25:3–11), Seow argues that Daniel has "understood Jeremiah

---

16. "He has read the passage and understood that such a prayer is called for before the restoration can begin." Newsom, *Daniel*, 291. Wilson sees the prayer "as an attempt to have Daniel fulfill the conditions for restoration set out in Jer. 29.12–14." Gerald Wilson, "The Prayer of Daniel 9: Reflection on Jeremiah 29," *JSOT* 48 (1990): 97.
17. Kwong (鄺炳釗), *Daniel*, 262.

properly" by recognizing and addressing the problem of Israel's sins, which led to the punishment of exile.[18]

As Daniel begins his prayer, he "confessed" (*yadah*, Heb.; vv. 4, 20) his and Israel's sins, just as Leviticus 26:40 instructs exiles to do. Confession is similarly emphasized in Hosea 14:2 ("Take words with you and return to the LORD") and in 1 John 1:9 ("If we confess our sins . . ."). In Leviticus 26:39–40, confession of sin stops the exiles from "wast[ing] away" because of their sins and their ancestors' sins and reverses God's escalating judgment (Lev 26:18, 21, 24, 28; cf. 16:21). Accordingly, Daniel confesses the sins of "our ancestors" (9:6, 8, 16). In the subsequent context in Leviticus 26, exilic confession of "sin" (*avon*, Heb.) is further linked to the humbling of Israel's "uncircumcised hearts" (v. 41; cf. 2 Chr 7:14) and the Lord "remember[ing]" his "covenant" with Abraham, Isaac, and Jacob (vv. 42, 45). This in turn has strong links with Jeremiah 31:31–34, which speaks of the "new covenant" written on the "heart," the forgiveness of "sin" (*avon*, Heb.), and the Lord no longer "remember[ing] sin."

Daniel addresses God as "LORD, the great and awesome God, who keeps the covenant and steadfast love to those who love him and keep his commandments" (Dan 9:4, author's translation). This address combines the ones used in Deuteronomy 7:9 and Deuteronomy 7:21 (cf. Neh 1:5), and the former can be traced further back to the Ten Commandments (Exod 20:6). Here and elsewhere, "Daniel's prayer draws heavily on traditional biblical language."[19] The theme of "covenant" in 9:4 is reinforced through Daniel's use of the covenant name of God, "the LORD" or "Yahweh" (cf. vv. 2, 8, 10, 13–14, 20), which appears only in Daniel 9 in the book of Daniel.[20] Widder explains that this "puts the covenant at the center of the chapter's events. It will be at the heart of everything Daniel confesses and requests in his prayer, and it will also be foundational to Gabriel's revelations in 9:20–27."[21] Similarly, "steadfast love" (*hesed*) only appears in Daniel 9:4 and 1:9. The covenant emphasis in Daniel 9 serves as an important link between the visions in the book of Daniel and the rest of the OT.

The beginning of Daniel's confession (vv. 5–7) has numerous parallels to 1 Kings 8:46–48 (itself dependent on Deut 4:29–30; 30:1–2) and suggests

---

18. Interestingly, Seow even sees the "main issue" and "main problem" not as one of chronology (because there is no "prayer for illumination"), but rather as one of sin. Seow, *Daniel*, 141.
19. Collins, *Daniel*, 350.
20. Collins, *Daniel*, 348.
21. Widder, *Daniel*, 463.

Daniel's familiarity with Solomon's dedicatory prayer for the temple in 1 Kings 8.[22] The verbs for "sinned," "done wrong," and "been wicked" in Daniel 9:5 are the same three used in 1 Kings 8:47 and in the same order (*hata, avah, rasha*, Heb.). Accordingly, the context in 1 Kings 8:46–48 is one of exile, in which the Israelites have been taken to enemy lands "far away or near" (*rahoq, qarov*, Heb., v. 46), which is the same language Daniel uses in 9:7. The verb used for "scattered" or "driven" (ESV; *nadach*, Heb.) in Daniel 9:7 is the same as in Jeremiah 29:14 and Deuteronomy 30:1, 4, suggesting an intentional relationship between these texts. 1 Kings 8:48 further describes praying towards Jerusalem and the temple, just as Daniel had done in 6:10.

Daniel confesses that the Israelites have turned away from the Lord's commandments (9:5) and "not listened to your servants the prophets" (v. 6). Reflecting on the Northern Kingdom's exile to Assyria, 2 Kings 17:13–14 likewise recalls the Lord sending "my servants the prophets," but Israel "did not listen" (NASB). The contexts of both prophecies of the seventy years in Jeremiah also refer to disobedience to prophets (Jer 25:4; 29:19). Daniel assigns guilt not only to his "ancestors" but also "our kings" and "our princes" (9:6, 8; cf. Jer 44:21), holding these leaders responsible while providing another link to the narrative of 1–2 Kings (cf. Dan 1:1–2), as 2 Kings 17:8 directly faults "kings" for leading Israel astray. Evidently, the perfect king who will fulfill the Davidic covenant had not yet come (2 Sam 7:12–14; 23:3–4). Indeed, the reader of the book of Daniel already knows to await the coming of the "one like a son of man" (7:13–14).

Daniel's confession not only highlights objective acts of sin and disobedience but also the subjective, emotional "shame" that the exiles bear.[23] The phrase used twice in Daniel 9:7–8 can be literally translated as "shame of face" (*boshet hapanim*, Heb.). A connection between "shame" and "face" appears in several other passages in the OT (2 Chr 32:21; Ps 44:15; Jer 7:19; cf. Ps 69:7; Isa 50:6; Jer 51:51). Many cultures in Asia also link shame and (public) face (e.g., in Chinese, *mianzi* [面子] and *lian* [臉] mean both "face" and "reputation"). Like Daniel, Ezra prays and repents for the exiles' sin of intermarriage while repeatedly mentioning their shame and disgrace (Ezra

---

22. Hamilton remarks that Daniel, "after invoking" the prayer in verse 4 (cf. 1 Kgs 8:23), "quotes" it in verse 5. James Hamilton, *With the Clouds of Heaven: The Book of Daniel in Biblical Theology* (Downers Grove: InterVarsity, 2014), 107. Cf. Widder, *Daniel*, 466; Bentzen, *Daniel*, 75.
23. "Shame is a powerful concept in biblical thought." Newsom, *Daniel*, 294. She cites both the social and psychological dimensions of shame in the OT.

9:5–7). In both Daniel's and Ezra's prayers, shame arises from their defeat and exile by foreign nations, which is deserved because of their sins. Moreover, they brought dishonor on the Lord's name in the eyes of the nations (cf. Deut 32:27; Ezek 36:20–23).

On the other hand, Daniel declares that the Lord is "righteous" (9:7). The contrast between the Lord's perfection and Israel's wickedness (cf. v. 14) is also central to the Song of Moses (Deut 32:4–5), a programmatic expression of God's dealings with Israel. As Daniel's confession proceeds, it is striking to see the many times that he says, "we have sinned" (vv. 5, 8, 11, 15) and that Israel has "not listened" (vv. 6, 10, 11, 14). Other verses express variations on the same theme, speaking of "our unfaithfulness" (v. 7) and how "we have rebelled" (v. 9), among others.[24] Daniel does not superficially say a few words about sin and move on but takes sin seriously as he repents. Rotohka points out that Daniel's repentance further includes "submission and obedience," based on verse 13 ("turning from our sins").[25]

Israel had specifically disobeyed the Lord's word ("your commands and laws," v. 5; "laws"/"your laws," vv. 10–11), and so just as "the Law of Moses" predicted, curse and disaster came upon them (vv. 11, 13; cf. Deut 29:18–21; 31:29). Thus, Daniel 9 explicitly mentions not only the book of Jeremiah (v. 2) but also the Pentateuch as extant Scripture bearing divine authority.[26] Texts such as Leviticus 26:33–38 and Deuteronomy 4:27; 28:63–64 warned that Israel's sins would result in exile, and Daniel recognizes the Lord's righteous judgment, not the nations themselves, as the primary cause (9:14).

Widder points out that verse 12 emphasizes the fulfillment of God's word.[27] The relatively uncommon Hebrew word used for how the Lord "watched over" (*shaqad*) the disaster that he brought on Israel (v. 14) likely alludes to texts in Jeremiah that use this word in the same way (Jer 31:28; 44:27).[28] At the beginning of the book and helping to set its course, Jeremiah 1:11–12 uses *shaqad*

---

24. Cf. Goldingay, *Daniel*, 249–250.
25. Rotohka, "Daniel," 1106. Verse 13 ends with the phrase "and giving attention to your truth." Newsom points out that the Hebrew verb *sakal* used here is unusual in this context and that it contributes to the theme of insight or wisdom in Daniel (1:4, 17; 9:13, 22, 25; 11:33, 35; 12:3, 10). Newsom, *Daniel*, 296.
26. Cf. Newsom, who refers to "the increasingly authoritative role of written Scripture." Newsom, *Daniel*, 295.
27. Widder, *Daniel*, 470.
28. Louis Hartman and Alexander Di Lella translate the phrase in verse 14 as, "Yahweh kept watch over the calamity," and explain, "The sense of this phrase, taken from Jeremiah 1:12; 31:28; 44:27, is that God kept his eye on the threatened calamity; he did not forget it." Hartman and Di Lella, *The Book of Daniel*, 242.

to declare that the Lord will watch over his word to fulfill it, whether through judgment in the near term (Jer 44:27) or the new covenant in the future (Jer 31:28). The strategic use of *shaqad* in Jeremiah suggests that it is a keyword that Daniel noticed in his study and then uses intentionally in his prayer.

In verses 15–19, Daniel makes his appeal to the Lord for mercy and restoration. He had briefly referenced the Lord as being "merciful" and "forgiving" in verse 9 but had kept the focus on confessing sin. Daniel's use of "now" in verses 15 and 17 signals a transition where he adds a request for salvation and forgiveness.[29] Accordingly, he mentions the Lord's mercy and forgiveness again in verses 18–19. Like Moses's intercession after the sin of the golden calf, Daniel cites the Lord bringing Israel ("your people") out of Egypt with "a mighty hand" (v. 15; Exod 32:11–12; Deut 9:26). In so doing, the Lord made a "name" for himself (v. 15) that ought not be dishonored (Exod 32:12; Deut 9:28). Just as Moses prayed that the Lord would "turn" from his "anger" (Exod 32:12; *shuv, af*, Heb.), Daniel prays that the Lord's "anger" (*af*, Heb.) would "turn away" (*shuv*, Heb.) from Jerusalem and the temple (v. 16).[30] Such judgment is threatened many times throughout Scripture (e.g., 1 Kgs 9:7; Jer 7:14, 34; Mic 3:12). At the same time, the restoration of Zion is also foretold repeatedly by the prophets (e.g., Isa 1:27; 2:2; Jer 3:17). The book of Daniel also emphasizes Jerusalem and the temple (1:1–2; 5:2–3; 6:10; 8:11–14).

Whereas Daniel ascribes "righteousness" to the Lord (9:7, ESV) and declares that he is "righteous" (v. 4) in punishing Israel, Daniel prays that the Lord's anger will subside according to "all your righteous acts" (v. 16). Divine righteousness or justice can thus play out in different ways (cf. Deut 32:4), and here Daniel has in mind *salvific* righteous acts in which the Lord delivers his people and punishes their enemies (e.g., Judg 5:11; 1 Sam 12:7; Ps 103:6).[31] House argues that Daniel believes in God's promises of restoration as found in the seventy year prophecies in Jeremiah and elsewhere.[32] His prayer for deliverance is not based on Israel's "righteousness" (v. 18; cf. Deut 9:4–6) but on God's "great mercy." The emphasis on the Lord's "name" (vv. 15, 17–19; cf. "scorn,"

---

29. Newsom, *Daniel*, 296.
30. Angukali Rotohka observes an additional parallel to Moses's appeal to God's glory in Numbers 14:16–19 during his intercession for Israel following their refusal to enter the Promised Land. Rotohka, "Daniel," 1106.
31. Cf. Widder, *Daniel*, 473.
32. House, *Daniel*, 155.

v. 16) shows that the plea is not based on "Israel's merit but for God's own sake."[33] This sentiment is also expressed in Isaiah 48:11 and Ezekiel 36:21–23.

9:20–27 GABRIEL ARRIVES AND EXPLAINS THE SEVENTY SEVENS

Daniel's testimony that he was confessing sin and petitioning on behalf of the temple (v. 20) offers a concise summary of the preceding prayer (vv. 3–19). If Collins is right that Daniel's study of Scripture in verse 2 is unique in the book in the way that it leads to revelation (see above), Plöger is also right that Daniel's preceding prayer (vv. 3–19), as a response to Scripture, plays a similarly important role.[34] According to verses 20–21, Gabriel, who had come in 8:15–26, comes to Daniel as he is in the middle of praying. The fact that an answer was given "as soon as [he] began to pray" (v. 23; cf. 10:12) shows the Lord's readiness to hear our prayers.[35] While not everyone will experience a dream or vision (see "Dreams and Visions," 19–21), we can all study the Scriptures and respond to them with prayer. Just as Daniel was "highly esteemed" (v. 23), so we who are in Christ are beloved children of God (1 John 3:1), who stand in grace and are encouraged to approach God in prayer (Rom 5:1–2; Heb 4:16).

Gabriel's arrival "about the time of the evening sacrifice" (v. 21) reinforces the importance of the temple in the divine plan while providing another link to Daniel 8 (e.g., the 2,300 "evenings and mornings" in vv. 14, 26). As before, Gabriel's purpose is to give Daniel understanding (9:22–23; cf. 8:16–17). Whereas the Israelites had not sought the Lord to "gain insight [*sakal*, Heb.] in your truth" (v. 13), Daniel prays humbly to the Lord and is about to "gain insight" (*sakal*, Heb.) into the "word" and "vision" (vv. 22–23). Once again, the point is not that Daniel's revelatory experience is normative, but as Collins notes, there is an analogy between Gabriel, who instructs Daniel, and the "wise" in Daniel 11:33, who give understanding to "many."[36] Indeed, the ordinary means of gaining insight includes the study of Scripture, prayer, and the ministry of the wise, who (like Daniel) have devoted themselves to studying and obeying the Scriptures.

---

33. Collins, *Daniel*, 350.
34. Otto Plöger, *Das Buch Daniel* (Gütersloh: Gerd Mohn, 1965), 135.
35. Lucas, *Daniel*, 241.
36. Collins, *Daniel*, 352. Cf. Newsom, *Daniel*, 298.

Gabriel explains that the "seventy years" Jeremiah spoke of (Jer 25:11–12; 29:10; Dan 9:2) will not be fulfilled in seventy calendar years but in "seventy sevens" (v. 24), or 490 units of time (commonly understood to be years).[37] In other words, it will take much longer than an actual seventy-year period before "the desolation of Jerusalem" ends (v. 2) and the "holy city" and "Most Holy Place" are restored (v. 24). Collins believes that Gabriel "departs from the plain sense of the text" in Jeremiah and provides a "reinterpretation."[38]

Newsom, on the other hand, raises the possibility of "double reading," in which the consonants of a Hebrew word are read with a different set of vowels, since vowels were not part of the written text at that time.[39] In this case, "seventy" (*shiv'im*, Heb.) can also be read as "sevens/weeks" (*shavu'im*, Heb.). Whether or not double reading is involved, the writing on the wall in Daniel 5 also involved the doubling of an important Aramaic word related to numbers, *mene* (5:25–26, "*mene, mene, tekel, parsin* . . . *mene*: God has *numbered* [*menah*, Aramaic] the days of your reign").[40] Whereas Newsom attributes double reading to exegetical practices of the second century BC, such wordplay is not only part of Daniel 5:25–28 itself but also other extant Scripture (e.g., Gen 49:8; Num 24:18; Jer 1:11–12).[41] In other words, it is traceable to the composition of the Bible itself, including its opening chapters in Genesis.[42]

As mentioned above, both the original context of Jeremiah's second prophecy of the seventy years in Jeremiah 29:10–14 and especially the four-kingdom scheme in Daniel 2 and 7 suggest that eschatological salvation "in the last days" (2:28; 10:14) still lies in the distant future. Indeed, the connection between the restoration of Jerusalem after "seventy years" (Jer 29:10) and Israel seeking the Lord "with all your heart" (Jer 29:13), not to mention what is likely an *enduring* "hope" and "future" (Jer 29:11), suggests an additional link to the "new covenant" written "on their heart" in Jeremiah 31:31, 33. Accordingly, just as Jeremiah 31:34 declares, "I will forgive their iniquity and their sin I

---

37. For example, Collins, *Daniel*, 352; Newsom, *Daniel*, 299.
38. Collins, *Daniel*, 352.
39. Newsom, *Daniel*, 299. She sees the "sevenfold" punishment in Leviticus 26:18 as "one possible intertext," which provides a precedent for multiplying the seventy years by seven.
40. The LXX (i.e., Theodotion) and Vulgate do not repeat *mene* but only mention it once in Daniel 5:25 ("*mene, tekel, parsin*").
41. For wordplay on "Judah" in Genesis 49:8 and "Seir, his enemies, will be a possession" in Numbers 24:18, see Chen, *Messianic Vision of the Pentateuch*, 46, 115, 138, 222.
42. "In few other places in ancient literature does one find so many wordplays and associations with personal names. This is easiest to identify in the larger narratives of Genesis 1–4 and 6–9." Richard Hess, *Studies in the Personal Names of Genesis 1–11* (Winona Lake: Eisenbrauns, 2009), 109.

will remember no more," so Gabriel explains that, Daniel's confession notwithstanding, it will actually take "seventy sevens" to "finish transgression," "put an end to sin," and "atone for iniquity" (9:24, Heb.).

Thus, just as Jeremiah's message to the exiles was that their return home was not imminent (i.e., "within two years," Jer 28:3, 11), so Daniel learns that despite the fall of Babylon and the passing of several decades of exile, the fulfillment of the seventy years is not imminent either.[43] The implications for today's readers, who can look *back* on much of the period of "seventy sevens," are likewise to remain faithful and hopeful in view of the end coming at an unknown time (Acts 1:7). Furthermore, the numbers seven and seventy can be used symbolically in the Bible (e.g., Gen 4:15, 24; Exod 15:27; Matt 18:21–22), and numerical symbolism is attested to elsewhere in Daniel (e.g., 7:2–3).[44]

Final victory over sin coincides with the "seal[ing] up" of "vision and prophecy" (9:24). Collins explains, "The immediate referent is Jeremiah's prophecy, but the allusion probably includes all prophecy that is construed as eschatological."[45] Newsom interprets "seal" in verse 24 as authentication rather than concealment (based on 1 Kgs 21:9; Jer 32:10, 11, 44).[46] Since Gabriel also mentions "everlasting righteousness" in Daniel 9:24, House believes that this "amounts to God's kingdom coming on earth (see 2:44) and the fulfilment of prophecy."[47] This would be consistent with the many texts in Daniel that proclaim God's everlasting kingdom (e.g., 2:35, 44; 4:3, 34; 6:26; 7:14, 27). Thus, we have reason to expect that Daniel 9:24–27 is consistent with the rest of the book, Jeremiah's original prophecies of the seventy years, and the broader framework of OT prophetic eschatology, particularly in light of the emphasis on authoritative Scripture in Daniel 9:2, 11, 13 (see "Biblical Allusions in the Book of Daniel," pp. 123–124).

This is sufficient grounds for rejecting the argument that the period of "seventy sevens" was fulfilled during the Maccabean era (i.e., "anointed one" in v. 26 = high priest Onias III; "ruler" in v. 26 = Antiochus IV Epiphanes).[48] It is

---

43. Chen, *Wonders from Your Law*, 293–295.
44. Lucas, *Daniel*, 248.
45. Collins, *Daniel*, 354.
46. Newsom, *Daniel*, 303. Cf. Lucas, *Daniel*, 242.
47. House, *Daniel*, 158.
48. Hartman and Di Lella, *The Book of Daniel*, 253–254. Collins, along with others, distinguishes between the "anointed one" who comes in verse 26 and the "anointed one" who comes in verse 25 after the first seven "sevens" (i.e., Joshua the high priest, though Zerubbabel and even Cyrus [Rashi] have also been proposed), a differentiation supported by Masoretic accents (cf.

hard to see how the Maccabean era could have experienced final atonement for sin and everlasting righteousness (thus answering Daniel's prayer for forgiveness in vv. 16, 19), much less fulfilled the highest prophetic hopes, since there was no new covenant, eschatological Messiah, nor everlasting kingdom of God.[49]

On the other hand, we have already seen above how Jeremiah predicts final forgiveness of sin in connection with the new covenant (Jer 31:31–34). This covenant is bound up with the continued existence of Israel as a nation and the restoration of Jerusalem (Jer 31:35–40), which is linked to the Messianic kingdom (Jer 23:5–6). As in Daniel 9:24, Isaiah also speaks of forgiveness of sin (Isa 44:22) and everlasting righteousness (Isa 32:15–17), sometimes in connection with the coming of the Messianic king (Isa 9:6–7; 32:1; 53:5–6, 8, 11–12). Thus the parallel between the sin-bearing Suffering Servant, who is "cut off from the land of the living" (Isa 53:8), and an "anointed one," who "will be cut off" after the sixty-ninth seven (Dan 9:26) may not be accidental.[50] The terms "anointed one" (*mashiach*, Heb.) and "ruler" (*nagid*, Heb.) are used to describe a Davidic king in several key texts ("anointed one," 1 Sam 2:10; Ps 2:2; "ruler," 1 Sam 13:14; 2 Sam 7:8; Isa 55:4), though these terms can also be used in other ways.[51]

There are many issues in Daniel 9:25–27 that remain unclear, such as the purpose of the first seven "sevens" (a jubilee cycle, Lev 25:8–10) and the details of the destruction and desecration of the final "seven." Shepherd does not take the enemy in Daniel 9:27 to be Antiochus IV but "the unidentified end-time 'Gog'" from Ezekiel 38:14–16 (cf. Num 24:7 LXX).[52] The violence and

---

ESV, "there shall be seven weeks" between the command to build Jerusalem and the coming of an anointed one; likewise JPS, NRSV). Collins, *Daniel*, 356–357. The effect of this interpretation is to muddle the Messianic picture, because there are two priestly anointed ones coming at different times rather than one royal Messiah climactically coming after the sixty-ninth seven.
49. Cf. Rotohka, "Daniel," 1107; Block, "Old Testament Apocalyptic," 47–48. For different views of precisely what sin is in view, see Newsom, *Daniel*, 301–302. Collins, while not excluding Israel's sins, thinks that the emphasis should be on the Gentile desecration of the temple. Collins, *Daniel*, 354.
50. Cf. Shepherd, *Daniel in the Context of the Hebrew Bible*, 98. Chen notes the additional parallel to the stone "cut" without human hands in Daniel 2:34, 45 and rejects Ginsberg's view that Daniel 12:3 is the earliest interpretation of Isaiah 53, a corporate interpretation no less. Chen, *Wonders from Your Law*, 304. In personal conversation, Seth Postell has also pointed out that Jeremiah 11:19 is evidence for an individual interpretation of the Suffering Servant.
51. Block takes Daniel 9:25–26 as "the only unambiguous reference to the Messiah . . . in the entire Old Testament." Block, "Old Testament Apocalyptic," 47. Although I believe there are others, this statement still shows Block's confidence in a Messianic interpretation of this passage. He also interprets the rock in Daniel 2 and the son of man in Daniel 7 Messianically (44–47).
52. Shepherd, *Daniel in the Context of the Hebrew Bible*, 97.

desecration committed by the "ruler" in Daniel 9:26–27 also recalls the "little horn" in Daniel 7 (vv. 8, 11, 20–22, 24–25), which the above commentary takes to be an eschatological Satanic enemy, as foretold by 2 Thessalonians 2:3 and 1 John 2:18. Regardless of the precise identity of this "ruler," the important thing is that he too will meet his "end" (Dan 9:27). In God's sovereignty and wisdom, "desolations have been decreed" (v. 26), but so has this enemy's defeat (v. 27; cf. Isa 10:22–23).[53] This reinforces the important theme of the triumph of the kingdom of God throughout the book of Daniel. We also learn from Gabriel that the rebuilding of Jerusalem (9:25) and the temple during the Second Temple period does not mean that the end is near, since in God's plan, the temple is evidently going to be destroyed or desecrated and restored multiple times (cf. 8:11–14; Matt 24:2, 15).

---

53. Cf. Widder, *Daniel*, 488. Regarding lexical and thematic parallels to Isaiah 10:22–23 (e.g. decree, end, flood), see Lester, *Daniel Evokes Isaiah*, 70–72. I would further note the Messianic importance of Isaiah 10:21 ("A remnant will return . . . to Mighty God"), given "Mighty God" as a title for the Messiah in Isaiah 9:6.

DANIEL 10

BATTLE IN THE HEAVENS

Chinese mythology tells of an epic battle between the legendary ruler Huangdi (or "Yellow Emperor"/ 黃帝) and his archenemy, the monstrous part-man, part-beast Chiyou.[1] According to legend, Huangdi was an extraordinary human being from the early days of Chinese civilization.[2] Huangdi fought righteously to establish order and peace, but Chiyou wanted anarchy, violence, and conflict. Huangdi tried to persuade Chiyou to desist but ultimately had to use force to defeat him.[3] Their battle also involved gods of wind, rain, and drought.[4] Von Glahn explains that this victory "became a metaphor for the triumph of order over anarchy, a basic motif in Chinese religious culture."[5] Legends further ascribe supernatural attributes to Huangdi, such as one that describes him riding on an ivory chariot drawn by dragons while ruling over spirits, animals, and deities of fire, wind, and rain.[6] Huangdi is thus portrayed as "the supreme lord of the divine and mortal realms."[7] Indeed, his battle with Chiyou took place on both the physical and spiritual planes.

Belief in the interconnection between physical and spiritual warfare was also common in the ANE.[8] Aslan describes "cosmic war" as reflecting an earthly battle that corresponds to a parallel heavenly battle between metaphysical

---

1. Richard von Glahn, *The Sinister Way: The Divine and the Demonic in Chinese Religious Culture* (Berkeley: University of California Press, 2004), 39–41.
2. von Glahn adds, "Huangdi also figured in Han legend as a god of storms and rain." von Glahn, *Sinister Way*, 39. Cf. Kevin McSpadden, "How 3 legendary figures shaped foundations of ancient China," 11 Sept 2024, https://www.scmp.com/news/people-culture/article/3277818/how-3-legendary-figures-shaped-foundations-ancient-china. He writes, "Descriptions of Huangdi intertwine seemingly historical accounts with mythological elements."
3. von Glahn, *Sinister Way*, 40.
4. See *Shanhai Jing* (山海經: 大荒北經), available online: https://ctext.org/shan-hai-jing/da-huang-bei-jing/zh. For English translations, see Anne Birrell, *The Classic of Mountains and Seas* (London: Penguin, 1999), 186–187; https://ancientchinesemythology.wordpress.com/2013/08/21/nv-ba-%E5%A5%B3%E9%AD%83-the-drought-goddess/.
5. von Glahn, *Sinister Way*, 40.
6. von Glahn, *Sinister Way*, 41.
7. von Glahn, *Sinister Way*, 41.
8. Reza Aslan, "Cosmic War in Religious Traditions," in *The Oxford Handbook of Religion and Violence*, ed. Mark Juergensmeyer, Margo Kitts, and Michael Jerryson (New York: Oxford University Press, 2013), 260–261.

forces, such as good and evil.[9] In the OT, the theme of the Lord as warrior and his participation in battle fall under this category (e.g., Exod 15:3–12). The little horn in Daniel 8:10 that "threw some of the starry host down to the earth" likewise hints at cosmic war (see commentary). In Daniel 10, Daniel will learn from an angel that Israel's conflicts with Persia and later Greece are indeed cosmic (vv. 13, 20).

Daniel 10 begins the last and longest literary unit in Daniel, Daniel 10–12, which Collins calls "The Final Revelation."[10] House notes the vast temporal scope of these chapters, beginning from the third year of Cyrus (10:1) and continuing all the way to the resurrection of the dead (12:2).[11] As Wildgruber observes, whereas each chapter in Daniel 1–9 is its own literary unit that corresponds to a particular narrative or vision, Daniel 10–12 involves a continuous action sequence that spans all three chapters, such that its meaning transcends its chapter divisions.[12] Daniel 10 may be divided into three sections: the setting for the vision (v. 1), Daniel's vision of the angel and reaction (vv. 2–9), and the angel's dialogue with Daniel (vv. 10–21).

10:1 SETTING: THE THIRD YEAR OF KING CYRUS OF PERSIA

The setting for the visionary experience in Daniel 10–12 is "third year of Cyrus king of Persia" (v. 1; i.e., 536 BC), which is the latest date reference in the book.[13] Subsequent to Darius's first year (9:1–2; i.e., 539 BC) and Cyrus's edict around the same time (see commentary), this date maintains the chronological ordering of the visions in Daniel 7–12.[14] At the same time, Collins notes that here, as elsewhere in Daniel, "the release of the Jewish exiles in the first year of Cyrus is ignored."[15] It is true that the rebuilding of Jerusalem is mentioned in Daniel 9:25, but silence concerning this release fits the book's ultimate emphasis on the eschatological future and Israel's eschatological salvation rather than the Second Temple period (cf. 2:28, 34–35, 44; 7:13–14, 18, 27; 9:24).

Unlike Daniel 8 and 9, which are reported by Daniel in the first person (8:1; 9:2), Daniel 10:1 reverts to the third person (as in 7:1 and elsewhere). Similar to Daniel 7:2, Daniel 10:2 embeds Daniel's first-person testimony ("I,

---

9. Aslan, "Cosmic War in Religious Traditions," 260.
10. Collins, *Daniel*, xi, 361, *passim*.
11. House, *Daniel*, 165.
12. Regina Wildgruber, *Daniel 10–12 als Schlüssel zum Buch* (Tübingen: Mohr Siebeck, 2013).
25. Collins, for example, treats Daniel 11:1–2a along with Daniel 10. Collins, *Daniel*, 362.
13. Newsom, *Daniel*, 328.
14. Though note that Daniel 7 is not in chronological order with respect to Daniel 5–6.
15. Collins, *Daniel*, 372.

Daniel") into this third person framework (cf. 8:1, 15; 9:2).[16] Daniel 10:1 also refers to Daniel's Babylonian name, Belteshazzar, which was used earlier in 1:7; 2:26; 4:8–9, 18–19; 5:12 (see "What's in a Name?," pp. 9–10), which House sees as a reminder of "his long service in exile."[17] Seow further observes that although Babylon has fallen, "Daniel is still known by this captive name," a reminder of Israel's ongoing captivity.[18]

As in Daniel 2:22–23, a "word" (Heb.) is "revealed" (*galah*, Heb.; cf. *gelah*, Aramaic) to Daniel in 10:1, forming an inclusio with respect to Daniel's revelatory experiences (see commentary, v. 14). Newsom notes the connection to the "mystery" in Daniel 2 that also concerns "the hidden course of history."[19] Like Nebuchadnezzar's first dream and interpretation (2:45) and other divine messages (8:26; 9:13), this divine message is described as being "true" (10:1), and therefore it can be relied upon, unlike the words of mere men.

The divine message concerns "a great war" (v. 1). Although Newsom believes that the Hebrew word translated as "war" (*tsava*) refers to Daniel's "struggle" to understand the message, this word is commonly used in contexts of war (e.g., Num 1:3; 1 Chr 7:4).[20] Although there are examples of *tsava* that can mean "work" or "service" (e.g., Job 7:1; 10:17; 14:14; Isa 40:2), these are still physical struggles rather than internal, mental struggles.[21] Thus both ancient and modern translations render it as "war," or the like (e.g., "conflict," ESV), which fits the cosmic war described in Daniel 10–12.[22]

10:2–9 DANIEL'S VISION OF THE ANGEL AND REACTION

Leading up to the vision, Daniel "mourned for three weeks" (v. 2). The reference to "weeks" recalls the seventy "weeks" from 9:24–27. Yet unlike those partially symbolic "weeks" of years, these are "weeks of days" (10:2–3, Heb.).[23] Daniel's mourning found expression through fasting. He did not fast from all food, but from "choice food," "meat," and "wine" (v. 3). He also did not

---

16. Widder, *Daniel*, 496.
17. House, *Daniel*, 167.
18. Seow, *Daniel*, 154.
19. Newsom, *Daniel*, 329. Cf. Hartman and Di Lella, *The Book of Daniel*, 278.
20. Newsom, *Daniel*, 329. Similarly, Collins associates the word with Daniel's experience rather than the vision itself, stating, "The service is presumably that of Daniel in receiving the vision." Collins, *Daniel*, 372.
21. These are the passages cited by Bentzen, which in turn are cited by the lexicon HALOT. Bentzen, *Daniel*, 70. This standard reference may have influenced some commentators.
22. Lucas, *Daniel*, 58, 274.
23. Widder, *Daniel*, 506. Cf. Tremper Longman III, *Daniel*, NIV Application Commentary (Grand Rapids: Zondervan, 1999), 247.

take care of his skin in typical fashion (v. 3). Based on the use of the same verb in 2 Samuel 14:2 (*suk*, Heb.), Collins explains that Daniel abstaining from anointing himself "is a traditional sign of mourning" (cf. 2 Sam 12:20).[24] Widder reasonably asserts that anointing would have been a common practice in that dry climate.[25]

Daniel's mourning and fasting in verses 2–3 is another link back to Daniel 9, where Daniel also prayed, fasted, and put on sackcloth and ashes (9:3). According to Daniel 10:12, Daniel is seeking "understanding," presumably concerning "the last days" (10:14, Heb.), and Collins concludes that Daniel's fasting here prepares him for receiving revelation.[26] Recalling his refusal to eat the royal food in Daniel 1:8–16, Daniel again demonstrates self-control regarding his physical appetites. A shared Medo-Persian setting (9:1; 10:1) and the focus on a "word"/"vision" (9:23; 10:1; cf. ESV) further strengthens the connection between Daniel 9 and 10–12.

Seow points out that Daniel 9 began with Daniel studying "the *word* of the LORD given to Jeremiah" (9:2), proceeds to report that "a *word* went out" in response to Daniel's prayer (9:23), which results in a "word" reaching him (9:23), and now in Daniel 10, he receives another "word" (10:1; *davar*, Heb.).[27] Accordingly, the revelations in both passages are primarily verbal rather than image-based (see Daniel 11; cf. commentary, 5:7–8; 7:1).[28]

The reference to the twenty-fourth day of the *first* month in Daniel 10:4 shows that the three-week fast also took place during this month, the month of Passover (Exod 12:2).[29] Although Cyrus's edict during his first year did result in a new exodus of sorts (Ezra 1:1–6), Daniel's fasting shows that the

---

24. Collins, *Daniel*, 373.
25. Widder, *Daniel*, 506.
26. Collins, *Daniel*, 372. Newsom thinks that Daniel mourns over the revelation from Daniel 9 ("the calamitous but mysterious events that were revealed to him"). Newsom, *Daniel*, 329. Rotohka mentions the continued distress of the Israelites, including opposition to the building of the temple. Rotohka, "Daniel," 1108. Commentators tend to distinguish Daniel's penitential fasting in Daniel 9 from his fasting in Daniel 10, but the seventy sevens of 9:24 is an all-encompassing framework for the future that culminates in atonement for Israel's sins and as such encompasses the details prophesied in Daniel 10–12 (see commentary, 9:24). Even if Daniel's fast in Daniel 10 is not explicitly connected to repentance, sin is at least indirectly related through his continuing exile and waiting for deliverance.
27. Seow, *Daniel*, 154.
28. Widder, *Daniel*, 497.
29. House thinks that Daniel was keeping the Passover along with those in Jerusalem and mentions a possible connection between Daniel's fasting and the "bread of affliction" eaten during the Feast of Unleavened Bread (Deut 16:3). House, *Daniel*, 167–168.

greatest exodus is still yet to come (cf. 9:15).[30] His location by the Tigris river (10:4) recalls this Edenic river from Genesis 2:14, and Wildgruber sees this reference, like "Shinar" in Daniel 1:2 (Heb.), as echoing the early chapters of Genesis and situating Daniel's experience within a grander story (cf. Gen 10:10; 11:2; 14:1, 9).[31]

The visionary account itself begins in Daniel 10:5–6. Daniel sees a "man" dressed in linen and wearing a belt of fine gold (v. 5). Linen was worn by priests during certain ceremonies (Lev 6:10; 16:4, 23, 32).[32] It is not only the man's clothing that is glorious but also his "body," including his face, eyes, and limbs, and even his voice (v. 6). Newsom shows how the description of the "man"/angel has numerous parallels to descriptions of supernatural beings in Ezekiel (linen: Ezek 9:2–3, 11; 10:2, 6, 7; loins: Ezek 1:27; 8:2; topaz: Ezek 1:16; 10:9; torches and lightning: Ezek 1:13; burnished bronze: Ezek 1:7; voice like sound of a multitude: Ezek 1:24).[33] She argues that Ezekiel's accounts "were treated like mosaic tiles that could be recombined in various ways," which Daniel "creatively recontextualizes."[34]

Like Paul on the Damascus road (Acts 9:7; cf. 22:9), Daniel is the only one among his group to see the vision (10:7). Widder believes that the presence of companions shows Daniel's special status as recipient of this revelation.[35] After his companions flee in fear (v. 7), Daniel is "left alone, gazing at this great vision" (v. 8). Like Ezekiel in Ezekiel 1:28, he has no strength and lies face down on the ground, even as he hears a voice speaking (v. 9).

10:10–21 THE ANGEL'S DIALOGUE WITH DANIEL

As in Ezekiel 2:1–2, the vision is preparatory for a verbal message that the prophet must hear after arising from the ground. Such a sequence suggests the importance of this verbal message, which applies to all, compared to the unusual experience that led up to it, which is unrepeatable. Daniel was not

---

30. Cf. Widder, *Daniel*, 507.
31. Wildgruber does not see "Tigris" exclusively as a historical reference and mentions its "legendary far distance." Wildgruber, *Daniel 10–12*, 27–28. For "Shinar," she notes the connection to the Tower of Babel and the theme of humanity living in chaos and in opposition to God.
32. Note the prominence of linen for the Day of Atonement.
33. Newsom, *Daniel*, 331.
34. Newsom, *Daniel*, 331.
35. Widder, *Daniel*, 508.

only face down on the ground but also in a "deep sleep" (v. 9; cf. 8:18; Gen 15:12) when a hand touches him and sets him on his hands and knees (v. 10).[36]

At this point, Daniel is addressed as "highly esteemed" (v. 11; cf. v. 19), just as he was in 9:23. Both times Daniel was engaged in humble prayer and fasting, a repetition that reminds readers that those who humble themselves before the Lord will be honored by him (Isa 57:15; Luke 14:11; 18:14; Jas 4:10).

The angel has come to give Daniel understanding, but he must stand up first (v. 11). Evidently, being on his hands and knees (v. 10), though an improvement over being face down (v. 9), is not enough. Just as Ezekiel receives strength to stand as he is being spoken to (Ezek 2:2), so Daniel stands up when the angel speaks to him (v. 11; cf. v. 19). Thus, while there certainly is a place for humbling ourselves completely before God, as both Daniel and Ezekiel do initially, the requirement that they stand before hearing more suggests God's desire for fellowship with them and also that their God-given dignity and capacities need to be activated when receiving his word.

Though standing, Daniel is also trembling (v. 11), and the angel encourages him not to be afraid (v. 12), a common exhortation to those who have similar encounters (e.g., Gen 15:1; Judg 6:23; Luke 1:13).[37] The angel tells Daniel that his prayers were heard from "the first day that you set your mind to gain understanding and to humble yourself before your God" (v. 12). This is a great encouragement to us when answers to our prayers are delayed. The Lord has heard us from the moment we started praying and knows what we need before we ask him (Matt 6:8).

The reason for the angel's delayed arrival is because he has been detained for three weeks (cf. vv. 2–3) in the spiritual realm by the "prince of the kingdom of Persia" (v. 13, ESV). Just as Job did not know that his suffering arose from Satan's conversations with God (Job 1:6–12; 2:1–6), Daniel does not know until now that the answer to his prayers has been delayed because of a conflict in the unseen world. Indeed, if not for the help of the chief prince, the angel Michael (v. 13), the messenger angel presumably would have been detained even longer.

---

36. Widder discusses the possibility that this "hand" may belong to another figure than the "man" in linen (v. 5), pointing out that "determining how many beings are involved in Daniel's vision and what role each play is difficult." Widder, *Daniel*, 509. She believes that the man in linen does all the talking while the other angel is the one who strengthens Daniel. Cf. Lucas, *Daniel*, 277. For the purposes of this commentary, I treat the speaking angel and the strengthening angel as the same angel, without being dogmatic.
37. Collins, *Daniel*, 374.

The existence of the "prince of the kingdom of Persia" as well as the "kings of Persia" (v. 13, ESV) in the spiritual realm demonstrates that earthly kingdoms and conflicts can have counterparts in the heavenly world (i.e., cosmic war), as discussed in the introduction to this chapter. Rotohka explains that South Asians "believe in the spirit world" and "can grasp this two-tiered view of reality."[38] She adds that this text "should give us courage in dark times" because "the events we see are only part of the story," and "God is involved in our lives in more ways than just listening and acting upon our prayers in ways that we can see."[39]

The angel further informs Daniel that he has come to explain "what will happen [*qara'*, Heb.] to your people in the last days" (v. 14, Heb.).[40] This expression and its usage are strikingly similar to Deuteronomy 31:29, where Moses predicts Israel's future idolatry and "the disaster that will happen [*qara'*, Heb.] to you in the last days" (Heb.). Both Daniel 11 and the Song of Moses in Deuteronomy 32 proceed to predict the ascendance of the nations and Israel's suffering at their hands (see Deuteronomy 32; Dan 11:16, 22, 30–36, 41). Both prophecies, however, ultimately end with the Lord's defeat of these enemies and salvation of his people (Deut 32:40–43; Dan 11:45–12:3). Though without reference to exile, the patriarch Jacob also foretold "what will happen [*qara'*, Heb.] to you [i.e., his sons, and hence the nation Israel] in the last days" in Genesis 49:1 (Heb.), even linking this eschatological era to an eschatological king, the Lion of Judah (Gen 49:8–12).[41]

The phrase "in the last days" appeared once earlier in Daniel 2:28, where Nebuchadnezzar learns that his dream is about "what will be in the last days" (Heb.). As discussed in the commentary, the destruction of the statue by a rock that becomes a gigantic mountain "in the last days" links Daniel 2 to the glorified, gigantic Mount Zion "in the last days" of Isaiah 2:2–4. Both texts are situated toward the beginning of their respective books and as such help set

---

38. Rotohka, "Daniel," 1109.
39. Rotohka, "Daniel," 1109.
40. Regarding the meaning and translation of this phrase, see Chen, *Messianic Vision of the Pentateuch*, 109–114; Dempster, "'At the End of the Days,' 118–141. Collins believes that the phrase "typically refers to some decisive change at a future time," that is, "a definitive change in the future but not to an end of history." Collins, *Daniel*, 161. Collins recognizes that some uses are indeed eschatological (Isa 2:2; Mic 4:1; Hos 3:5; Ezek 38:16) but thinks that Daniel 10:14 refers to the Hellenistic period, an interpretation which may have influenced his understanding of the phrase. The concept of "change" in Collins's definition, however, seems foreign to the Hebrew phrase itself. His questioning of "end of days" as a translation also does not sufficiently engage the meaning of the Hebrew word *acherit* ("end").
41. Sailhamer, *Pentateuch as Narrative*, 235.

an eschatological course for each book. Through its use at key macrostructural junctures in the Pentateuch (Gen 49:1; Num 24:14; Deut 4:30; 31:29), "in the last days" similarly frames the Pentateuch in eschatological terms.[42]

The use of "in the last days" in Daniel 10:14 reinforces the book of Daniel's connection (via 2:28) both to its usage elsewhere in the OT and to OT eschatology generally. Since Daniel 10–12 is a literary unit (with 10:14 having an introductory function) and Daniel 2 contains the first vision in the book, the phrase "in the last days" functions as a sort of (bilingual) inclusio around the visions of the book of Daniel, which encompass almost the entire book.[43] The structural and theological significance of "in the last days" within Daniel is thus comparable to its significance in the Pentateuch.

The angel's explanatory comment, "for still the vision is for the [i.e., those] days" (v. 14, author's translation) seems to merely reinforce the prophetic nature ("vision") and future orientation of the message he is about to share in Daniel 11. At the same time, this statement from Daniel 10:14 is nearly identical to Habakkuk 2:3, "For still the vision is for the appointed time" (author's translation), which likewise speaks of an eschatological "vision" (*hazon*, Heb.).[44] Both statements begin with the same three Hebrew words in the same order (*ki 'od hazon* ["for still the vision"]), with the only difference being the last Hebrew word ("days" rather than "appointed time"). Even though "appointed time" (*mo'ed*, Heb.) is not used in Daniel 10:14, its appearance in Daniel 11:27, 35; 12:7 suggests that the broader influence of Habakkuk 2:3 on Daniel 10–12 includes this term. Focusing on the citation of Habakkuk 2:3 in Daniel 11:27 ("for still the end is for the appointed time," author's translation), Fishbane notes the common themes of both foreign invasion as well as falsehood (*kazav*, Heb.) and argues that Daniel's "vision" can be seen as fulfilling Habakkuk's "vision."[45] This is the very relationship that Daniel's "vision" in Daniel 9 (*mar'eh*, Heb., v. 23) has to Jeremiah's prophecy of the seventy years (Dan 9:2, 24).

After the angel finishes his initial words (vv. 11–14), Daniel bows his face to the ground again (v. 15; cf. v. 9). He is speechless, but as before he receives an angelic touch (v. 16; cf. v. 10), this time on his lips, which enables him to

---

42. Sailhamer, *Pentateuch as Narrative*, 35–37.
43. As noted in the commentary on Daniel 10:1 above, the mention of a "word" that is "revealed" to Daniel forms a similar inclusio, such that both inclusios are mutually reinforcing.
44. Michael Shepherd, *A Commentary on the Book of the Twelve: The Minor Prophets* (Grand Rapids: Kregel, 2018), 324–325.
45. Fishbane, *Biblical Interpretation*, 492.

speak. Daniel explains that he has no "strength" (v. 17), as was the case in verse 8, but the angel touches him yet again and strengthens him (v. 18). Daniel thus receives a total of three angelic "touches" (*naga'*, Heb., vv. 10, 16, 18), a clear reminder of human frailty (cf. v. 19). Although Daniel's weakness is due to his visionary experience, the Bible teaches that we are always but dust (Gen 3:19; Ps 103:14) and a breath (Ps 144:4), subject to aging, illness, and death. Christians likewise experience the Lord strengthening us again and again (Prov 24:16; 2 Cor 12:9), sometimes even in a short span of time like Daniel.

After strengthening Daniel, the angel continues speaking (vv. 19–21; cf. vv. 11–12). He again calls Daniel "highly esteemed" and encourages him not to be afraid (v. 19; cf. vv. 11–12). Daniel also needed repeated encouragement (vv. 11, 19), just as we often do. Similar to verse 11, he receives strength through the angel's words (cf. Ezek 2:2) and is able to receive further revelation. The angel explains that the aforementioned struggle with "the prince of Persia" (v. 20; cf. v. 13) is not over, and he must go back and fight more. Furthermore, there is also "the prince of Greece" who will come. Thus, there is not only a heavenly counterpart to the Persian kingdom but also to the Greek kingdom, suggesting still more such counterparts in an ongoing "great war" (v. 1). Again, it is the archangel Michael who leads the fight against these powers (v. 21; cf. v. 13).

Whereas the angel's words reveal the existence of spiritual conflicts that correspond to earthly ones, even more things are left unsaid, such as the details of this war in the heavenly realm, the precise relationship of Daniel's prayers to this war (cf. 2 Cor 10:3–4; Eph 6:18), the nature of the "kings" (plural) of Persia and their relationship to the "prince of Persia" (cf. Dan 11:2), the nature and origin of angelic hierarchy (e.g., Michael, as "one of the chief princes"), and more.[46] Evidently, these things are not for Daniel to know, but the angel will shortly reveal many other things, as we will see in Daniel 11.

---

46. Cf. Widder, *Daniel*, 511. Based on Deuteronomy 32:8–9 (LXX) and 4QDeut^n, which have "angels of God" and "sons of God," respectively, instead of "sons of Israel," Collins thinks that the prince of Persia is a "patron angel." Collins, *Daniel*, 375.

DANIEL 11

WAR AFTER WAR UNTIL

THE END COMES

World War II is widely considered the bloodiest conflict in human history, with one source estimating a death toll of sixty-six million.[1] Given the great value of even one human life, since we are all created in the image of God (Gen 1:27), it is impossible to even come close to understanding the loss from this war. As mentioned in the introduction to the commentary on Daniel 1, my grandparents were also affected. Most of the deaths from World War II were in Asia, particularly in the Soviet Union and China, but also Indonesia, Japan, and India, among other places. Indeed, several of the deadliest wars in world history took place in Asia, many of them in China.

Violence and bloodshed can be traced all the way back to Cain and Abel in Genesis 4, and "enmity" still further back to the conflict between Eve and the serpent (Gen 3:15). Thus, the prophet Isaiah's vision that "they will beat their swords into plowshares and their spears into pruning hooks" (Isa 2:4) is as relevant as ever, with war still raging in some parts of the world. We still await the final consummation of the seed of the woman's victory over the serpent (Gen 3:15; Ps 110:1; Heb 2:8).

As explained in the commentary on Daniel 10, Daniel 10–12 is a literary unit and concludes the book of Daniel. Although certainly valuable in and of itself, Daniel 10 also serves as an introduction to Daniel 11, in which the angel's main message is revealed. This message continues the report of "a great war" (Dan 10:1) raging both in the heavens and on earth. Whereas Daniel 10 reveals the existence of a heavenly battle, one that even involves angelic powers such as the "prince of Persia," "kings of Persia," and "prince of Greece" (10:13, 20, Heb.), Daniel 11 focuses on earthly wars involving Persia (v. 2), Greece (v. 2), and more. Some of these wars do not overtly involve God's people, but some do (see vv. 16, 28, 30–36).

---

1. Alberto Lucas López and Kaya Lee Berne, "Peaks of Brutality," https://www.nationalgeographic.com/magazine/graphics/graphic-wwii-and-the-100-deadliest-events-in-history-feature. This estimated figure can vary greatly, whether lower or higher.

Daniel 11 begins with a brief prediction about the Persian kingdom (vv. 1–2), continues with a similarly brief prophecy about the Greek kingdom (vv. 3–4), and proceeds with a lengthy discussion of the kings of the North and South (vv. 5–35). Finally, the angel foretells an end-time king who opposes both God and Israel (vv. 36–45).

11:1–2 THE PERSIAN KINGDOM

The historical setting for Daniel 11 is the same as Daniel 10 – the third year of Cyrus, king of Persia (10:1). Daniel 11:1 should be grouped with the last verses of Daniel 10 (the chapter division is unhelpful here) as this verse explains the timing of 10:21 to be "the first year of Darius the Mede," which is when the angel began to fight alongside Michael the archangel. This Medo-Persian king was also mentioned in Daniel 5:31 as having taken over the kingdom after Babylon fell (cf. 6:1–28). Thus, the angel's entry into this battle took place at a time of major transition from one empire to another. Although the nature of Michael's struggle at this moment is not explained, Widder points out that the parallel reference to "the first year of Darius . . . a Mede" in Daniel 9:1 "invites us to consider a relationship between the two [visions]."[2] Noting that Cyrus's decree to rebuild the temple also happened at that time, she "wonders if other heavenly princes really wanted the Jews restored to their land."[3] What is clear is that this transitional time saw a flurry of significant activity on earth and in heaven that transcends the Second Temple period.

Daniel 11:2 begins the bulk of the angelic message to Daniel, which the angel calls "truth" (*emet*, Heb.; cf. 8:12, 26; 9:13; 10:1). This emphasizes the reliability of divine revelation, as the same word was just used in Daniel 10:21: "I will tell you what is written in the Book of Truth [*emet*, Heb.]." Collins explains that the Book of Truth "evidently contains the course of history."[4] Although this book is probably not identical to revealed Scripture, written words that bear divine authority recall Daniel's study of Jeremiah in Daniel 9:2 and his devotion to "the law of his God" in 6:5.[5]

The angel explains that, after Cyrus (10:1), "Three more kings will arise in Persia, and then a fourth" (11:2). This clarifies the earlier reference to the

---

2. Widder, *Daniel*, 513. Several links between Daniel 9 and Daniel 10–12 are already noted in the commentary on Daniel 10:2–3, 11, 14. The first year of Darius the Mede is yet another.
3. Widder, *Daniel*, 513.
4. Collins, *Daniel*, Hermeneia, 376.
5. For more on the theme of writing in Daniel, see commentary on Daniel 5–6. Daniel 7:10 also mentions "books" used by the Ancient of Days for judgment.

heavenly "kings of Persia" in 10:13 (Heb.). Conflicting theories for the identities of these four kings have been set forth, including Cyrus, Darius, Xerxes, and Artaxerxes (Collins), Cambyses, Smerdis, Darius, and Xerxes (Jerome), and Artaxerxes I, Darius II, Artaxerxes II, and Artaxerxes III (Plöger).[6] In addition to the rejection of predictive prophecy by critical scholars, the main difficulty here is that "history knows of many more than four Persian kings after Cyrus," and therefore scholars such as Widder take the number "four" to be "symbolic for the totality of Persian kings."[7] Newsom points out the great wealth of Persia's last king, Darius III Codomannus, whom Collins takes to be the king who fights Greece in Daniel 11:2.[8]

11:3–4 A MIGHTY KING FROM GREECE

Given the conclusion of the Persian kingdom and the introduction of "the kingdom of Greece" in verse 2, the "mighty king" in verse 3 is naturally understood as a Greek king (cf. 8:20–21; 10:20). His "great dominion" (v. 3, ESV) and its eventual breakup into lesser kingdoms towards "the four winds of heaven" (v. 4) suggests identification with the third beast in Daniel 7:6 (a leopard) and especially the goat in 8:5–8, which began with a "large horn" that was later broken off and replaced with four horns that "grew up toward the four winds of heaven" (see commentary). As 8:21–22 explained, these things represent the "first king" of Greece, his kingdom, and the four lesser kingdoms that succeed his. As before, commentators agree that 11:3–4 refers to Alexander the Great and the division of his kingdom after his death (323 BC).[9] Daniel 11:4 further predicts that his successors will not be "his descendants," which is in fact what happened when the kingdom was divided among his generals.[10]

11:5–35 KINGS OF THE NORTH AND SOUTH

In the complicated aftermath of the breakup of Alexander's kingdom, Ptolemy came to power in Egypt (i.e., south) and Seleucus in Syria (i.e., north), and the Ptolemaic kings fought with the Seleucid kings six times between 274–163 BC.[11] Accordingly, verses 6–8 say that one from the South invades the fortress

---

6. For these theories, see Collins, *Daniel*, 377. Michael Shepherd seems to lean towards Jerome's view. Shepherd, *Daniel in the Context of the Hebrew Bible*, 100.
7. Widder, *Daniel*, 523.
8. Newsom, *Daniel*, 339; Collins, *Daniel*, 377.
9. Collins, *Daniel*, 377.
10. Widder, *Daniel*, 524; Collins, *Daniel*, 331, 377–378; Newsom, *Daniel*, 339–340.
11. Newsom, *Daniel*, 340.

of "the king of the North" and takes plunder to "Egypt."[12] However, "the king of the South" and "the king of the North" do not merely refer to two individual kings but to the Ptolemaic kings and Seleucid kings of this period. As Newsom remarks, "The identities of the individual kings are assimilated into the symbolic figures of the king of the south (Ptolemies) and the king of the north (Seleucids)."[13] Widder further explains, "These are the kings of interest in Dan 11 because they represent the dynasties that warred over 'the land between,' Palestine."[14] The land of Israel, including the exiles who returned, will thus be caught in the middle (vv. 16, 28, 30–36), and this is presumably why this prophetic message is being given to Daniel and the Lord's people. There will be much war, sacrilege, and suffering, but evil kings will ultimately fall, just as 2:21 declares: "He changes times and seasons; he deposes kings and raises up others." Daniel himself was no stranger to these trials, and God's people can likewise take heart when caught in such crossfire.

The prophecies about Ptolemaic and Seleucid relations in Daniel 11:5–35 are exceptionally precise. Widder calls Daniel 11 "an extraordinary prophecy" with an "astounding" amount of detail, "such that a reader can fill in the specific names and identify the specific events of nearly everything described."[15] On the other hand, critical scholars attribute such accuracy to this actually being history written after the fact and then presented as predictive prophecy (*vaticinium ex eventu*, as it is classically called in Latin).[16] As elsewhere in Daniel and throughout the Bible, I take prophecy at face value as indicative of God's omniscience, sovereignty over history, and revelation.

While differing presuppositions of scholars do matter, commentators of varying theological persuasions essentially agree on the referents of Daniel 11:5–35. In verse 5, the "king of the South" is Ptolemy I Soter, and "one of his commanders" is Seleucus I Nicator, the first of the Seleucid kings.[17] Whereas the time frame of verse 5 is 315–312 BC, the marriage alliance in verse 6 takes

---

12. As Collins points out, the Old Greek version of Daniel repeatedly glosses "South" as "Egypt" (vv. 5, 6, 9, 11, 14, 15, 25, 29, 40), whereas the Hebrew only explicitly mentions "Egypt" in verse 8 and alongside other countries in verses 42–43. Collins, *Daniel*, 378.
13. Newsom, *Daniel*, 340.
14. Widder, *Daniel*, 524.
15. Widder, *Daniel*, 523. See the helpful table in Newsom, though she interprets verses 36–45 as referring to Antiochus IV Epiphanes, in contrast with this commentary. Newsom, *Daniel*, 338–339.
16. For example, Newsom observes, "The detailed history [n.b.] of Seleucid-Ptolemaic relations begins here." Newsom, *Daniel*, 340.
17. Collins, *Daniel*, 380; Newsom, *Daniel*, 340; Widder, *Daniel*, 525; Shepherd, *Daniel in the Context of the Hebrew Bible*, 100.

place in 250 BC.[18] The opening phrase of verse 6 ("After some years") reflects the passage of time, and in fact it is the successors of Ptolemy I and Seleucus I who will be involved in this alliance. In particular, the granddaughter of Ptolemy I and daughter of Ptolemy II (kings of the South), Berenice, will marry Antiochus II, the grandson of Seleucus I and son of Antiochus I (kings of the North). Verse 6 suggests that this marriage will be unsuccessful, and Berenice and her son (the heir-apparent) were indeed later murdered.[19]

The one "from her family line" who will arise against the king of the North in verse 7 is Berenice's brother, Ptolemy III.[20] History confirms that he attacked the Seleucids in 246 BC and took plunder to Egypt, just as verses 7–8 foretell.[21] The taking of gods broadly parallels the plundering of the temple in Daniel 1:2.[22] After "some years" (v. 8) of relative peace, Seleucus II invaded Ptolemy's kingdom in 242 BC.[23]

The "sons" of Seleucus II (v. 10) refer to Seleucus III and Antiochus III the Great.[24] Seleucus III's reign (226–223 BC) was cut short by assassination.[25] Verses 10–19 focus on the reign of Antiochus III (223–187 BC), as the shift to the singular partway through verse 10b suggests ("he will surely come and flood and pass over," Heb.).[26] Verses 11–12 predict the Battle of Raphia (217 BC) between Antiochus III and Ptolemy IV, in which Ptolemy will be victorious, but then will become proud, to his own demise.[27]

Collins points out that "flood and pass over" in verse 10 (Heb.) is used of the Assyrian invasion of Judah in Isaiah 8:8 and also that "it will not stand and will not be of advantage to him" in verse 17 (Heb.) is very similar to Isaiah 7:7 ("it will not stand and it will not be," Heb.).[28] Fishbane notes the frequent use of the verb "to flood" (*shataf*, Heb.) to characterize Assyria in Isaiah 28:15,

---

18. Newsom, *Daniel*, 340–341.
19. Widder, *Daniel*, 525; Newsom, *Daniel*, 341; Collins, *Daniel*, 378.
20. Collins, *Daniel*, 378; Newsom, *Daniel*, 341; Widder, *Daniel*, 525.
21. Widder, *Daniel*, 525.
22. Newsom describes "godnapping" in the ANE as "symbolizing that the defeated nation's deities were powerless against the victor and his gods." Newsom, *Daniel*, 341. The Assyrians' boast in 2 Kings 18:33–35 and Isaiah 36:18–20 implies the same.
23. Collins, *Daniel*, 378; Shepherd, *Daniel in the Context of the Hebrew Bible*, 100. Cf. Newsom, *Daniel*, 341.
24. Shepherd, *Daniel in the Context of the Hebrew Bible*, 100.
25. Newsom, *Daniel*, 341–342; Collins, *Daniel*, 378.
26. Seow, *Daniel*, 172.
27. Newsom, *Daniel*, 342–343.
28. Collins, *Daniel*, 378, 381.

17–18 and the foreign powers in Daniel 11:10, 22, 26, 40 (cf. 9:27).[29] He also observes the theme and language of "destruction decreed" in Isaiah 10:23 (note "flood," v. 22 [Heb.]; 28:22; Dan 9:27; 11:36).[30] Fishbane concludes that Daniel 11 casts the Seleucids as "the fulfilment of the old doom prophecies spoken concerning Assyria . . . . More significant, one may presume, was the fact that the great Isaianic oracles against Assyria had *not yet* been fulfilled."[31] Teeter argues further that eighth-century Assyria has been "absorbed into a larger pattern" (i.e., literary strategy) in Isaiah that extends into the future and beyond Assyria itself.[32]

Perhaps it is no coincidence that these Isaianic contexts all involve Messianic themes: "Immanuel" (Isa 7:14; 8:8); the remnant's repentance towards "Mighty God" (Isa 10:21; cf. "Mighty God" in 9:6); and the laying of Zion's cornerstone as the foundation (Isa 28:16; cf. 8:14). The allusions in Daniel 11 to extant prophetic texts situate it within the framework of OT prophecy and its fundamental presupposition of God's sovereignty over history and perfect foreknowledge throughout the Bible (see "Biblical Allusions in the Book of Daniel," pp. 123–124).

The regrouping of the king of the North "after several years" (v. 13) predicts the aggression of Antiochus III the Great during 212–205 BC, in which he took control of much territory.[33] The many who "will rise against the king of the South" (v. 14) may refer to the rebellion of provinces subject to Egypt, internal revolt within Egypt itself, Philip of Macedon's coalition with Antiochus in the Fifth Syrian War, and/or support for Antiochus in Syria and Palestine.[34] The "violent among your own people" (v. 14) refers to rebellious Israelites, but the exact fulfillment is unclear.[35] Regarding their rebellion "in fulfillment of the vision, but without success" (v. 14), Newsom suggests that "some Jews

---

29. Fishbane, *Biblical Interpretation*, 490. Writing earlier, Seeligmann emphasizes the dependence of Daniel 9:27 and Daniel 11 on Isaiah, Numbers, and Habakkuk. I. L. Seeligmann, "Voraussetzungen der Midraschexegese," in *Supplements to VT* (Leiden: Brill, 1953), 150–181. More recently, see Andrew Teeter, "Isaiah and the King of As/Syria in Daniel's Final Vision: On the Rhetoric of Inner-Scriptural Allusions and the Hermeneutics of 'Mantological Exegesis,'" in *A Teacher for All Generations: Essays in Honor of James C. VanderKam*, ed. Eric Mason (Leiden: Brill, 2012), 169–199. Daniel 11:10, 22, 40 associates flood-like power with "the king of the North." Destruction also comes from the "north" in Jeremiah 1:14–15; 6:22; 25:9.
30. Fishbane, *Biblical Interpretation*, 490.
31. Fishbane, *Biblical Interpretation*, 491 (emphasis in original).
32. Teeter, "Isaiah and the King of As/Syria in Daniel's Final Vision," 196.
33. Collins, *Daniel*, 379; Newsom, *Daniel*, 343. Adapting Newsom's characterization of a "compressed allusion," it can be considered a compressed prediction.
34. Collins, *Daniel*, 379. Newsom, *Daniel*, 343.
35. Collins, *Daniel*, 379–380.

may have interpreted the upheavals of the Fifth Syrian War in eschatological terms . . . however, this . . . movement failed because the appointed time had not in fact arrived."[36] The "vision" and its "appointed time" is decided by God himself (vv. 27, 35; 10:14).

The "fortified city" that Antiochus III captures in verse 15 is Sidon, which gives him control over Palestine.[37] His freedom to "do as he pleases" and the fact that "no one will be able to stand against him" in verse 16 shows his unstoppable power (cf. v. 3; 8:4), including over "the Beautiful Land" (cf. vv. 41; 8:9), the land of Israel.[38] Antiochus III would indeed give his daughter, Cleopatra, in marriage to Ptolemy V for political reasons, but this did not end up benefiting him (v. 17).[39] Just as verses 18–19 foretell, Antiochus sought to conquer "coastlands" but was defeated twice by Rome (the "commander" being Lucius Cornelius Scipio), and he was later killed in 187 BC.[40] Thus, despite the seeming invincibility of Antiochus III the Great earlier (v. 16), he will perish (v. 19). His successor in verse 20 is Seleucus IV, who had to pay tribute to Rome and was assassinated in 175 BC.[41] Thus, the fourth kingdom in Daniel 2 and 7 is on the rise.

Newsom characterizes the struggles between North and South as following a "pattern of alternating aggression and dominance."[42] However, the prophecies of Antiochus III the Great in verses 10–19, and especially Antiochus IV Epiphanes in verses 21–35, show that "the Seleucid kingdom is depicted as the more powerful and the one that will ultimately upset history's natural balance."[43] Antiochus IV Epiphanes is the "contemptible person" in verse 21, and his coming was predicted earlier in Daniel 8:9–12, 23–25. The prophecy that he will not be "given the honor of royalty" but will seize the kingdom "through intrigue" (v. 21) is fulfilled when he usurps the throne as the younger brother (not the son) of Seleucus IV.[44]

Collins interprets the detail about "an overwhelming army" being "swept away [or "flooded"] before him" in verse 22 "as a general introductory statement

---

36. Newsom, *Daniel*, 344.
37. Newsom, *Daniel*, 338, 344; Collins, *Daniel*, 380.
38. Newsom, *Daniel*, 344. Collins further cites his reception in Jerusalem. Collins, *Daniel*, 380–381.
39. Newsom, *Daniel*, 345; Collins, *Daniel*, 381.
40. Newsom, *Daniel*, 345–346; Collins, *Daniel*, 381.
41. Collins, *Daniel*, 381–382; Newsom, *Daniel*, 346.
42. Newsom, *Daniel*, 341.
43. Newsom, *Daniel*, 340.
44. Collins, *Daniel*, 382; Newsom, *Daniel*, 346.

that anticipates the effect of Antiochus's reign."[45] This fits the allusive, theological use of the Hebrew verb *shataf* (to flood) discussed above. On the other hand, the destruction of "a prince of the covenant" predicts the murder of the high priest Onias III in 172 BC.[46] Antiochus IV's deception is predicted again in verse 23 ("deceitfully"; cf. v. 21), and the "agreement" here may be with Eumenes II, king of Pergamum.[47] Antiochus IV Epiphanes surpassing "his fathers" and "his forefathers" anticipates his unprecedented power (v. 24).

The detailed prophecies about Antiochus IV Epiphanes continue with his first (vv. 25–28) and second invasion of Egypt (v. 29), involving Ptolemy VI.[48] During the first invasion, Ptolemy VI is defeated (v. 25) and undermined by his courtiers (v. 26).[49] Later Ptolemy VI has a face-to-face meeting with Antiochus (v. 27).[50] On his way back to Syria, Antiochus attacks Jerusalem (v. 28).[51] According to 1 Maccabees 1:20–24 (NRSV), he entered the temple, plundered it, "shed much blood," and "spoke with great arrogance." Antiochus IV invades Egypt again (v. 29) in 168 BC but without success due to the intervention of Rome, or "ships of Kittim" (v. 30, ESV), which is understood by historians to refer to a Roman delegation arriving by sea and led by Gaius Popillius Laenas.[52]

The seemingly innocuous phrase, "ships of Kittim," is loaded with inner-biblical significance as it is nearly identical to "ships from the hand of Kittim" in Numbers 24:24 (Heb.). This connection has generated scholarly interest for a long time, at least since Montgomery.[53] Bentzen sees "ships of Kittim" in Daniel 11:30 as setting this "dramatic event [i.e., confrontation] as a fulfillment of Num 24:23ff."[54] Seeligmann links this allusion with other

---

45. Collins, *Daniel*, 382.
46. Collins, *Daniel*, 382; Widder, *Daniel*, 527. Goldingay and other scholars (such as Newsom, Collins) equate this "prince [or ruler] of the covenant" (*negid berit*, Hebrew) with the "anointed one" who is "cut off" in Daniel 9:26. Goldingay, *Daniel*, 262, 299. Such commentators also tend not to equate this "anointed one" in verse 26 with the "anointed one" in verse 25, who is also called a "ruler/prince" (*nagid*). In this approach, Onias III would not actually be called a "prince" in Daniel 9:25–26. In contrast, I argue in the commentary for a Messianic interpretation of Daniel 9:25–26.
47. Collins, *Daniel*, 382. Newsom, *Daniel*, 346–347.
48. Widder, *Daniel*, 527–528.
49. Newsom, *Daniel*, 347–348.
50. Newsom, *Daniel*, 348.
51. Newsom, *Daniel*, 348.
52. Hartman and Di Lella, *The Book of Daniel*, 297–298. Collins explains how the Old Greek translation of Daniel glosses "ships of Kittim" as "Romans" (Ῥωμαῖοι), as well as additional evidence from Qumran. Collins, *Daniel*, 384.
53. Montgomery, *Daniel*, 455.
54. Bentzen, *Daniel*, 81.

allusions to Isaiah and Habakkuk in Daniel 11 (and 9:27) and concludes that this is "probably the finest example of biblical interpretation in the Bible."[55] Fishbane sees Daniel 11:30 as "a citation from the concluding oracle of Balaam," which is "understood in the Daniel apocalypse as an allusion to the humiliation of Antiochus IV (in 168 BCE)."[56] Newsom believes "Dan 11:30 interprets the events in light of a passage from Num 24:24."[57]

A closer look at the respective contexts of Numbers 24:24 and Daniel 11:30 reveals that both contexts are situated "in the last days" (Num 24:14; Dan 10:14), with the former preceded by an important Messianic prophecy concerning "a star from Jacob" (Num 24:17). For Shepherd, Antiochus IV Epiphanes is thus set "within the context of 'the end of the days,'" even though he experiences only "a minor foretaste" of what the final enemy will experience before the Messiah (Dan 11:36–45).[58] Shepherd further believes that "it is entirely possible that the author intends Antiochus to serve as a pre-figuration" of this future figure.[59]

Numbers 24:23–24 is still difficult, to be sure, but Daniel 11:30 helpfully relates at least some of its content to a sacrilegious, violent "king of the North." Numbers 24:22 mentions the ascendance of "Assyria" (Heb.), which some link to Syria (i.e., "the North"), and Numbers 24:24 predicts how "ships from Kittim" will afflict "Assyria" (Heb.).[60] Indeed, this implies the existence of an "Assyria" contemporaneous with Rome.

---

55. Seeligmann classifies this under the category of "adaptation" and, even more specifically, "actualization." Here he is referring to "an actualizing commentary on Isaiah's prophecy concerning Assyria." Seeligmann, "Voraussetzungen der Midraschexegese," 171.
56. Fishbane, *Biblical Interpretation*, 491.
57. Newsom, *Daniel*, 349.
58. Shepherd, *Daniel in the Context of the Hebrew Bible*, 102. Situating Antiochus in "the end of the days" fits the usage of this phrase elsewhere, which suggests that it starts sometime during the exile (e.g. Deut 31:29). Cf. Sailhamer, *The Meaning of the Pentateuch*, 337–341.
59. Shepherd, *Daniel in the Context of the Hebrew Bible*, 110, note 109. This is an endnote for a statement on page 103.
60. For Assyria and Syria, see Teeter, "Isaiah and the King of As/Syria in Daniel's Final Vision," 187–199. Numbers 24:24b also teases the reader: who is the "he" (lit.) that will go to destruction, Antiochus IV Epiphanes or the Antichrist? Numbers 24:23 LXX further begins with a plus, parallel to the oracles in verses 20 and 21, "and seeing [g]og" (see *BHS* apparatus; Göttingen LXX apparatus lists text group *b* in support of "Gog" reading). For the character of pluses in *b*, including "substituting synonyms," "substantial semantic variation," and glosses "for greater precision," some of which are "influenced by the near context," see John William Wevers, *Text History of Greek Genesis* (Göttingen: Vandenhoeck and Ruprecht, 1974), 37. This textual evidence for "gog" is not strong, but it does fit the contextual use of "Gog" in Numbers 24:7 LXX by clarifying who [g]og is (i.e., the last enemy), including linking him to "the last days" (Num 24:14). In this case, the "he" in Numbers 24:24b could be Gog, who may or may not be involved with the ships of Kittim, which could still concern Antiochus IV Epiphanes. If verses

In any case, the resistance of the ships of Kittim to Antiochus IV Epiphanes will lead him to "turn back and vent his fury against the holy covenant" (Dan 11:30). His opposition to the "covenant" was already mentioned in Daniel 11:22, 28 and appears again in verse 32. He will also "desecrate the temple," "abolish the daily sacrifice," and "set up the abomination that causes desolation" (v. 31), just as Daniel 8:9–14 predicts.[61] Shepherd is careful to distinguish this "abomination" from the one in Daniel 9:27.[62]

Antiochus's mistreatment of God's people is emphasized in verses 30–35. He will encourage apostasy (v. 30), sometimes by using "flattery" (v. 32; cf. vv. 21, 34). However, "the people who know their God" will resist (v. 32), though "they will fall by the sword or be burned or captured or plundered" (v. 33). Their reception of "a little help" (v. 34) may refer to real, though incomplete, deliverance.[63] The faithful are also referred to as "wise," and they "instruct many" but sometimes also suffer defeat or "stumble" (vv. 33, 35).[64] At the same time, their suffering will result in their purification, or we might say, sanctification (v. 35; cf. 12:10).[65] Collins further explains "that the wisdom they impart corresponds to the apocalyptic wisdom of the book."[66] Newsom specifies this wisdom as the theological messages of the four kingdoms in Daniel 7 (cf. Daniel 2), the rise and fall of mighty kings (Daniel 8), the true meaning of Jeremiah's prophecy of the seventy years (Daniel 9), and the details of Daniel 11.[67] Indeed, this is the wisdom (*sakal* [Hiphil], Heb.) that

---

23–24 are taken as concerning Gog, then this would support an eschatological interpretation of Daniel 11:30. Cf. Jerome's traditional view that Daniel 11:21–45 (not just vv. 36–45) is about the Antichrist, though often in a typological sense (with Antiochus IV Epiphanes serving as type, except in vv. 44–45). See Mary Reaburn, "St Jerome and Porphyry Interpret the Book of Daniel," *Australian Biblical Review* 52 (2004): 9–13.

61. Collins believes that Antiochus IV Epiphanes attacked Jerusalem twice, whereas Newsom cites recent analysis to argue that he only attacked Jerusalem once. Collins, *Daniel*, 383–384; Newsom, *Daniel*, 350.

62. Shepherd writes, "The language of the two passages differs markedly, and the two figures appear in two different places in the book's sequence of kingdoms [i.e., one in the third kingdom, the other in the fourth]." Shepherd, *Daniel in the Context of the Hebrew Bible*, 102. On page 98, Shepherd explains that "the daily sacrifice" mentioned in Daniel 8:11–13 and 11:31 is not mentioned in 9:27, which uses "sacrifice" and "offering." Also, the Hebrew text of Daniel 9:27 does not necessarily refer to "an abomination that causes desolation" (NIV) but could instead be translated, "on the wing of abominations shall come one who makes desolate" (ESV).

63. Keil and Delitzsch, *Daniel*, 801.

64. Newsom, *Daniel*, 352.

65. Cf. Collins, *Daniel*, 386; Newsom, *Daniel*, 353. For the use of "purify" in this way (*barar*, Heb.), see Isaiah 52:11. For "refine" (*tsaraf*, Heb.) as removing dross, see Isaiah 1:25; 48:10. For "make spotless" (*lavan*, Heb.) as meaning cleansing from sin, see Isaiah 1:18; Psalm 51:7.

66. Collins, *Daniel*, 385.

67. Newsom, *Daniel*, 352.

Daniel possesses and that God's people need as well (1:4, 17; 9:13, 22, 25). Wildgruber has further pointed out the use of *sakal* in Psalm 2:10 ("Therefore, you kings, be wise") as part of a broader "inner biblical discourse [involving the book of Daniel and Psalms 1–2] concerning the relationship between Israel and the nations."[68]

The wise, then, are those who know that the "King of heaven" (4:37) rules over history and every earthly kingdom. They also know that his own kingdom will crush all earthly ones and will never be destroyed (2:34–35; 6:27). As a result, the wise await the worldwide rule of the son of man (7:13–14), though it may mean suffering and even death. The focus on God's people in Daniel 11:30–35 suggests that we should seek to be among the "wise" who "know their God" (vv. 32–33, 35) and resist evil because of our hope in the kingdom of God. As Daniel 11 implies, nothing happens outside of the Lord's sovereignty over time (e.g., vv. 27, 29, 35, 40), and the time will come when his kingdom triumphs.

11:36–45 THE LAST ENEMY KING

Critical scholars believe that verses 36–45 are likewise about Antiochus IV Epiphanes. This view can be traced all the way back to Porphyry, whom Jerome responded to his commentary on Daniel.[69] On the other hand, some conservative commentators, such as Widder and Shepherd, point out that the designation "the king" in verse 36 is not used of the kings of the North and South.[70] The introduction of a unique king here would not be out of place, since verse 36 begins a new section in the discourse, with the preceding verses focused on the faithful (vv. 32–35). Sailhamer argues that this individual king battles both "the king of the South" and "the king of North" in verse 40, which would imply that he is distinct from these kings and Antiochus IV

---

68. Regina Wildgruber, *Daniel 10–12*, 298. She notes how the nations raging in Psalm 2:1 parallels the behavior of the nations in Daniel, especially Daniel 10–12. The "righteous" in Psalm 1 further parallel the "wise" in Daniel. There are also blessing statements in Psalm 1:1, Psalm 2:12, and Daniel 12:12, as well as references to Zion in Psalm 2:6 and Daniel 11:45.
69. Collins explains that modern scholarship sees verse 40 as the transition from "prophecy after the fact" to erroneous prediction, whereas Porphyry takes verse 45 to be accurate history. Collins, *Daniel*, 25, 388.
70. Widder takes a both-and interpretation of Antiochus and the Antichrist. Widder, *Daniel*, 528–529; Shepherd, *Daniel in the Context of the Hebrew Bible*, 103. On the other hand, House, a conservative, takes verses 36–45 to be about Antiochus, that is, as proceeding chronologically, encompassing events beyond 168 BC, and providing a "general description" of what happens to Antiochus from 171–164 BC. House, *Daniel*, 178.

Epiphanes, in particular, who was a king of the North.[71] On the other hand, it is also possible to read verse 40 as a battle involving only the king of the South and the king of North, where the Antichrist is the final "king of the North."[72]

This king's "do[ing] as he pleases" (v. 36) shows that he will be the culmination of other kings who have done the same (vv. 3, 16; 8:4).[73] His arrogance, boasting, and blasphemy (vv. 36–37) equate him with the little horn from the fourth beast/kingdom in Daniel 7:8, 11, 20–21, 24–25. The reference to "what has been determined" (11:36) or "decreed" (ESV) connects to the enemy and the troubles "decreed" at the end of the seventy sevens (9:26–27). Commentators agree that this king's disregard for "the gods of his ancestors," "the one desired by women" (i.e., Tammuz-Adonis), or "any god" does not fit Antiochus IV Epiphanes.[74] On the other hand, this king's worship of strength (11:38) fits the biblical profile of Habakkuk 1:11. He will wage a final war that will involve the Promised Land (Dan 11:41, 45), but "he will come to his end, and no one will help him" (v. 45; cf. Num 24:24). His death in the land of Israel coheres with other texts that predict an eschatological battle there (Ezek 38:14–23; 39:1–5; Joel 3:12–16; Zech 14:1–4).

Thus, this final king will meet his end, just as all the others foretold in Daniel 11 will. The comfort and encouragement to believers is that the kings of this earth rise and fall, but the Lord rules over even the worst of them and will bring about his plans in his time. We, his people, will have to endure much at times, but our ultimate destiny is salvation, even resurrection, as Daniel 12 reveals.

---

71. Sailhamer, *NIV Compact Bible Commentary*, 412–413. The referent of the pronouns "he" and "him" are mostly consistent in verses 36–40, except in verse 38. Verse 38 uses an untranslated resumptive pronoun "him" that refers to "a god unknown to his ancestors." The phrase, "instead of them," at the beginning of verse 38 is the other exception, where the (singular) pronoun refers to the gods in verse 37.
72. Cf. Shepherd, *Daniel in the Context of the Hebrew Bible*, 103; Keil and Delitzsch, *Daniel*, 807–808. Of course, some who read verse 40 as involving only these two kings take the king of the North as Antiochus.
73. Widder, *Daniel*, 529.
74. Newsom, *Daniel*, 355; Collins, *Daniel*, 387; Shepherd, *Daniel in the Context of the Hebrew Bible*, 103. Critical scholars attribute this to inaccuracy. See note 69 above.

DANIEL 12

SHINING LIKE THE STARS

Many Buddhists believe in reincarnation, which the official website of the Dalai Lama describes in this way, "Sentient beings come to this present life from their previous lives and take rebirth again after death."[1] From this perspective, birth is not a real beginning, and death is not the end either. Predating Buddhism, the Chinese practice of ancestor worship assumes the continued existence of the spirits of the deceased.[2] This traditional belief is also reflected in modern culture, such as in the *Kung Fu Panda* movie series, in which characters such as Oogway, Po, and others pass into the spirit realm.

Although the Bible does not teach that sentient beings have previous lives, it does affirm the existence of human afterlife. As the most famous verse in the Bible declares, those who believe in Jesus Christ "shall not perish but have eternal life" (John 3:16). There are indeed many passages in the NT that promise eternal life for Christians. On the other hand, some have wondered whether this teaching can be found in the OT. As we will see below, Daniel 12:2 dispels all doubt by predicting the resurrection of the dead, which leads to eternal life for some but eternal reproach for others.

As noted previously, Daniel 10–12 is a literary unit, and Daniel 12 concludes both this unit and the book of Daniel as a whole. This means that the struggles between the kings of the North and South in Daniel 11, especially the prophecies about the final enemy king in verses 36–45, are essential background for Daniel 12. Daniel 12:1–4 foretells the final victory of God's people, and Daniel 12:5–13 describes Daniel's last encounter with angels.

12:1–4 FINAL VICTORY

Daniel 12:1 picks up right where Daniel 11:45 leaves off. Whereas some commentators interpret the king in Daniel 11:36–45 as referring to Antiochus IV Epiphanes just as Daniel 11:21–35 does, this commentary interprets the king in verses 36–45 to be the Antichrist/Gog. This interpretation bears on

---

1. https://www.dalailama.com/messages/retirement-and-reincarnation/reincarnation.
2. Ori Tavor, "Ancestor Worship," 24 October 2024, https://www.oxfordbibliographies.com/display/document/obo-9780199920082/obo-9780199920082-0171.xml.

the precise meaning of "At that time" in Daniel 12:1, which then refers to the end of history rather than the second century BC (cf. 10:14, "in the last days," Heb.). Widder points out the fourfold repetition of the word "time" in the Hebrew text of Daniel 12:1 (cf. ESV), which is an important theme in Daniel 11 and elsewhere in Daniel.[3] This theme contributes to the theological message that "God is the one in control of time" and that "'the time' toward which the entire book has been driving finally arrives with the fulfillment of this prophecy."[4] This time is "the time of the end," as it is described in Daniel 11:35, 40; 12:4, 9.[5]

At this eschatological moment, Michael the archangel will arise and help Israel (12:1). The precise aid that he provides is unspecified, but the verb "arise" (*'amad*, Heb.) suggests a turning point that contrasts with the "arising" of various earthly kings in Daniel 11 (vv. 2, 3, 7, 16, 20, 21).[6] In its focus on the earthly scene, Daniel 11 had not mentioned Michael, but his leading role in the heavenly realm had already been cited in Daniel's vision in Daniel 10. Daniel 10:13, 21 highlight Michael's battle with the angelic princes of Persia and Greece, describing him as "your prince" (i.e., Israel's). Accordingly, he "protects *your* people" in Daniel 12:1 (emphasis added). Thus, the reality of a cosmic war simultaneously raging on both the earthly and heavenly planes is brought into focus again.[7] The encouragement to believers is that we are not alone and that God's holy angels are involved in this battle also (cf. 2 Kgs 6:16–17).

The unprecedented "time of distress" (*'et tsarah*, Heb.) in Daniel 12:1 likewise refers to the last enemy king's blasphemy, destruction, and violence in Daniel 11:36–45. Daniel 11:41 had described this king's invasion of Israel, and 11:44 referred to his destruction of "many." Newsom believes that this "time of distress" in 12:1 alludes to Jeremiah 30:7.[8] Shepherd points out the related phrase, "day of distress" (*yom tsarah*, Heb.), in other texts such as Nahum 1:7 and Habakkuk 3:16.[9] These two texts may be traced further back to Deuteronomy 32:35 in the Song of Moses, which prophesies of a "time"

---

3. Widder, *Daniel*, 530.
4. Widder, *Daniel*, 530.
5. Shepherd, *Daniel in the Context of the Hebrew Bible*, 102–104. See also the discussion of Daniel 8:17–19 in this commentary. Collins calls this moment "the time of the decisive heavenly intervention." Collins, *Daniel*, Hermeneia, 390.
6. Widder, *Daniel*, 530. Cf. Collins, *Daniel*, Hermeneia, 390.
7. Newsom, *Daniel*, 360.
8. Newsom, *Daniel*, 360.
9. Shepherd, *Daniel in the Context of the Hebrew Bible*, 103.

and "day of disaster" when the Lord brings vengeance on enemies but shows compassion to his servants.[10] Just as Jeremiah 30:7 refers to an unprecedented "time of distress" (Heb.) from which "Jacob . . . will be saved," so Daniel 12:1 predicts that "your people . . . will be delivered." The description of the unprecedented distress in Daniel 12:1 ("such as has not happened from the beginning of nations") may further allude to the day of the Lord in Joel 2:2 ("such as never was in ancient times") and the Passover in Exodus 11:6 ("worse than there has ever been").[11]

Daniel 12:1 clarifies the identity of those who will be saved as "everyone whose name is found written in the book." This commentary has pointed out the recurring theme of writing throughout the book of Daniel (e.g., 5:5–8, 24–28; 6:8–9, 13; 9:2, 11, 13; 10:21). Final judgment by the Ancient of Days is characterized as involving "books" (7:10), and other biblical passages refer to a book listing the names of the saved (e.g., Exod 32:32–33; Ps 69:28; Isa 4:3; Mal 3:16).[12] The great white throne passage in Revelation 20 accordingly describes the final judgment of humanity based on both "what they had done as recorded in the books" and "the book of life" containing the names of those spared (vv. 12, 15).

Daniel 12:2 proceeds to predict the resurrection of the dead, "Multitudes who sleep in the dust will awake." Collins refers to the "virtually unanimous agreement" among scholars that this verse refers to resurrection and that it is "the only generally accepted reference to resurrection" in the OT.[13] Newsom argues for dependence on Isaiah 26:19 ("Your dead will live, Lord; their bodies will rise – let those who dwell in the dust wake up") and Isaiah 66:24 ("The worms that eat them will not die, the fire that burns them will not be quenched, and they will be loathsome").[14] Noting the "physically graphic nature" of these two texts, she concludes, "It seems likely that Daniel envisions a bodily resurrection," even though Daniel 12:2 does not directly say so.[15]

---

10. Chen, *Wonders from Your Law*, 162–163.
11. All three passages negate the Hebrew verb *hayah* in the Niphal stem to describe catastrophic divine judgment.
12. Collins, *Daniel*, 391; Newsom, *Daniel*, 361; Shepherd, *Daniel in the Context of the Hebrew Bible*, 103.
13. Collins, *Daniel*, 391–392.
14. Newsom, *Daniel*, 364.
15. Newsom, *Daniel*, 364. Cf. Kevin Chen, "Resurrection in the Old Testament," in *A Handbook on the Jewish Roots of the Christian Faith*, ed. Craig Evans and David Mishkin (Peabody: Hendrickson, 2019), 250–255; Kevin Chen, *Messianic Vision of the Pentateuch*, 124–129.

The eschatological context of the preceding verses suits this resurrection being for the sake of final judgment ("some to everlasting life, others to shame and everlasting contempt," v. 2). The promise of "everlasting life" (cf. Pss 21:5; 133:3) is significant because it shows that death is not the end for believers, particularly those who are faithful unto death in the book of Daniel (7:21, 25; 8:12–13, 24; 11:32–35). Not only do their earthly lives bring honor to God, but they themselves will be raised from the dead and enjoy their reward.

The reality of resurrection hope that transcends death is also important because the faithful tend to be delivered from death in Daniel 1–6, but less so in Daniel 7–12. Concerning these matters, the theology of Daniel is thus rich and multilayered, both depicting God's power and wisdom to save in this life, but "even if he does not" (3:18), and actually even if he does, also declaring that our ultimate hope is the promise of resurrection unto eternal life. We will share in the life of "him who lives forever" (4:34; 12:7; cf. 6:27) and inhabit "a kingdom that will never be destroyed" (2:44; cf. 6:26; 7:14). This inheritance is something earthly kings can only wish for (2:4, 21; 3:9; 5:10; 6:6, 21).

The flip side of the resurrection of the righteous in Daniel 12:2 is the resurrection of the wicked unto "shame and everlasting contempt." In relation to God's justice, the punishment of the wicked is equally as important as the rewarding of the righteous (Deut 32:4, 35). The book of Daniel as well as the annals of history testify to numerous wicked people, some of them rulers, and their crimes cry out for justice (cf. Gen 4:10). Similar to the theme of deliverance for the faithful, the book of Daniel records instances in which judgment falls on a wicked ruler in this life (e.g., Belshazzar in Daniel 5), but final judgment is a certainty either way. Daniel 12:2 emphasizes the eternal dishonor that the wicked will bear, presumably in contrast with the glory they may have enjoyed for a period of time (e.g., 8:8, 10–11; 11:36, 42).

Daniel 12 proceeds by focusing on the righteous, who "will shine like the brightness of the heavens" and "like the stars for ever and ever" (v. 3). The phrase, "Those who are wise," ties back to Daniel 11:33, 35, where the wise "instruct many" and endure severe suffering "until the time of the end," which arrives in 11:40 and continues into 12:1–3. As the commentary on 11:33, 35 explains, the wise are those who understand the apocalyptic wisdom of the book of Daniel and teach it to others.

Ginsberg recognizes a parallel between how the wise make many righteous (*tsadaq* [Hiphil], *rabbim*, Heb.) and are exalted in Daniel 12:3 and how the Suffering Servant is also exalted and makes many righteous (*tsadaq* [Hiphil], *rabbim*, Heb.) in Isaiah 52:13; 53:11.[16] Another lexical parallel is that the Servant will "act wisely" (Isa 52:13), which uses the same Hebrew word *sakal* (in the same verbal stem, Hiphil) that is used to refer to the "wise" in Daniel 11:33, 35; 12:3, 10. Lester points out that these allusions to Isaiah practically frame Isaiah 52:13–53:12 and evoke the entire Servant Song.[17] Based on the fact that the Servant dies (Isa 53:8–10, 12), Newsom further argues that the Servant's exaltation in Isaiah 52:13 "can also be understood as a resurrection from death," which provides one more link to Daniel 12:2–3.[18]

Whereas Ginsberg equates the wise in Daniel 12:3 with the Suffering Servant and so adopts a corporate interpretation of this Servant, it is also possible to see the wise as extending the work of this Servant, much like the "servants" in the subsequent context of Isaiah (54:17; 56:6; 63:17; cf. the Servant's "offspring" in 53:10).[19] In this case, it is still the Suffering Servant who "will justify many" (53:11), and the wise will teach others about this Messiah, who was "cut off" (Dan 9:26, Heb.) to atone for sin (9:24) and will rule over God's everlasting kingdom (7:13–14).[20]

The exaltation of the wise is described in terms of the everlasting glory of the sky and the stars.[21] Stars are also mentioned in Daniel 8:10, where they represent the heavenly host who are battling with the goat's little horn, often identified as Antiochus IV Epiphanes. Widder detects a contrast with Antiochus, who reached for the stars and triumphed for a time but ultimately fell.[22] Relatedly, Collins sees the comparison of the wise to stars as implying their association and keeping company with angels.[23]

Perhaps more significant is the allusion to the Abrahamic covenant promise that Abraham's descendants will become "as numerous as the stars in the sky" (Gen 15:5; 22:17; 26:4; Exod 32:13). These passages not only share the

---

16. H. L. Ginsberg, "The Oldest Interpretation of the Suffering Servant," *VT* 3 (1953): 402. Cf. Montgomery, *Daniel*, 472.
17. Lester, *Daniel Evokes Isaiah*, 96–99.
18. Newsom, *Daniel*, 364. Cf. Bentzen, who sees the resurrection in Isaiah 53 as individualized. Bentzen, *Daniel*, 85.
19. Cf. W. A. M. Beuken, "The Main Theme of Trito-Isaiah: 'The Servants of YHWH,'" *JSOT* 47 (1990): 67–87.
20. Collins wants to distinguish between their teaching many in Daniel 11:33 and their making many righteous in Daniel 12:3, but there is a possible double meaning with the Hebrew verb *zahar*, which does mean "shine" here, but elsewhere means "teach" or "warn" (e.g., Exod 18:20; Ezek 3:17–21). Collins, *Daniel*, 393.
21. Newsom, *Daniel*, 364.
22. Widder, *Daniel*, 531.
23. Collins, *Daniel*, 393–394.

term "stars" (*kokavim*, Heb.) but also the comparative preposition "like/as" (*ke*, Heb.) as well as the theme of sky. Even though these verses focus on the number of these stars rather than their shining, Abram's initial reception of this hope in Genesis 15:5 comes at night and involves him actually going outside and looking at these stars. Their shining, then, can be assumed, and therefore it is not out of line to highlight this connection in Daniel 12:3. Eschatological Zion is also called to "shine" in Isaiah 60:1, and both the Lord and his Messiah do the same (e.g., Deut 33:2; 2 Sam 23:3–4). Thus, Daniel 12:2–3 weaves together both Isaiah 53 and key Abrahamic covenant texts.[24]

The lengthy vision that began in Daniel 10 concludes in 12:4 with Daniel being instructed to "seal the words of the scroll." Goldingay believes that this statement near the end of the book may apply not only to the final vision of Daniel 10–12 but also to the book of Daniel as a whole.[25] Newsom explains this sealing in terms of authentication and protection from tampering, though for the reader "the book is now unsealed."[26] Its contents concern "the time of the end" (cf. v. 9; 11:35, 40; also "in the last days" [Heb.] in 2:28; 10:14). Several interpreters see "Many will go here and there [*shut*, Heb.] to increase knowledge" in Daniel 12:4 as an allusion to Amos 8:12, which likewise describes people who "wander [*shut*, Heb.] from north to east, searching for the word of the Lord, but they will not find it."[27]

12:5–13 DANIEL'S LAST ENCOUNTER WITH ANGELS

The lengthy vision (10:12–12:4) has concluded, but Daniel has one last interaction with angels in Daniel 12:5–13. This passage begins with him seeing two other angels standing on opposite sides of the river (v. 5), which Daniel 10:4 identified as the Tigris.[28] Daniel does not immediately engage the conversation, but first hears one of the angels ask, "How long will it be before these astonishing things will be fulfilled?" (v. 6). The "astonishing things" (*pele'*, Heb.) may refer especially to the "unheard-of things" (*pala'*, Heb.) spoken

---

24. Elsewhere I refer to this phenomenon as "braiding" and to passages that link to multiple texts as "nexus passages." See Chen, *Wonders from Your Law* (for braiding, see pp. 121, 128–129, 138).
25. Goldingay, *Daniel*, 309.
26. Newsom, *Daniel*, 365.
27. For example, Newsom, *Daniel*, 365; Collins, *Daniel*, 399; Seow, *Daniel*, 189–190. However, the nature of this allusion is debated.
28. For further discussion, see Seow, *Daniel*, 192; Collins, *Daniel*, 373, 399.

against God by the final enemy king in Daniel 11:36.[29] Commentators have noted how this question parallels Daniel 8:13–14, where a "holy one" also asks "how long" it will take for a particular vision to be fulfilled.[30] Blasphemy and persecution of God's people also elicit responses in Daniel 7:19–22, 28; 8:27.

The "man clothed in linen," who had appeared gloriously in Daniel 10:5–6, responds, saying, "It will be for a time, times and half a time" (12:7). This Hebrew phrase has essentially the same meaning as the Aramaic phrase that is translated "a time, times and half a time" in Daniel 7:25.[31] In Daniel 7, this refers to the length of time in which "the holy people are delivered into his hands," which is a reference to the boastful, violent, little horn of the fourth beast/kingdom (7:7–8, 19–25). Daniel 12:7 also mentions God's people enduring extreme suffering. The breaking of their "power" or "hand" (v. 7, Heb.) precedes their eschatological deliverance, as foretold in Deuteronomy 32:36 ("their strength [Heb., 'hand'] is gone").[32] Collins draws an additional connection to "the last half-week of years in 9:27."[33] Daniel 12:6–7 thus weaves together the fourth beast's little horn from Daniel 7, the enemy who will arise during the seventieth seven from Daniel 9, and the final enemy king from Daniel 11.

Daniel, however, does not understand and asks a follow-up question in verse 8. He seems to want further information about what will happen after what was described in verse 7.[34] However, his request is denied as the man dressed in linen says, "Go your way" (v. 9). Nothing else will be revealed at this time (v. 9). Some believe that "roll up" (*satam*, Heb.) and "seal" (*hatam*, Heb.) in verse 9 emphasize mystery and secrecy, unlike in verse 4.[35] The angel may also be redirecting Daniel to the "words" and the "scroll" that *were* revealed and that he was supposed to "roll up" and "seal . . . until the time of

---

29. Commentators often point out the connection to the use of the same Hebrew root in Daniel 8:24, where it characterizes Antiochus IV Epiphanes. Whereas they also see Daniel 11:36 as Antiochus, this commentary distinguishes between him and the final enemy king in Daniel 11:36–45.
30. For example, Lucas, *Daniel*, 296.
31. Cf. Shepherd, *Daniel in the Context of the Hebrew Bible*, 104.
32. Collins takes the shattering of power to refer instead to the downfall of the oppressor in Daniel 11:45. Cf. Collins, *Daniel*, 399.
33. Collins, *Daniel*, 399.
34. Widder, *Daniel*, 537; Collins, *Daniel*, 400.
35. Hartman and Di Lella, *The Book of Daniel*, 313; Newsom, *Daniel*, 367.

the end" (v. 4). Either way, verse 10 explicitly circles back to Daniel 11:35, which foretells how the "wise" will be "refined, purified and made spotless."[36]

The repetition of the terms "wise" (*sakal*, Heb.), "refine" (*tsaraf*, Heb.), "purify" (*barar*, Heb.), and "make spotless" (*lavan*, Heb.) in Daniel 12:10 in the context of "the time of the end" (12:9) in these two key texts (cf. 11:35) at the end of the book of Daniel suggests one of its main applications: our need to endure trials for the sake of sanctification (1 Pet 4:1; cf. 1 Thess 4:3). The ultimate purpose of the book is not to satisfy our curiosity about the future but to declare God's sovereignty over it (Dan 2:21) and the coming kingdom of the son of man (7:13–14). Though questions, study, and even debate about its contents have their place, the book of Daniel was primarily written to motivate and call us to be wise and to be ready to endure suffering from earthly kingdoms because of our hope in God's coming kingdom. In so doing, we will be increasingly sanctified, demonstrate our understanding, and bear witness to the mystery of this kingdom (cf. 2:30).

Daniel 12:11–12 provides the reader "one last puzzle."[37] Following the instructions to Daniel in verses 9–10, the flow of thought shifts to "the daily sacrifice" and "the abomination that causes desolation" (v. 11). The removal of this sacrifice (*tamid*, Heb.) had been mentioned in Daniel 8:11–13 and 11:31 with reference to Antiochus IV Epiphanes's desecration of the temple. An "abomination" (*shiquts*, Heb.) or "transgression" (*pesha*, Heb.) that causes "desolation" (*shamam*, Heb.) is likewise found in Daniel 8:13 and 11:31. The commentary on 9:27 and 11:30–31 argued that the desolation during the seventieth seven is distinct from the desolation caused by Antiochus.

On the surface, it seems strange that the eschatological emphasis of the preceding verses would be muddled by changing the subject to Antiochus. However, there may be a clue in the two enigmatic lengths of time: 1,290 days (v. 11) and 1,335 days (v. 12). These numbers have long puzzled scholars, and the commentary below is meant to be tentative. Without pursuing it further, Hartman and Di Lella note that if a month is counted as thirty days, then 1,290 days is precisely forty-three months, and 1,335 days is 44.5 months.[38] Building upon this, Newsom points out that if forty-two months is taken as a reference, which can be justified by the importance of this length

---

36. In view of the unusual use of the *weyiqtol* verb form in the surrounding context (e.g., 11:5–7, 11, 15–19, 22, 25, 28, 30, 36, 42, 45), these three verbs at the beginning of Daniel 12:10 are not necessarily jussives.
37. Newsom, *Daniel*, 368.
38. Hartman and Di Lella, *The Book of Daniel*, 314.

of time in Daniel (7:25; 8:14; 9:27; 12:7), then forty-three months adds one extra month and 44.5 months adds 2.5 months, which aligns with "a time, [two] times, and half a time."[39] If this intriguing line of reasoning is followed, then Daniel 12:11–12, while referencing the persecution under Antiochus, ultimately pronounces a blessing on those who endure suffering under the last enemy king for "a time, times and half a time" (12:7; 7:25; 9:27).

Of course, Daniel 12:1–3 has just declared that all whose names are written in the book of life will be delivered, resurrected to everlasting life, and will shine like the stars forever. As for Daniel, and for all others who live in the meantime, we are to "go your way till the end" (v. 13; cf. v. 9). Collins interprets Daniel's "rest" and "rising" as his death and eventual resurrection, respectively, and concludes that his destiny is among the wise, "who rise to eternal life."[40] Indeed, all who heed the message of the book of Daniel and endure "a time, times and half a time" will "shine . . . like the stars for ever and ever" (12:3, 7).

---

39. Newsom, *Daniel*, 368.
40. Collins, *Daniel*, 402. Cf. Newsom, *Daniel*, 368.

SELECTED BIBLIOGRAPHY

Albertz, Rainer. "The Social Setting of the Aramaic and Hebrew Book of Daniel." In *The Book of Daniel: Composition and Reception*, vol. 1. Edited by John Collins and Peter Flint. Leiden: Brill, 2001.

Alexander-Knotter, Mirjam. "Rembrandt's Hebrew." *Jahrbuch der Berliner Museen* 51 (2009): 25–32.

Anderson, Bernard. "Exodus Typology in Second Isaiah." In *Israel's Prophetic Heritage: Essays in Honor of James Muilenberg*. Edited by Bernard Anderson and W. Harrelson. New York: Harper, 1962.

Anderson, Steven, and Rodger Young. "The Remembrance of Daniel's Darius the Mede in Berossus and Harpocration." *BibSac* 173 (2016): 315–323.

Arnold, Bill. "Wordplay and Narrative Techniques in Daniel 5 and 6." *JBL* 112 (1993): 479–485.

Aslan, Reza. "Cosmic War in Religious Traditions." In *The Oxford Handbook of Religion and Violence*. Edited by Mark Juergensmeyer, Margo Kitts, and Michael Jerryson. New York: Oxford University Press, 2013.

Avalos, Hector. "The Comedic Function of the Enumerations of Officials and Instruments in Daniel 3," *CBQ* 53 (1991): 580–588.

Bailey, Benjamin, and Sunny Lie. "The Politics of Names among Chinese Indonesians in Java." *Journal of Linguistic Anthropology* 23 (2013): 21–40.

Baldwin, Joyce. *Daniel*. TOTC. Downers Grove: InterVarsity, 1978.

Bar, Shaul. *A Letter That Has Not Been Read: Dreams in the Hebrew Bible*. Translated by Lenn Schramm. Cincinnati: Hebrew Union College, 2001.

Bauckham, Richard. *The Climax of Prophecy*. Edinburgh: T&T Clark, 1993.

Beaulieu, Paul-Alain. "The Babylonian Background of the Motif of the Fiery Furnace in Daniel 3." *JBL* 128 (2009): 273–290.

Begbie, Jeremy. *Resounding Truth: Christian Wisdom in the World of Music*. Grand Rapids: Baker, 2007.

Bennett, William. "Where did Eastern Lightning's Leaders Come From?" 2 April 2014. *China Source*. https://www.chinasource.org/resource-library/articles/where-did-eastern-lightnings-leaders-come-from/.

Bentzen, Aage. *Daniel*. 2nd ed. Tübingen: Mohr Siebeck, 1952.

Beuken, W. A. M. "The Main Theme of Trito-Isaiah: 'The Servants of YHWH.'" *JSOT* 47 (1990): 67–87.

Birrell, Anne. *The Classic of Mountains and Seas*. London: Penguin, 1999.

Block, Daniel. "Preaching Old Testament Apocalyptic to a New Testament Church." *Calvin Theological Journal* 41 (2006): 17–52.

Chan, Sabrina S., Linson Daniel, E. David de Leon, and La Thao. *Learning Our Names: Asian American Christians on Identity, Relationships, and Vocation*. Downers Grove: InterVarsity, 2022.

Chen, Christopher S. *Evil Empire? Government Officials as Proponents of the Gospel in Luke-Acts and Beyond*. Eugene: Wipf and Stock, 2025.

Chen, Kevin. *The Messianic Vision of the Pentateuch*. Downers Grove: InterVarsity, 2019.

———. "Resurrection in the Old Testament." In *A Handbook on the Jewish Roots of the Christian Faith*. Edited by Craig Evans and David Mishkin. Peabody: Hendrickson, 2019.

———. *Wonders from Your Law: Nexus Passages and the Promises of an Exegetical Intertextual Old Testament Theology*. Downers Grove: InterVarsity, 2024.

Clayton, Thomas. "Building the New Cambodia: Educational Destruction and Construction under the Khmer Rouge, 1975–1979." *History of Education Quarterly* 38 (1998): 1–16.

Clermont-Ganneau, M. "Mene, Tekel, Peres, and the Feast of Belshazzar." Translated by Robert Rogers. *Hebraica* 3 (1887): 87–102.

Collins, John. *Apocalypse, Prophecy, and Pseudepigraphy: On Jewish Apocalyptic Literature*. Grand Rapids: Eerdmans, 2015.

———. "Apocalyptic Genre and Mythic Allusions in Daniel." *JSOT* (1981): 83–100.

———. *The Apocalyptic Imagination: An Introduction to Jewish Apocalyptic Literature*. 2nd ed. Grand Rapids: Eerdmans, 1998.

———. *Daniel: A Commentary on the Book of Daniel*. Hermeneia. Minneapolis: Fortress, 1993.

———. *Daniel: With an Introduction to Apocalyptic Literature*. Grand Rapids: Eerdmans, 1984.

Conway, William Martin, ed. *Literary Remains of Albrecht Dürer*. Cambridge: Cambridge University Press, 1889.

Coxon, Peter. "The Great Tree of Daniel 4." In *A Word in Season: Essays in Honor of William McKane*. Edited by James Martin and Philip Davies. Sheffield: JSOT Press, 1986.

———. "The 'List' Genre and Narrative Style in the Court Tales of Daniel." *JSOT* 35 (1986): 95–121.

Davis, Dale Ralph. *The Message of Daniel: His Kingdom Cannot Fail*. The Bible Speaks Today Series. Downers Grove: InterVarsity, 2013.

Day, John. *God's Conflict with the Dragon and the Sea: Echoes of a Canaanite Myth in the Old Testament*. Reprint. Eugene: Wipf & Stock, 2020.

Dempster, Stephen. "'At the End of the Days' (בְּאַחֲרִית הַיָּמִים) – An Eschatological Technical Term? The Intersection of Context, Linguistics and Theology." In

Selected Bibliography

The Unfolding of Your Words Gives Light: Studies on Biblical Hebrew in Honor of George L. Klein. Edited by Ethan Jones. University Park: Eisenbrauns, 2018.

Dockery, David. *Renewing Minds: Serving Church and Society through Christian Higher Education.* Rev. ed. Nashville: B&H Academic, 2008.

Doukhan, J. B. "Allusions à la création dans le livre de Daniel." In *The Book of Daniel in Light of New Findings.* Edited by A. S. Van Der Woude. Leuven: Leuven University Press, 1993.

Driver, S. R. *The Book of Daniel with Introduction and Notes.* Cambridge: University Press, 1901.

Dunn, Emily. *Lightning from the East.* Leiden: Brill, 2014.

Elman, Benjamin. *A Cultural History of Civil Examinations in Late Imperial China.* Berkeley: University of California Press, 2000.

Fewell, Danna Nolan. *Circle of Sovereignty: A Story of Stories in Daniel 1–6.* Sheffield: Almond Press, 1988.

Fishbane, Michael. *Biblical Interpretation in Ancient Israel.* Oxford: Clarendon, 1985.

Flores, Esteban. "Indoctrination or Education? Inside North Korean Schools in Japan." *Harvard International Review* 39, no. 1 (2018): 9–12.

Gandhi, Mahatma. *Gandhi on Non-Violence: Selected Texts from Mohandas K. Gandhi's Non-Violence in Peace and War.* New York: New Directions, 1965.

Ginsberg, H. L. "The Oldest Interpretation of the Suffering Servant." *VT* 3 (1953): 400–404.

Goldingay, John. *Daniel.* WBC. Dallas: Word, 1989.

Grillo, Jennie. "From a Far Country: Daniel in Isaiah's Babylon." *JBL* 136 (2017): 363–380.

Grossman, Jonathan. *Creation: The Story of Beginnings.* Translated by Sara Daniel. New Milford: Maggid, 2019.

Haberman, David. *People Trees: Worship of Trees in Northern India.* Oxford: Oxford University Press, 2013.

Hamilton, James. *With the Clouds of Heaven: The Book of Daniel in Biblical Theology.* Downers Grove: InterVarsity, 2014.

Hamilton, Victor. *The Book of Genesis: Chapters 1–17.* Grand Rapids: Eerdmans, 1990.

Hansen, Valerie. "The Kitan-Liao and Jurchen-Jin." In *Routledge Handbook of Imperial Chinese History.* Edited by Victor Cunrui Xiong and Kenneth Hammond. London and New York: Routledge, 2019.

Hartman, Louis, and Alexander Di Lella. *The Book of Daniel.* Anchor Bible. Garden City: Doubleday, 1978.

Henze, Matthias. "The Use of Scripture in the Book of Daniel." In *A Companion to Biblical Interpretation in Early Judaism*. Edited by Matthias Henze. Grand Rapids: Eerdmans, 2012.

Hess, Richard. *Studies in the Personal Names of Genesis 1–11*. Winona Lake: Eisenbrauns, 2009.

Hilton, Michael. "Babel Reversed – Daniel Chapter 5." *JSOT* 66 (1995): 99–112.

Holm, Tawny. "The Fiery Furnace in the Book of Daniel and the Ancient Near East." *Journal of the American Oriental Society* 128 (2008): 85–104.

House, Paul R. *Daniel*. TOTC. Downers Grove: InterVarsity, 2018.

Houtman, Cornelius. "What Did Jacob See in His Dream at Bethel? Some Remarks on Genesis XXVIII 10–22." *VT* 27 (1977): 337–351.

Howard, David M., Jr. *Joshua*. New American Commentary. Nashville: B&H, 1998.

Hugenberger, Gordon. "The Servant of the Lord in the 'Servant Songs' of Isaiah: A Second Moses Figure." In *The Lord's Anointed: Interpretation of Old Testament Messianic Texts*. Edited by P. E. Satterthwaite, R. S. Hess, and G. J. Wenham. Grand Rapids: Baker, 1994.

Ireland, Daryl. *John Song: Modern Chinese Christianity and the Making of a New Man*. Waco: Baylor, 2020.

Jenkins, Philip. *The Lost History of Christianity: The Thousand-Year Golden Age of the Church in the Middle East, Africa, and Asia – and How It Died*. New York: HarperOne, 2008.

Kane, Daniel. *The Kitan Language and Script*. Leiden: Brill, 2009.

Keener, Craig. *Miracles: The Credibility of the New Testament Accounts*, vol. 2. Grand Rapids: Baker, 2011.

Keil, C. F., and Franz Delitzsch. *Daniel*. Vol. 9, *Commentary on the Old Testament*. Reprint. Peabody: Hendrickson, 1996.

Kilcourse, Carl. *Taiping Theology: The Localization of Christianity in China, 1843–64*. New York: Palgrave Macmillan, 2016.

Kim, Daewoong. "Biblical Interpretation in the Book of Daniel: Literary Allusions in Daniel to Genesis and Ezekiel." PhD diss., Rice University, 2013.

Kratz, Reinhard. "The Visions of Daniel." In *The Book of Daniel: Composition and Reception*, vol. 1. Edited by John Collins and Peter Flint. Leiden: Brill, 2001.

Kuykendall, Michael. "Numerical Symbolism in the Book of Revelation: A Weakness of Modern Bible Versions." *Themelios* 47, no. 3 (2022): 472–489.

Kwong, Andrew P. C. (鄺炳釗). *Daniel*. Tien Dao Bible Commentary. Hong Kong: Tien Dao, 1989.

Lacocque, Andre. "Allusions to Creation in Daniel 7." In *The Book of Daniel: Composition and Reception*, vol. 1. Edited by John Collins and Peter Flint. Leiden: Brill, 2001.

Selected Bibliography

Lefevre, Amy Sawitta. "For Thailand, a portrait is crucial for preparations of succession." 20 April 2016. https://www.reuters.com/article/lifestyle/for-thailand-a-portrait-is-crucial-to-preparations-for-succession-idUSKCN0XI002/.

Lester, G. Brooke. *Daniel Evokes Isaiah: Allusive Characterization of Foreign Rule in the Hebrew-Aramaic Book of Daniel.* London: T&T Clark, 2015.

Lin, Hang. "Examination Essays, Paratext, and Confucian Orthodoxy: Negotiating the Public and Private in Knowledge Authority in Early Seventeenth-Century China." In *Early Modern Privacy: Sources and Approaches.* Edited by Michaël Green, Lars Cyril Nørgaard, and Mette Birkedal Bruun. Leiden: Brill, 2022.

Longman, Tremper, III. *Daniel.* NIV Application Commentary. Grand Rapids: Zondervan, 1999.

Lucas, Ernest C. *Daniel*, Apollos Old Testament Commentary. Downers Grove: InterVarsity, 2002.

McAllister, Ray. "Clay in Nebuchadnezzar's Dream and the Genesis Creation Accounts." *Journal of the Adventist Theological Society* 18 (2007): 122–129.

McConville, J. Gordon. "Ezra-Nehemiah and the Fulfillment of Prophecy." *VT* 36 (1986): 205–224.

McSpadden, Kevin. "How 3 legendary figures shaped foundations of ancient China." 11 Sept 2024. *South China Morning Post.* https://www.scmp.com/news/people-culture/article/3277818/how-3-legendary-figures-shaped-foundations-ancient-china.

Meadowcroft, Tim. "Metaphor, Narrative, Interpretation, and Reader in Daniel 2–5." *Narrative* 8 (2008): 257–278.

Miyazaki, Ichisada. *China's Examination Hell: The Civil Service Examinations of Imperial China.* Translated by Conrad Schirokauer. New Haven: Yale University, 1981.

Mong, Ambrose. *A Better World is Possible: An Exploration of Western and Eastern Utopian Visions.* Cambridge: James Clarke & Co, 2018.

Montgomery, James A. *Daniel.* International Critical Commentary. Edinburgh: T&T Clark, 1927.

Morales, L. Michael. *Who Shall Ascend the Mountain of the Lord? A Biblical Theology of Leviticus.* Downers Grove: InterVarsity, 2015.

Motyer, J. Alec. *The Prophecy of Isaiah.* Downers Grove: InterVarsity, 1993.

Mounce, Robert. *The Book of Revelation.* New International Commentary on the New Testament. Grand Rapids: Eerdmans, 1997.

Munson, Paul. "A Biblical View of Music." In *The Worldview Study Bible.* Edited by David Dockery and Trevin Wax. Nashville: Holman Bible Publishers, 2018.

Newsom, Carol. *Daniel.* Old Testament Library. Louisville: Westminster John Knox, 2014.

Noonan, Benjamin. "Daniel's Greek Loanwords in Dialectal Perspective." *BBR* 28 (2018): 575–603.

Noort, Ed. "Gandhi and the World of the Hebrew Bible: The Case of Daniel as Satyagrahi." *Religions* 13 (2022): 1–18.

Oppenheim, Adolf Leo. "The Interpretation of Dreams in the Ancient Near East. With a Translation of an Assyrian Dream-Book." *Transactions of the American Philosophical Society* 46 (1956): 179–373.

Philip, Finny. "1 Corinthians." In *South Asia Bible Commentary*. Edited by Brian Wintle. Grand Rapids: Zondervan, 2015.

Plöger, Otto. *Das Buch Daniel*. Gütersloh: Gerd Mohn, 1965.

Polaski, Donald. "*Mene, Mene, Tekel, Parsin:* Writing and Resistance in Daniel 5 and 6." *JBL* 123 (2004): 649–669.

Portier-Young, Anathea E. "Languages of Identity and Obligation: Daniel as Bilingual Book." *VT* 60 (2010): 98–115.

Postell, Seth. "Does the Book of Psalms Present a Divine Messiah?" In *Reading the Psalms Theologically*. Edited by David Howard, Jr. and Andrew Schmutzer. Bellingham: Lexham, 2023.

Prinsloo, G. T. M. "Two Poems in a Sea of Prose: The Content and Context of Daniel 2.20–23 and 6.27–28." *JSOT* 59 (1993): 93–108.

Qureshi, Nabeel. *Seeking Allah, Finding Jesus: A Devout Muslim Encounters Christianity*. Grand Rapids: Zondervan, 2016.

Reaburn, Mary. "St Jerome and Porphyry Interpret the Book of Daniel." *Australian Biblical Review* 52 (2004): 1–18.

Rindge, Matthew. "Jewish Identity under Foreign Rule: Daniel 2 as a Reconfiguration of Genesis 41." *JBL* 129 (2010): 85–104.

Roche, Evita. "The largest banyan tree in the world is located in India." 21 April 2022. *Condé Nast Traveler*. https://www.cntraveller.in/story/kolkata-west-bengal-largest-banyan-tree-in-the-world/.

Rotohka, Angukali. "Daniel." In *South Asia Bible Commentary*. Edited by Brian Wintle. Grand Rapids: Zondervan, 2015.

Sailhamer, John. *The Pentateuch as Narrative*. Grand Rapids: Zondervan, 1992.

———. *The Meaning of the Pentateuch*. Downers Grove: InterVarsity, 2009.

———. *NIV Compact Bible Commentary*. Grand Rapids: Zondervan, 1994.

Scheetz, Jordan. *The Concept of Canonical Intertextuality and the Book of Daniel*. Eugene: Pickwick, 2011.

Seeligmann, I. L. "Voraussetzungen der Midraschexegese." In *Supplements to Vetus Testamentum*. Leiden: Brill, 1953.

Segert, Stanislav. "Aramaic Poetry in the Old Testament." *Archív Orientální* 70 (2002): 65–79.

Seow, C. L. *Daniel*. Louisville: Westminster John Knox, 2003.

Selected Bibliography

———. "From Mountain to Mountain: The Reign of God in Daniel 2." In *A God So Near: Essays on Old Testament Theology in Honor of Patrick D. Miller*. Edited by Brent Strawn and Nancy Bowen. Winona Lake: Eisenbrauns, 2003.

Shepherd, Michael B. *A Commentary on the Book of the Twelve: The Minor Prophets*. Grand Rapids: Kregel, 2018.

———. *Daniel in the Context of the Hebrew Bible*. New York: Lang, 2009.

———. "Daniel 7:13 and the New Testament Son of Man." *WTJ* 68 (2006): 99–111.

Suchard, Benjamin. "The Greek in Daniel 3: Code-Switching, Not Loanwords." *JBL* 141 (2022): 121–136.

Sung, John (宋尚節). 我的見證 (My Testimony). Rev. ed. Hong Kong: Hong Dao, 1975.

Tavor, Ori. "Ancestor Worship." Last modified 24 October 2024. https://www.oxfordbibliographies.com/display/document/obo-9780199920082/obo-9780199920082-0171.xml.

Teeter, Andrew. "Isaiah and the King of As/Syria in Daniel's Final Vision: On the Rhetoric of Inner-Scriptural Allusions and the Hermeneutics of 'Mantological Exegesis.'" In *A Teacher for All Generations: Essays in Honor of James C. VanderKam*. Edited by Eric Mason. Leiden: Brill, 2012.

Ünaldi, Serhat. *Working Towards the Monarchy: The Politics of Space in Downtown Bangkok*. Honolulu: University of Hawai'i Press, 2016.

Van Der Toorn, Karel. "Scholars at the Oriental Court: The Figure of Daniel Against Its Mesopotamian Background." In *The Book of Daniel: Composition and Reception*, vol. 1. Edited by John Collins and Peter Flint. Leiden: Brill, 2001.

von Glahn, Richard. *The Sinister Way: The Divine and the Demonic in Chinese Religious Culture*. Berkeley: University of California Press, 2004.

von Rad, Gerhard. *Old Testament Theology*. Translated by D. M. G. Stalker. Peabody: Prince, 2005.

Vu, Hoang Minh. "Recycling Violence: The Theory and Practice of Reeducation Camps in Postwar Vietnam." In *Experiments with Marxism-Leninism in Cold War Southeast Asia*. Edited by Matthew Galway and Marc Opper. Canberra: ANU, 2022.

Waltke, Bruce. *Genesis: A Commentary*. Grand Rapids: Zondervan, 2001.

Wevers, John William. *Text History of Greek Genesis*. Göttingen: Vandenhoeck and Ruprecht, 1974.

Widder, Wendy. *Daniel: A Discourse Analysis of the Hebrew Bible*. Zondervan Exegetical Commentary on the Old Testament. Grand Rapids: Zondervan, 2023.

———. "The Court Stories of Joseph (Gen 41) and Daniel (Dan 2) in Canonical Context: A Theological Paradigm for God's Work among the Nations." *OTE* 27 (2014): 1112–1128.

Wildgruber, Regina. *Daniel 10–12 als Schlüssel zum Buch*. Tübingen: Mohr Siebeck, 2013.

Wilson, Gerald. *Psalms – Volume 1*. NIV Application Commentary. Grand Rapids: Zondervan, 2002.

———. "The Prayer of Daniel 9: Reflection on Jeremiah 29." *JSOT* 48 (1990): 91–99.

Wiseman, Donald J. *Notes on Some Problems in Daniel*. London: Tyndale Press, 1965.

Wolters, Al. "Untying the King's Knots: Physiology and Wordplay in Daniel 5." *JBL* 110 (1991): 117–122.

———. "The Riddle of the Scales." *Hebrew Union College Annual* 62 (1991): 155–177.

Wood, Barry. *Invented History, Fabricated Power*. London: Anthem Press, 2020.

Yonglin, Jiang. *The Great Ming Code/Da Ming lü*. Seattle: University of Washington Press, 2005.

———. *The Mandate of Heaven and The Great Ming Code*. Seattle: University of Washington Press, 2011.

Zakovitch, Yair. *"And You Shall Tell Your Son . . .": The Concept of the Exodus in the Bible*. Jerusalem: Magnes, 1991.

Asia Theological Association
54 Scout Madriñan St. Quezon City 1103, Philippines
Email: ataasia@gmail.com Telefax: (632) 410 0312

OUR MISSION

The Asia Theological Association (ATA) is a body of theological institutions, committed to evangelical faith and scholarship, networking together to serve the Church in equipping the people of God for the mission of the Lord Jesus Christ.

OUR COMMITMENT

The ATA is committed to serving its members in the development of evangelical, biblical theology by strengthening interaction, enhancing scholarship, promoting academic excellence, fostering spiritual and ministerial formation and mobilizing resources to fulfill God's global mission within diverse Asian cultures.

OUR TASK

Affirming our mission and commitment, ATA seeks to:

- **Strengthen** interaction through inter-institutional fellowship and programs, regional and continental activities, faculty and student exchange programs.
- **Enhance** scholarship through consultations, workshops, seminars, publications, and research fellowships.
- **Promote** academic excellence through accreditation standards, faculty and curriculum development.
- **Foster** spiritual and ministerial formation by providing mentor models, encouraging the development of ministerial skills and a Christian ethos.
- **Mobilize** resources through library development, information technology and infra-structural development.

To learn more about ATA, visit www.ataasia.com or facebook.com/AsiaTheologicalAssociation

Langham Literature, along with its publishing work, is a ministry of Langham Partnership.

Langham Partnership is a global fellowship working in pursuit of the vision God entrusted to its founder John Stott –

> *to facilitate the growth of the church in maturity and Christ-likeness through raising the standards of biblical preaching and teaching.*

Our vision is to see churches in the Majority World equipped for mission and growing to maturity in Christ through the ministry of pastors and leaders who believe, teach and live by the word of God.

Our mission is to strengthen the ministry of the word of God through:
- nurturing national movements for biblical preaching
- fostering the creation and distribution of evangelical literature
- enhancing evangelical theological education

especially in countries where churches are under-resourced.

Our ministry

Langham Preaching partners with national leaders to nurture indigenous biblical preaching movements for pastors and lay preachers all around the world. With the support of a team of trainers from many countries, a multi-level programme of seminars provides practical training, and is followed by a programme for training local facilitators. Local preachers' groups and national and regional networks ensure continuity and ongoing development, seeking to build vigorous movements committed to Bible exposition.

Langham Literature provides Majority World preachers, scholars and seminary libraries with evangelical books and electronic resources through publishing and distribution, grants and discounts. The programme also fosters the creation of indigenous evangelical books in many languages, through writer's grants, strengthening local evangelical publishing houses, and investment in major regional literature projects, such as one volume Bible commentaries like the *Africa Bible Commentary* and the *South Asia Bible Commentary*.

Langham Scholars provides financial support for evangelical doctoral students from the Majority World so that, when they return home, they may train pastors and other Christian leaders with sound, biblical and theological teaching. This programme equips those who equip others. Langham Scholars also works in partnership with Majority World seminaries in strengthening evangelical theological education. A growing number of Langham Scholars study in high quality doctoral programmes in the Majority World itself. As well as teaching the next generation of pastors, graduated Langham Scholars exercise significant influence through their writing and leadership.

To learn more about Langham Partnership and the work we do visit **langham.org**

www.ingramcontent.com/pod-product-compliance
Lightning Source LLC
Chambersburg PA
CBHW072030170426
43200CB00025B/2447